LEN

Gerald Howat was educate[...] [...]versity and Exeter College, [...] degree in nineteenth-centu[...] [...] Royal Historical Society an[...] [...]en several books of an historical nature.

He is the author of seven cricket books including five biographies, that of Learie Constantine winning a literary award. He is a regular contributor to various cricket journals.

Gerald Howat has played MCC cricket and still appears for his local club, Moreton in Oxfordshire, of which he became president in 1990. He is a fully qualified umpire and his younger son, Michael, won a cricket Blue at Cambridge.

LEN HUTTON

GERALD HOWAT

Mandarin

A Mandarin Paperback

LEN HUTTON

First published in Great Britain 1988
by Heinemann Kingswood
This revised and updated edition published 1990
by Mandarin Paperbacks
Michelin House, 81 Fulham Road, London sw3 6rb

Mandarin is an imprint of the Octopus Publishing Group,
a division of Reed International Books Limited

A CIP catalogue record for this title
is available from the British Library

ISBN 0 7493 0863 X

Printed and bound in Great Britain
by Cox and Wyman Limited, Reading, Berks.

For Ian and Gillian Bossenger,
my son-in-law and daughter

Contents

Illustrations

Acknowledgements

The M25 almost became a familiar friend as I drove regularly from Oxfordshire to Kingston-on-Thames to discuss the shape of this book with Sir Leonard and Lady Hutton, to whom I am grateful for their willingness to search their memories, answer questions, complete chronological sheets, lend photographs and entertain me. There are those who would argue that a biographer should stand apart from his living subject and produce what may be called 'an unauthorized biography'. I do not subscribe to that opinion and from the moment right at the start when Lady Hutton said, 'You are not writing a book to please us', I felt completely free in my interpretation of their lives. It is more than fifty years since Sir Leonard and Lady Hutton first met and her contribution to his career has a significant part to play in a biography of him. Other members of the family who welcomed me and informed me included Richard and Charmaine Hutton, his son and daughter-in-law; Mrs Florence Firth, his sister; Mrs Mary Hutton, his sister-in-law and Mr Robin Hutton, his cousin.

Many people put their recollections of Sir Leonard at my disposal and to them my thanks are due: L. E. G. Ames, CBE; Alan Barker; P. W. Barker, CBE; C. J. Barnett; A. V. Bedser, CBE; Sir Donald Bradman, AC; J. G. W. Davies, OBE; A. R. Gover; T. W. Graveney, OBE; Dr Sidney Hainsworth, CBE; J. Hardstaff; C. G. Howard; George Johnson; I. W. Johnson, MBE; Reg Law; Roger Mann; P. B. H. May, CBE; Keith Moss; Tom Naylor; Roland Parker; Gerald Pawle; Netta Rheinberg, MBE; Carol Rymer; Colin Shakespeare; the late R. G. Sinfield; P. A. Snow, OBE; E. W. Swanton, OBE; B. J. Thompson; C. Washbrook; A. J. Watkins; Roland Wilkinson; R. E. S. Wyatt; N. W. D. Yardley. I recall also a fascinating day spent with the late W. E. Bowes just before he died.

For assistance and for access to archive material I acknowledge the help of the following institutions and individuals: the Yorkshire County Cricket Club (Joe Lister); BBC Television (Jeff Goddard); MCC (Colonel John Stephenson and Stephen Green); the Bodleian Library, Oxford; the British Museum Newspaper Section; *The Times* (Marcus Williams). Dr Richard Cashman and B. D. Young kindly undertook some work on my behalf in Australian newspaper sources,

Acknowledgements

as did the Hon. Gloria Valère in Trinidad. Mrs H. Hewitson lent me a most informative scrapbook.

There are others to whom I also have obligations. Brian Croudy of the Association of Cricket Statisticians provided the details of Sir Leonard's first-class career, taking the opportunity to make some corrections from the accepted records in *Wisden* for 1956. Anthony Woodhouse read through the entire manuscript with the vigilant and knowledgeable eye of a member of the Yorkshire Committee. Norman Lilley, of the Queensway Studio, Thame, Oxfordshire, assisted me in the preparation of the photographs. My secretary, Nora Harragin, in undertaking her first book for me, survived and – I hope – enjoyed the experience and introduced me to the new technology. My wife, Dr Anne Howat, compiled yet another index.

Parts of this book were written on the farm of my son-in-law and daughter, Ian and Gillian Bossenger, in Kentucky. They provided ideal working conditions and excused me (more or less) from duties on the farm, and in return I dedicate this book to them.

Margot Richardson has been thoroughly professional in seeing the book through the press – a valued friend from previous enterprises.

North Moreton   GERALD HOWAT
Oxfordshire
1988

Author's Note

Sir Leonard Hutton died in 1990. In this paperback edition the opportunity has been taken to notice the events in his life between 1988 and 1990 and to make some minor changes in the text. I am indebted to Tony Lewis for his Foreword.

GERALD HOWAT

Foreword

On Thursday 13 September 1990 I stood for a few moments' silence in the middle of the Warwickshire County Cricket ground. As Chairman of Glamorgan, I had been invited to join the Warwickshire Chairman, Mr Bob Evans, at the side of the cricket square alongside our club teams which were engaged in the current championship match. In Kingston-upon-Thames, Surrey, on that day, the funeral service of Sir Leonard Hutton was being held in St Peter's Church.

The small crowd at Edgbaston also stood. They were acknowledging that Len Hutton had been pillar of their cricket-loving lives. Part of me was sad at his passing, more of me was thankful for his life and artistry with the bat. A part of me was stunned by the fact that the Len Hutton era was over.

He was the cornerstone of England in the 1940s and 1950s of my boyhood and youth – the captain who opened the batting and held out when others crumbled, the first professional leader of England. I tried to play his deft late cut and plagued my father for a pair of Len Hutton autograph batting gloves, the ones with the brown and white sausage fingers. We pulled our caps down over the right eye and in our fantasies scored 364 runs against the Australians . . . up against Mrs Jones's gate on the road.

His ultimate honour – though he would not have known it – was to be the most prized cigarette card in the school. Three of Yardley for one Hutton, four of Bakewell, Mitchell, Turnbull or anyone else. Perhaps two of Compton. But Hutton like Bradman was a golden possession.

At some time or other my generation of cricket lads had all, in the imagination, been Len Hutton, and as long as Sir Leonard went about his gentlemanly way and sat proudly on the presidential seat of his beloved Yorkshire he glowed inside us. The chill about standing in silence that day at Edgbaston was that we knew that part of us had died with him.

I saw him bat only once, but then it was not in his prime nor in a proper match. It was a game played on the Fenner ground in Marfleet, Hull, for the benefit of the Yorkshire wicket-keeper Jimmy Binks in the mid-1960s. He was about 50 years old. Gerald Howat writes of the tension Sir Leonard felt in these matches: the great expectations of him.

The pitch was uncomfortable for batting, uneven in bounce and responding to spin. I was out and retreated to the pavilion to loud applause only because Sir Leonard Hutton was walking out to replace me.

He stopped me and spoke. 'Is that a good bat?'

'Yes. It goes well.'

'Can I borrow it?' he asked with a smile.

We did a public swop. He batted against the serious bowling of the Yorkshire spinners. I did not bother to remove my pads, I just sat and watched every precious moment. What time he had: what touch. There was an occasional smile but the concentration was absolute when the bowler ran in. He eased the ball behind square on the leg side, and played the ball easily into gaps on the off and treated us to the late cut, steered fine, using the speed of the ball for its power.

I should say that I saw him play twice, because earlier, as recorded in Wisden of 1961, Sir Leonard and I were opponents in a first-class match. He was in the Col. L. C. Stevens XI against Cambridge University at the Saffrons, Eastbourne. Alas on a perfect pitch he was bowled 'through the gate' second ball by our Essex off-spinner Alan Hurd.

We were disappointed but Sir Leonard was obviously disturbed too because we found him at the lunch interval still with his pads on trying to work out how the ball had got past him, or so he was modest enough to say.

That was his only innings in the match but he was to play one more first-class innings in his career, noted a few pages along in that same Wisden. At Dublin in September he scored 89, opening the batting for MCC against Ireland. Normal service had been resumed.

It was in 1962 that I came to know Sir Leonard Hutton better because Richard, his son, and I were at Christ's College, Cambridge together and in the same 1962 cricket team. Sir Leonard took time to watch some matches at Fenners and certainly helped me as captain to get the best from Richard whose talents were not immediately obvious. Being Sir Leonard must have been the toughest job of the lot. Wherever he went to the end of his life he was recognised and feted – tiring work – but with his gentlemanly demeanour and twinkle in his eye he could charm the day with one smile or with one of his famous *non sequiturs*.

I sat next to him at dinner not many days before he died. It was at the Holiday Inn in Swiss Cottage, London and a young journalist on his other side had been unburdening himself of the flaws he saw in the modern game. He set the stage for a thesis from Sir Leonard, flipped his napkin, took a swill of wine and waited for the great man to reply.

Len nodded as if to say that he had understood these many points, then leaned forward towards the young man, opened the wide eyes and said – 'D'you know. D'you know . . . er . . . what stocks and shares are you buying these days?'

His life is a fascinating story and of course, the legend will grow.

Tony Lewis
September 1990

1

A Moravian Upbringing

1916–32

'That lad will play for England if he goes on like that.'
Voice heard on the sands at Morecambe, 1923

Seventeen-year-old Henry Hutton was feeling pleased with himself.
He had taken six wickets against Pudsey Mount Zion and they were all
out for 16. Then it was Fulneck's turn to bat in this Sunday School
match on the small sloping field looking across the valley to Tong and
Sykes Wood. Henry made the eleventh 'duck' of the afternoon and
Fulneck failed, by four runs, to reach their target. One day Henry's
youngest son, Leonard, would make his only appearance in a Sunday
School match on the same little ground just outside his own front
door. Fulneck and Henry Hutton had their successes even if that
Saturday afternoon in August 1893 was not one of them. Sunday
School cricket had its place on the rungs of the ladder which led to the
Yorkshire Council, the Bradford League and Yorkshire County
Cricket Club. Henry and all his four sons would play for Pudsey St
Lawrence in the Bradford League; Leonard would go on to play for
Yorkshire and England.

The Huttons were one of the oldest Fulneck families. They had been
there ever since the arrival of Benjamin Hutton towards the end of
the eighteenth century. Benjamin was born in Perth in 1763 and
unwittingly heeded the advice given in the year of his birth by Samuel

1

Johnson to James Boswell: 'the noblest prospect which a Scotchman sees is the high road that leads him to England'. He became an itinerant trader, leaving his home on the edge of the Highlands and making his way across the border to Northumberland and then to Yorkshire. He married a girl from Tong called Hannah Tempest and they had made their home among the small Moravian community in Fulneck, a few miles west of Leeds on the edge of Pudsey.

The Moravians were the earliest Protestant sect in fifteenth-century Europe, a century before the Protestant movements identified with Martin Luther and John Calvin. From their beginnings in Bohemia, under the leadership of John Hus, they found their way to Saxony where Count Zinzendorf gave them religious shelter before he brought them to England in the 1730s and more particularly to Yorkshire and to Fulneck. There they established traditions of Christian discipline, hard work, self-sufficiency and a simple and unworldly faith. Those first 'English' Moravians in Fulneck built a row of two-storey terraced houses of solid West Riding stone around whose walls have grown up clematis and roses. Facing them, across the single street of the settlement, they built a school for boys and a school for girls, separated by a church, all three of them tributes to the classical elegance, dignity and formalism of the eighteenth century. From the start, the community set out to be self-contained and self-supporting. Glovers, tailors (such as Benjamin Hutton), weavers, joiners and hosiers manufactured their goods to create a sense of industry, good craftsmanship and prosperity which is still apparent in the 1980s, though many of today's Moravians go to Pudsey or Leeds to work.

Of Benjamin and Hannah's six children, Edmund, born in 1804, the only surviving son, became a butter trader, making weekly trips over the Dales to Otley market to sell his wares. He had married Ann Galloway of Scott Hill and two of their children, Robert and William, are of some concern to us. Robert became first a leather merchant and then a Moravian minister and the father of Joseph Edmund (1868–1937) who also became a Moravian minister, the leading historian of the Moravian movement and a leg-break bowler. Joseph's son Robin became a master at the school and the author of its history in its bicentenary year. He was a second cousin of Leonard Hutton whom he used to watch at Headingley.

William, Robert's younger brother and the grandfather of Leonard, was born in 1845, a few years after the death of his grandfather Benjamin. He became a builder, eventually a master-builder, and a prosperous man in the Pudsey of the second half of the nineteenth century. His marriage to Elizabeth Milner in 1870 would bring an important cricketing 'strain' into the Huttons, for Elizabeth's brother, Seth Milner, was a well-known local cricketer often participating in matches on which large sums of money were placed – something a little different from the virtues of the Moravians. In due course Seth encouraged his young nephews to play cricket and his young nieces to enjoy it. We should remember the nieces: they will become the much-loved aunts of Leonard.

Henry, the third son of William and Elizabeth, whom we have already met playing for Fulneck against Mount Zion, was born in 1876. He joined his father in the building business, besides finding time to play as an all-rounder for Pudsey St Lawrence. When he was approaching forty, just before the first world war, there was a decline in the family fortunes. High labour rates and fixed pricing on contracts for projects such as the Trinity Methodist Church in Pudsey and the Majestic Hotel in Harrogate had caused his father to lose money. When William died in 1910 Henry carried on with the business, tendering, for example, to build the Boys' Brigade Hall in Fulneck in 1912 for £255. Then the effects of the first world war, the post-war depression and his own poor health led him first to sell the property in Pudsey known as the Hutton terrace and eventually to sell the business altogether.

Henry had married Lily Swithenbank at the turn of the century and they set up home in No. 5 Fulneck, one of the eighteenth-century terraced houses, rented for a modest sum from the church. Henry, no longer with a business of his own, became a foreman-joiner and bricklayer and it was into a household of modest circumstances, with something of a struggle to keep up appearances, that Leonard, the youngest of their five children, was born on 23 June 1916. 'I was lucky in my parents,' Sir Leonard recalled, 'in a home which was strict but caring'. He was lucky too in the devotion of his three aunts, Mary, Florence and Louise, who lived almost next door. For fifty years Louise made weekly collections for the National Savings Movement, starting in the year of her nephew's birth at the height of the first world war. This she combined with being a teacher in an elementary school. All the sisters were interested in Gilbert & Sullivan and would organize performances in Fulneck. Their nephew looked back with affection and respect on the contribution which they made to the life of the community. They also encouraged his cricket, giving him a bat which cost 2/6d for his second birthday and books such as Noble's *The Game's the Thing* and Hobbs's *Playing for England* as Christmas presents. Later they kept scrapbooks of his early years playing for Yorkshire.

3

Leonard did not go to the Fulneck Boys' School because the fees would have been far beyond the means of his parents. Instead, he went in 1921 to Littlemoor Council School in nearby Pudsey. His younger cousin, Robin, did go to Fulneck School because, as the son of a Moravian minister, he could be educated there without fees. The lives of the two cousins were different in several ways. Robin had a privileged if restricting one at the Fulneck School, with crocodile walks on Sundays, shirts with stiff collars and an 'exeat' needed to go to tea with the aunts across the road. Leonard was free to roam the fields and venture into the great world of Pudsey. Each had a little to envy in the other's way of life. Something which would bring them together, indeed the whole Fulneck community of children whether at the School or not, would be the celebration in Fulneck in 1932 of the bicentenary of Moravianism in Yorkshire. Everyone had to dress up and take a part, even a rather shy sixteen-year-old on the edge of the Yorkshire 2nd XI and his cousin preparing for his School Certificate.

To have a cricket ground at one's back door and not to be able to play on it must have seemed frustrating to young Leonard, for at the Fulneck School cricket was the principal sport. Its most distinguished cricketer had been Major Booth, the son of a prosperous Pudsey grocer, who not only went on to play both for Pudsey Britannia and for Pudsey St Lawrence but became a successful all-rounder for Yorkshire and England. Major was his name and he fell in action on the Somme as a second-lieutenant. Hutton played his own cricket at Fulneck across the road in the field or up the hill behind the house on the playing fields of Fulneck Girls' School where the minister, Charles Mellowes, would give him some coaching in the evenings. He would sometimes watch the Boys' School XI and notice a curious position in the field-setting peculiar to Fulneck School. This was called a 'rampage', a sort of deep square leg or deep extra cover who would field the balls which ran down the slope out of sight on to the road.

One of Leonard's recollections of Littlemoor school was of being moved up from the seven-year-olds to the nine-year-olds by a headmaster who felt he had ability. Unfortunately, the class teacher whom he then acquired failed to rouse his interest, for he had already made up his mind that he wanted to devote his energies to playing cricket.

Cricket at the school took place in the concrete playground with a shed acting as a wicket. The other boys, such as Norman Armitage and Roland Wilkinson, would not let him bat first as the playground rules allowed you to bat until you were out, and they feared they would never get a turn. Every so often a teacher would organize a match on the field at Roker Lane against Greenside, Primrose Hill or St Joseph's Schools, and each side would make about 50 runs. In these matches, Leonard opened the batting with Roland, who would receive the advice, 'You stop 'em and I'll get 'em.' Kit was a problem but Leonard would help out by bringing along his elder brothers' old bats with the ends cut off for size. Football held little appeal for him, though it was a playground occupation in the winter months, and in any case what ambitions he had ended when his mother burnt his boots after he came home with a severe gash on his knee. At home, it was cricket all the year round if he could persuade anyone to play with him on the concrete area behind his house. Only once, as we have noticed, did he play for the Sunday School side on the field across the road: it would be playing cricket at Pudsey in the family tradition which would claim him from the age of 11 onwards. How important cricket was to Pudsey he had first realized a year or two earlier when he was taken by his father to join the thronging crowds welcoming Herbert Sutcliffe back after his successes in the MCC tour of Australia in 1924–25. Little could Leonard have known what an effect on his own life Sutcliffe would have.

He was a contented boy so long as he had his cricket bat and his weekly copy of *The Magnet*. The only thing he recalled being envious of was the Rolls-Royce driven by a local mill-owner! He attended the Moravian Church, heard Mr Mellowes's forty-minute sermons, joined the Boys' Brigade and played billiards in the Young Men's Institute. Once a year the family would go for a week in August to Morecambe, Blackpool or Whitby for a holiday. Leonard's luggage always included a bat and a surviving photograph shows a small boy in cap, blazer and long socks batting on the sands, rather formally dressed for the beach but already holding the bat the way he would hold it throughout his career. His father heard someone say, 'That lad will play for England if he goes on like that.'

Apart from such occasional visits to Lancashire, Leonard's life as a child was centred on Yorkshire, and more precisely, Fulneck. His abiding memory would be of the peacefulness, 'a place with a quality and importance of its own' and a place he remembered as a 'paradise' – the name, indeed, of one of its settlement buildings. And so it seemed when I visited Fulneck, turning off the busy road from Leeds through Pudsey to enter an oasis of calm. A highly skilled potter still continued the tradition of craftsmanship; the small museum faithfully reflected the way of life of Moravians; the minister showed me the church registers testifying to the Hutton associations; the buildings, terraces and gardens of the school looked serenely towards the sloping valley and the distant hills; the churchyard with its flat stones (a symbol that no person shall be higher than another) was an engraved reminder of the lives of six generations of Moravians in Fulneck. A picture of Fulneck proudly graced Sir Leonard Hutton's home near London and not all the splendid cricket enclosures of his later years blotted out the memory of the little sloping ground outside his front door where the Sunday School side played and where he would practice.

Fulneck was his home for twenty-three years – the years of his childhood, early successes and initial fame – until he left it on his marriage a few days after the outbreak of the second world war. He grew up as a member of that close-knit, God-fearing community which had in the past two hundred years sent out Huttons to be leather merchants and joiners, ministers and teachers, tradesmen and printers, missionaries and doctors, surveyors, and dressmakers. One Hutton was a singer, another a judge of poultry, a third emigrated to the New World. The sheer variety of their activities and talents has its appeal.

The Fulneck community has made its own contribution to the English nonconformist tradition of service, endeavour, social reform and good works. To do whatever you had to do thoroughly and to the best of your ability was a precept Leonard Hutton absorbed and adhered to throughout his life. It may be related to the determination and concentration which was so essential a feature of his batting and to the courage and commitment he displayed as captain of England. Cricket has received its input, if less spectacularly, from nonconformity as well as from the Anglican cricket-playing parson. Indeed, the first historian of Yorkshire cricket, R. S. Holmes, was a nonconformist minister.

Yet it would not be in Fulneck itself that the young Hutton would blossom as a cricketer. Fulneck and its minister of the day can claim some credit for spotting his abilities, but it would be Pudsey's responsibility to develop them. Leonard's three elder brothers, Edmund, George and Reginald, all played cricket during his childhood and beyond for Pudsey St Lawrence, a mile or so away in Tofts Road. From infancy Leonard would be taken there by his aunts while, for his sister-in-law, Mary, going to watch the club on Saturday afternoons began in the early 1920s and still continued in the late 1980s. She and her famous brother-in-law would both become life members. As a small boy Leonard would turn up for junior practices in the evenings, playing with his friends Dick Milligan, Cyril Whitely and the rest. He would take his turn mowing and rolling the outfield to make good practice wickets, and then came the day in 1927 when the eleven-year-old made his first appearance for the 2nd XI against Saltaire when the club were one short. He was sent in at No.8 and found himself facing Saltaire's fast bowler. For just a ball or two the bowler relented before bowling as well as he could to the youngster, who made 12. Two years later, at 13, he appeared for the 1st XI, a boy playing in a man's world and playing before critical spectators who expected their money's worth. Sympathy would take second place to expectations.

By this time, another Pudsey influence had become important. On the hill behind Fulneck, in Woodlands Park Road, lived the Yorkshire and England cricketer, Herbert Sutcliffe, whose own career had begun at Pudsey Britannia, and young Hutton was encouraged to go to Sutcliffe's garden and be coached on his concrete strip. One bitterly cold day in February 1930 on the recommendation of Sutcliffe and of Richard Ingham, the Pudsey St Lawrence president, Hutton reported to the Yorkshire indoor shed at Headingley, one of a large number of youngsters whom George Hirst, the foundation stone of Yorkshire coaching, would be looking at. Hirst was a legendary figure who had first played for Yorkshire in 1891 and made twenty-four Test appearances for England against Australia and South Africa. After he retired from playing, he would spend the springs in the Yorkshire shed, the summers coaching at Eton College and the early autumns coaching in countless towns and villages throughout Yorkshire; schoolboys in the afternoons and older colts till dusk. Any boy of promise had his name noted, and an invitation to appear at Headingley would follow. 'You're the boy from Pudsey, aren't you?' was his kindly greeting to Leonard. 'Keep your eyes open, and watch. You'll be all right.'

Later in the same summer Leonard took the penny bus ride to Stanningley Bottom and made his way by tram to Headingley, a fourteen-year-old lad in short trousers munching his sandwiches and cream bun and sitting spellbound in the vast ground as Don Bradman in the third Test scored 309 not out in a single day's play. Bradman's eventual total of 334 would be something for him to eclipse in eight years' time.

Leonard's visit to Headingley had come just after his fourteenth birthday, and a few days before the end of the summer term when he was legally allowed to leave school. Whatever might be his own ultimate hopes, there was no tradition in his family of playing cricket for a living, though the advice of Herbert Sutcliffe and the judgment of George Hirst seemed to make it much more than a mere possibility.

7

But his parents considered he should learn a trade, and as a first step in that direction he spent a further year at Pudsey Grammar School learning technical drawing, quantitative work and electrical work, before beginning work alongside his father in the building firm of Trickett's of Bramley and subsequently with that of Joseph Verity. It was an experience he both enjoyed and took seriously. 'I was fascinated by timber and wood, and I liked creating things. The building industry is in me,' Sir Leonard remembered. As cricket made more and more demands he was lucky to have employers who gave him time off and who would later welcome him back in the winters before the second world war. For it was in the spring of 1932 that such demands began to take on a regular pattern when Hirst arranged for the Yorkshire fast bowler, Bill Bowes, to take a serious look at him in the winter shed at Headingley to see how he could cope with pace. Bowes detected a weakness in 'over-positioning himself with his footwork' which made him vulnerable to really fast bowling. Bowes called it 'one of the best faults in the game', and felt it was his only flaw in technique. At the end of the season, Hirst turned to Bowes with the comment, 'That's been worth every bit of trouble.' Hutton's ability to learn and remember what he was told made him an apt pupil and a rewarding one to teach; indeed, there came a point when Hirst felt there was nothing more to be taught to him as a batsman, and he asked Wilfred Rhodes to come and see him as a bowler.

Meanwhile, the winter of 1932 offered cricket on a wider front. Bowes was in Australia with the MCC side under Douglas Jardine's captaincy, and on the last day of the year Hutton read in his morning paper that Bowes had bowled Bradman for a duck. It was that dramatic event and the achievements of Harold Larwood and Bill Voce which sowed the seeds of the preference for fast bowlers which he would display as England captain twenty years later.

2

Yorkshire Apprentice
1933–36

'He may safely be entrusted with the task of regaining for
England records which Bradman has made his own.'
J. M. Kilburn, *Yorkshire Post*, 1934

There used to be a music hall joke in the Theatre Royal, Leeds in which
the comedian asked, 'Where is Leeds?' to receive the reply, 'Near
Pudsey.' Set between Leeds and Bradford, Pudsey became a municipal
borough at the turn of the century. Its fine parish church overlooks the
federation of Lowtown, Fartown and Chapeltown and its Georgian
and Victorian buildings, in whose creation William Hutton played a
part, are a testimony to its growth in the eighteenth and nineteenth
century.

The origins of cricket in Pudsey lie deep. In the early nineteenth
century the game was played in the streets and lanes with a tub-leg as
a bat, a stone called a hob serving as wickets and a ball made from a
taw (or marble) covered with a band. From these small beginnings
emerged a Pudsey team good enough to play the travelling All-
England XI in 1863 and lose by only seven runs. This side, begun by
William Clarke in 1846, did a great deal for the evolution of cricket in
the north of England. His XI would play against odds, travelling long
and uncomfortable journeys by train or coach-and-four and attracting
large crowds wherever they played. They were the missionaries of
the game to areas where it was primitive and undeveloped. As H. S.

Altham wrote in his *History of Cricket*, 'It was every cricketer's ambition to see them play, still more to be chosen to do battle with them, and a double-figure with the bat, or a wicket or two with the ball against the acknowledged champions of England, would win a man local renown for ever.' It might, indeed, win him rather more, for Clarke was always on the look-out for fresh recruits to join his professional side at £6 a match. Professionalism was by then becoming established in Yorkshire as a whole, and the county club dated from 1863. To the Yorkshire side, some thirty years later, went the first recruit from Pudsey, John Tunnicliffe, who would score over 20,000 runs for the county and share in a partnership of 554 with John Brown against Derbyshire – a record that Sutcliffe and Percy Holmes would beat in 1932.

Tunnicliffe had been a Pudsey Britannia player. In his day the rivalry between Britannia and St Lawrence became symbolized by geography, one the club for the low-enders in the town, the other for the top-enders. In 1912 the St Lawrence Club and the Britannia one both joined the recently formed Bradford League and the town of Pudsey thus associated itself with something which quickly became an essential part of the Northern and Midland cricket tradition. There was nothing in the south of England to compare with the stern endeavour, massive support and professionalism of leagues such as those established in Bradford, Lancashire or Birmingham. There evolved a cricket as demanding and rigorous for its performers as the claims of the mill-owner from Monday to Saturday; as stern and embracing as the voice of the pastor on Sunday. On the cricket field on a Saturday afternoon, no less a discipline and commitment was claimed and voiced by those who came in their thousands. The crowd would watch with a critical eye, make generous contributions to those who performed well and follow the fortunes of each other's teams in the evening editions. The leagues were a testing-ground of technique and temperament with the light of local publicity perpetually upon them.

It was into such a tradition that Leonard Hutton came when he joined Pudsey St Lawrence. In 1933 he became a regular member of the 1st XI, the year his brother Edmund was club captain, and he opened the batting with the former Yorkshire professional, Edgar Oldroyd. It was said that the older man was not too keen on going out to bat with such a youngster but soon accepted Hutton's worth. From Oldroyd, Hutton learnt the art of playing spin-bowling, of batting on a sticky wicket and of defence. Later, whether as partner or observer, he would learn from other great players such as Sutcliffe and Walter

Hammond. He had the ability to take what he wanted from the technique of others and make it his own.

The local press soon saw Leonard Hutton as one of the most promising batsmen in the Bradford League and Pudsey saw him as a future Tunnicliffe or Sutcliffe, especially after his performance in the first round of the Priestley Cup match with Bradford. In an afternoon punctuated by stoppages for rain, he batted through for 70 not out until the compulsory suspension of the innings at 153 for 4. Bradford scored 215 and the rules allowed Pudsey to resume their innings. Leonard secured for his side a victory by one wicket and for himself a score of 108 not out. The *Yorkshire Post* called it:

> a brilliant century: In Pudsey's final bid for victory, almost everything depended on Leonard Hutton, so frail did his partners prove to be, but he shouldered his responsibility like a veteran while batting with almost stoic composure in most exciting circumstances.

There, of course, is a clue to the future. Hutton's 'stoic composure' matched by economy of movement would be the foundation stone of many a long innings in years to come. The *Pudsey and Stanningley News* gives us the excitement of the last moments:

> Leonard cut the first ball of a new over from Douglas to the boundary. This made the scores equal and a great shout went up. Still the Saints were not out of danger. He had to be extremely careful with the next four deliveries. The last ball of the over he stopped with his bat. It went less than a couple of yards. 'Come on!' he shouted to his partner. Like a flash they were across the pitch. Pudsey had won! A still greater shout went up. The Pudsey supporters rushed on to the field to congratulate the two heroes, and particularly young Hutton who had batted throughout the innings for 108 not out, and he was carried to the pavilion shoulder high!
>
> It was a great day for Hutton. He played a magnificent defensive innings for over four hours, and though the rate of scoring was slow, he could not have served his side better. He never gave a single chance, and altogether he made thirteen boundary hits, including one out of the field.

A few days later on Bank Holiday Monday, 5 June, Pudsey and indeed all Yorkshire had something else to celebrate when Lancashire, the old enemy, were overwhelmed in the Roses match, succumbing for 93 and 92 to Bowes, George Macaulay and Hedley Verity and losing by an innings in two days. Yorkshire had won all eight of their County Championship matches and were far in front in the table.

Their only defeat over a 12-month period was by 19 runs at the hands of a strong Cambridge University side. But one young sixteen-year-old Yorkshireman might feel that cricket was a cruel game in which the luck seemed to go to every other Yorkshireman but him, for Leonard Hutton had followed up a duck on his 2nd XI debut for the county against Cheshire two weeks earlier, by another that Bank Holiday against Lancashire in the 2nd XI Roses match. His future Test partner, Cyril Washbrook, made 202 not out. He had another chance in the second innings when he made 41 not out, his first runs in the second-class County Championship and his first runs for Yorkshire. Later that week he made 11 against Staffordshire and got a press notice for his fielding.

On Saturdays he continued to appear for Pudsey and it was nearly three weeks before Yorkshire again required his services in the home and away matches against lowly Denbighshire, bottom of the table and due to lose all their matches in the season. His score of 86 not out at Brighouse in a tenth-wicket partnership of 72 with Leslie Heaton brought comments which were the first significant pointers to his future. The *Daily Mail* hailed him as 'another star from Pudsey' and the *Yorkshire Post* commented that he was 'now seriously being spoken of as Herbert Sutcliffe's successor'. A week later, in the return game at Colwyn Bay, played at Rydal School, he scored 128 off the Denbighshire bowling and made another century in the same week against Cheshire. These had been the first two matches in which he had opened for Yorkshire and his position as a potential opening batsman for the county may be dated from that point.

Against Staffordshire at Bramall Lane he faced the veteran England bowler, Sydney Barnes, now turned sixty, and he was 69 not out when rain ended the match. He had faced Barnes, said the *Leeds Mercury*, 'with a confidence and correctness which could hardly have been surpassed by Sutcliffe himself' – a Barnes 'whose bowling was little short of miraculous in conception'. In four matches Hutton had scored 401 runs for two dismissals and J. M. Kilburn in the *Yorkshire Post* featured him in an article on cricketers who had had a good week with the bat. He opened the batting against Durham, playing at Headingley only three years after he had been a schoolboy in the crowd watching Bradman score his 334 there, and he delighted in his first experience of batting on this and two other great grounds of the North of England, Park Avenue, Bradford and Old Trafford, Manchester. Runs came on each occasion though in the Lancashire match a blow on the nose caused by the ball ricocheting off the wicket-keeper would give him pain for years. Despite that memory, he would always enjoy visits to pre-war Old Trafford for the Lancashire hotpots and rice pudding served at lunch.

During an interval in the 2nd XI programme he travelled to Leicester as twelfth man for Yorkshire. He was able to watch Sutcliffe, Arthur Mitchell and his 2nd XI colleague, Cyril Turner, score substantially in Yorkshire's total of 550. And he learnt, in no uncertain terms, that Yorkshire's twelfth man was not expected to carry out the drinks in black shoes. By beating Northumberland, when Hutton made a half-century, Yorkshire's 2nd XI qualified to play Norfolk for the Minor Counties' title. As a result, for the first time ever, a county won both the 1st XI and the Minor Counties Championship, Hutton's contribution to the 2nd XI triumph being 699 runs for an average of 69.90. In lovely September sunshine the young Yorkshire side achieved a victory over Norfolk by 9 wickets; Hutton made exactly fifty, in his two innings together, and he had played for the first time in the same match as two Test colleagues of the future, Bill Edrich and Norman Yardley. But Yorkshire delight at the double triumph was set aside seven weeks later when a clerical error was found which revealed that the 2nd XI had lain 3rd, and not 2nd, in the championship and therefore had had no right to challenge Norfolk for the title. That privilege should have gone to Wiltshire but by late October it was too late to stage a new match. The 2nd XI championship of 1933 was, therefore, declared 'Not Decided' at a meeting at Lord's in December. Hutton's sympathies were for his county captain Colonel Raleigh Chichester-Constable, who had won the devotion of his largely teenage side. Chichester-Constable was a natural leader besides being a man with a personal record of bravery, for he had won a DSO in Flanders and would win another at Dunkirk. Within the context of Yorkshire cricket he knew what he was expected to do with his young players in the 2nd XI – to take them a stage beyond club cricket, to introduce them to the wider strategy of the game and to prepare them for the social relationships involved in living with other professionals on a day-by-day basis, week in and week out.

An assessment of Hutton at the end of the 1933 season may be made. He was still only seventeen, although a surprising number of newspapers spoke of him as eighteen. He was singled out by the *Yorkshire Post* as the most prominent of the county's young players, with a remarkably sound defence but some reluctance 'to open out at all when the state of the game demands it'. Opinion was near-unanimous that he would emerge as Sutcliffe's opening partner, especially as Yorkshire had ended the contract of Holmes. But some critics suggested that he should be kept in the wings for a year or two and that Sutcliffe should see through the immediate future with support from stalwarts such as Mitchell and Wilfred Barber. Indeed, said one critic, 'it is much too early to discuss him as the possible successor to Percy Holmes, despite his displaying the temperament and qualities of a potential first-wicket batsman in that grade.'

Pudsey St Lawrence thought differently. At the Annual General Meeting in the following February (1934) a speaker saw 'one of our own boys as the natural successor to Percy Holmes' and the chairman, Alderman Ingham, looked forward 'to next season and seeing Leonard in the first team for Yorkshire'. Only the secretary, Reginald Hutton, with family modesty, forbore from singing his praises, simply giving the statistic that Leonard had come second in the batting figures with 258 runs for an average of 23.45. Pudsey, typical of any local club, flourished because of the enthusiasm of its members and their supporters. The meeting reported that whist drives, draws and 'the efforts of the ladies' had raised £90 14s 7d and (how often has one heard it?) members were asked to give the ladies better support than they had done in the past. Among items of expenditure which the club incurred were the £157 paid to Oldroyd, the professional. Cricket equipment cost £21, printing £26 and wages and insurance £61. £110 had come from gate money and £82 from members' subscriptions, with a further £14 outstanding. Pudsey St Lawrence CC lost £10 16s 10d on the season. The meeting closed with plans for a bazaar in 1934 and high hopes of rising above their current place of 11th in the League.

Yorkshire, like Pudsey, viewed the coming season with optimism, although John Nash, the Yorkshire secretary (and a Pudsey man himself), writing in the Handbook for 1934, recognized that the victorious side which had won three championships running would undergo some change. Moreover, speaking at a pre-season lunch to the press, Brian Sellers, the captain, indicated that the visit of the Australians would deplete Yorkshire in over a dozen fixtures. He saw this as an opportunity for the younger players. Of those younger players, Hutton's name was again the most frequently quoted. In the event, only Yardley, of three other Colts, would achieve any great distinction – Kenneth Davidson deserted cricket for badminton in the United States, Turner (a 2nd XI stalwart) would prove a solid 1st XI batsman until just after the war, and William Harbord would remain a dependable 2nd XI amateur. Those who advocated Hutton had the evidence of his youth, temperament and record on which to base their judgments. 'Dare one suggest,' asked the *Daily Dispatch*, 'there is another Sutcliffe at hand?' George Hirst himself wrote in March to Lord Hawke, the Yorkshire president, indicating that he had discovered 'a very likely young cricketer' and he told a *Leeds Mercury* reporter that he was also impressed with Hutton as a leg-break bowler who flighted the ball with ease and could bowl a googly. When the twelve players were announced for the southern tour which would begin Yorkshire's season, there was no surprise at the selection of Hutton who, said the *Yorkshire Post*, 'would be observed with interest by the many good judges who had been impressed with his promise'.

Fenner's at the beginning of May can often be bitterly cold with a wind from the Urals sweeping across the North Sea and the flatlands of East Anglia. In recent years it has also proved cold comfort for young men thrust into the arena of first-class cricket against county players looking for early runs and wickets. Fifty years ago, the disparity was less evident; the Cambridge University side could anticipate two or three wins a season and, as we have seen, the XI of 1933 had defeated Yorkshire. But the side of 1934 had lost Kenneth Farnes and its strength lay in batting rather than bowling. Yorkshire won the toss, untypically the day was as hot as midsummer, and the undergraduates toiled as Sutcliffe, with the 120th century of his career, scored 152, Mitchell got 61, Barber 103 and Morris Leyland (always known to cricketers as Maurice) 51. Then came Hutton, the youngest player to appear for Yorkshire since Hirst in 1889, to make a debut in first-class cricket as statistically unflattering as he had done in second-class cricket a year earlier. As the *Yorkshire Post* put it, 'it may have been an understandable anxiety to get off the mark that sent him scampering down the pitch for a run that was not there'. Hutton had made no allowances for the speed with which Jack Davies would run him out from cover point – the same Davies who would leap to fame a week later by bowling Don Bradman for nought and who would, over fifty years later, become President of MCC. There was some consolation in getting his first wicket in first-class cricket.

The real consolation, however, came a week later on a hot day in the Parks when he scored a not out half-century against Oxford University. *Wisden* wrote, 'Sutcliffe had as opening partner a lad of 17 who came through his test so satisfactorily that he stayed three hours without making a mistake. Straight drives brought him most of his runs'. The critic in the Bradford *Telegraph and Argus*, writing his piece at the start of the day when Hutton was not out nought overnight wrote: 'I am not given to hysterics of exaggeration, but I will say that, given ordinary normal development with the years, Hutton is certain to play for England.' Later on, when Hutton had completed his half-century, he added: 'A very impressive innings indeed, in which one is justified in ignoring the clock, and an innings which completely vindicated everything I wrote about him earlier today.'

After a 2nd XI appearance in the Roses match, Hutton made his debut in a county championship match against Warwickshire at Edgbaston. Conditions were wet and cold and the crowd was sparse, but the occasion allowed him to make another half-century and to dismiss both the Warwickshire openers, taking a wicket with his second ball in championship cricket. The press was generous in giving him head-lines such as 'Memorable Day for Hutton' and 'Yorkshire's budding all-rounder', though the *Birmingham Post* thought that he scored too slowly in the circumstances of the game. Analysing his batting, Kilburn in the *Yorkshire Post* commented on his positioning, his defence and his ability to select the right ball to play – all qualities which he would retain throughout his career. His bowling also commanded attention for 'his exceptional ability to flight the ball, and the accuracy of his length'. Not everyone thought so. Gerald Pawle, the Northern correspondent of *The Cricketer* wrote, after watching him against Lancashire 2nd XI at Old Trafford:

I think he would do well to stick to his batting. Indeed, he does not consider himself a bowler though he possesses a peculiar aptitude for flighting the ball. However, his mentors are convinced that they have found in him the leg-break bowler Yorkshire have been looking for. He showed at Old Trafford a woeful lack of length, and when all is said and done, it doesn't matter a great deal how cunningly one flights a long hop.

By now he was beginning to meet many of the established players of the day, besides, of course, the Yorkshire side. Warwickshire introduced him to Bob Wyatt – a cricketer of courage and determination – but the experience to savour was seeing a Frank Woolley century at Headingley. It was batting he admired and felt it almost a crime to take the great left-hander's wicket himself. But take it he did before sharing in a first-wicket partnership of 267 with Barber, to which he contributed 70. After the match, the Kent captain, Percy Chapman, joined in the general appreciation of Hutton's patience and control but looked for more variety in his strokeplay. *The Times* correspondent, the following morning, put it more caustically:

He has an astonishing amount of patience. He is indeed a little too patient and if he occasionally allowed himself a moment of human weakness he might develop a stroke or two. His innings consisted of cautious and severely circumscribed movements of a straight bat.

This critic was Dudley Carew and he would prove less generous than others towards Hutton over the next year or two. In the middle of the Kent match, Hutton played alongside Woolley in an evening game for Leyland's benefit. Gradually he was learning the demands of time, travel and obligations to colleagues which went with being a professional cricketer.

It is perhaps the moment to consider how Hutton, still a few days under eighteen, approached the awesome stronghold of the Yorkshire dressing room. In playing for the Yorkshire 1st XI he had entered a new and forbidding world. To a seventeen-year-old, however talented, its atmosphere was a stern baptism of fire. As cricketers in the great Yorkshire tradition, they were heroes to him and to every other properly brought-up youngster, but at close quarters they were men with their own peculiarities and idiosyncrasies, sharing a common bond of talent and dedication but not at all willing to open their ranks to an outsider until he had proved his worth and served his articles. How would the young Hutton cope with the caustic wit of Macaulay or the bleak austerity of Mitchell? To miss a slip catch from the one might earn no more than an invitation to be a candidate for Madame Tussaud's. To share the slips with the other was simply to be asked what right had he to be a slip-fielder. Mitchell's austerity lay in his total reluctance to award praise or encouragement. After one particular burst of sarcasm, Hutton 'gave him a wide berth. He was too hard for me'; Sutcliffe described him as 'grim as a piece of stone from Baildon Moor'.

Sutcliffe himself, the young man's near neighbour and family friend in Pudsey, would come to praise his young protégé, almost to the point of embarrassment; Hedley Verity would become one of his closest friends; Bowes, the wise counsellor would urge the Yorkshire authorities not to play the young man in the 1st XI too often; Leyland would seek him out with words of consolation after he had been run out for 0 in his first game; Sellers, the best captain of Yorkshire since Lord Hawke, would give him advice and encouragement he would value. Finally came Turner, who had toiled long and hard himself to secure a 1st XI place, and who was the member of the side appointed to look after the junior. He would take Hutton to have a meal of steak and chips and then go to the Palladium or the old Holborn Empire when Yorkshire were playing in London. The two men, both non-drinkers, would sometimes go to the cinema two or three times a week in the evening of away matches in the provinces.

Something more should be said about Sutcliffe in these years. He was a man of strong personality of whom some Committee members, let alone the young Hutton, were not a little frightened. One such member recalled the selection of sides for a Scarborough Festival match. 'So-and-so *must* play,' Sutcliffe, the professional, told the Committee; he did! He set the tone for the behaviour of Yorkshire sides on and off the field and it was his authority, even more than that of a strong captain like Sellers, which dictated standards. Woe betide the Yorkshire player who failed to wear his blazer at the appropriate times! In his last years as a Yorkshire professional he was pursuing his own business interests and he would be seen in a hotel lounge in the evening, or in the pavilion after being dismissed, writing letters with the same calm efficiency with which he batted. To him, a Yorkshire cricketer had to be better than any other cricketer not only on the field but off it. He gave to the rough diamond of Yorkshire cricket a polished edge.

From these men Leonard Hutton would learn much as he listened and watched. The folklore of the Yorkshire cricket tradition was woven into the fabric of their lives and he was expected to don the mantle of discipline, hard work and dedication. To this was added the sense of Yorkshire optimism. In the world of the 1930s in which a pessimism born of factory closures and unemployment found very real expression in the county of Yorkshire, cricket expressed its exact reverse. Yorkshire expected to win, to be the best of all counties, to have a prescribed right to the championship. There is a modern parallel in the fortunes of Liverpool and Everton football clubs in the 1980s. The experience of this superiority, so natural a part of the Yorkshire scene, would later be invaluable to Hutton when he became captain of England; not the least of his contributions in that role was to remove the inferiority towards Australia which had dogged England sides after the second world war.

Gradually, the sense of awe he felt on joining the county side gave way to the recognition of friendship and the realization that he 'belonged to a fraternity sharing a special relationship'.

The support which that fraternity could give was demonstrated a few matches after the Kent game when he made his first appearance at Lord's and made an error of judgment which led to Barber letting himself be run out rather than Hutton. Out himself moments later and fearing the worst back in the dressing room, he found at once that he had nothing to contend with but a genial smile. The match itself had an exciting finish. Middlesex were set 51 to win, but against Bowes at his fieriest Middlesex lost 6 wickets for 37 before eventually scraping home by two wickets. Bowes earlier took 6 for 17 in what was Yorkshire's first defeat by Middlesex in seven years. Hutton remembered the match as one of high drama which attracted as much public interest as the Test match currently being played at Nottingham – in which three of the regular Yorkshire side were participating.

The return of these men from the Test side sent him back to the 2nd XI to make 67 runs against Staffordshire, and their departure for the Old Trafford Test gave him a chance again against Gloucestershire at Bristol. He was seeing one by one the county grounds of England with which he would become so familiar in the following 20 years. Bristol with its marquees and tents, gleaming white in the sunshine; flags flying and farmers discussing market prices was, he realized, a different world from Leeds or Bradford. It was also a world without motorways to whisk one there. Instead, a night journey sitting up from Leeds to arrive at Temple Meads at 6 a.m. was the prelude to going out to bat at Ashley Down's Phoenix Ground. He made 39 and 0, on the second occasion being run out. Yorkshire, slipping from their customary supremacy, lost again. Sellers' prediction of the effect of Test match calls was proving uncomfortably accurate. Hutton was disappointed not to play against Hammond whom he would come to admire so greatly, both as a player and as a man, but since Hammond chose his next match at Bristol to make a double-century, it was probably just as well for Yorkshire, though it denied Hutton a lesson in the art of battling.

He was continuing to prove that he had the self-control and personal discipline to bat for a sustained length of time, though the slowness of his scoring still drew its critics. Against Surrey, for example, he shared an opening partnership of 155 in two and a half hours with Mitchell, his own contribution being 35. All the time he was observing at close quarters his partners at the other end and his own chance came against Worcestershire at the end of July, when he made his maiden hundred. At the close of play on the first day he was 75 not out and on the second day he took his score to 196. In an innings which included 3 sixes and 21 fours, he became the youngest Yorkshireman to score a century. By four runs he missed the added distinction of making it a double-century and by being last out, the honour of carrying his bat through the innings. *The Cricketer* commented that he was 'ridding himself of his ultra-slow tactics which had caused so many people to think he was lacking in strokes'.

From that innings onwards, Hutton never doubted his own abilities. Neville Cardus wrote that he was mature at an age when most brilliant beginners were merely showing promise. Telegrams of congratulations poured in, including ones from George Hirst and from the Yorkshire players engaged in Gentlemen v. Players at

Lord's. The County Committee, nurturing their young plant, promptly dispatched him to the 2nd XI for most of August, where Middlesborough, Redcar and New Brighton had their last chance to see him before he would command a 1st XI place as of right. He kept company with Yardley, still a schoolboy at St Peter's, York, and his future county and England captain. A century against Cheshire virtually ended his career in the 2nd XI – he played once in 1935 – and gave him a 2nd XI average for 1934 of 74.50. Shortly afterwards, back in the 1st XI, his season as a whole ended when he made two half-centuries against Gloucestershire at Scarborough and was twice dismissed by Tom Goddard. In the final averages he came immediately below the four pillars of Yorkshire batting, Mitchell, Sutcliffe, Leyland and Barber. He had scored over 800 runs and he had more than satisfied expectations. Yet at this stage it is worth noting that in figures the other newer players in the side, Davidson and Turner, were very close. *Wisden* guardedly recognized that he might outstrip them. The *Yorkshire Post* came out trenchantly in his favour:

> To seek faults in such a cricket prodigy savours of base ingratitude. In this eighteen-year-old batsman Yorkshire have surely found a future Colossus of the game. He may be safely entrusted with the task of regaining for England records which Bradman has made his own.

The writer, J. M. Kilburn, would over the years see Hutton more than any other journalist and he went on to emphasize that the player was under instructions 'to make use of every moment in acquiring experience' and was successfully meeting the requirement. *The Cricketer* called him 'the best batsman in England for his age' and its correspondent, Gerald Pawle, believed he had put behind him his policy of caution:

> It has been fascinating to watch the evolution of his batting style from impregnable defence and little else to a judicious blend of defence and attack marked by beautifully timed off-drives and hooks. He is never boring at the wicket owing to his superb footwork.

Despite all the success which had come his way and, by and large, a flattering press, Leonard Hutton remained a modest and unassuming young man. Pawle contributed a short character sketch of him to *The Cricketer*:

> He is the most retiring and unconceited personality that anyone could meet. The acclamation of thousands holds no apparent significance for

him and although he has tasted success to turn the heads of most boys of his age, he leaves one with the impression that his League games on Saturday afternoons are as important to him as his matches in a more exalted sphere.

Yorkshire hopes for Hutton were expressed both by Lord Hawke, the president, and Sellers, the captain, at the County AGM in January 1935, Sellers (a future England selector) going so far as to say that he would pick Hutton for Australia were a side being chosen. All this was enough to inspire Hutton to give his best in the indoor nets and to look forward to the spring southern tour. But he was not in the best of health and some breathing difficulties were related to his injury at Old Trafford two years earlier. Instead of setting off to play MCC at Lord's, he went to a nursing home to have a nose operation and, instead of opening the batting with Sutcliffe, he had to be content with reading Sutcliffe's book *For England and Yorkshire*, published in May 1935, in which was written:

We have more men that we can use but there is in Yorkshire these days one young man who is going, I firmly believe, to be called by both England and Yorkshire and that before so very long. I am especially happy about Len Hutton because he came from Pudsey but chiefly I am happy because he is a batsman of a calibre quite unusual. He is a certainty for a place as England's opening batsman. He is a marvel – the discovery of a generation. At the age of 14 he was good enough to play for most county sides. He has as many shots as a Bradman or a Hammond. His technique is that of a maestro. I shall not be surprised to find him attracting as much attention as any batsman, including the great Don, for his style and his polished skill must triumph. I have seen no likelier cricketer in the making and I have, season by season, seen the hundreds of youngsters who arrive from all parts of the county for trial at the nets.

Sutcliffe's praise of Hutton was so expansive that it has been quoted almost in its entirety. Lord Hawke, in his foreword to the book, uttered a note of caution: 'I hope he has not formed too high an opinion of Hutton's ability, whose future the cricket world is watching with intense interest.' Hutton was somewhat ill at ease with the extravagance of Sutcliffe's eulogy and privately wished he had not said it for it focused the spotlight of attention on him. Both Hawke and Sir Home Gordon, who saw the manuscript, had tried to persuade Sutcliffe to omit such a glowing testimony.

By mid-May Hutton had joined the Yorkshire side for the second half of their three-week tour, making 44 at Cambridge and an important 35 not out against Gloucestershire to help his county to an eight-wicket win in a long, low-scoring game. Conditions at Gloucester were difficult and the spin-bowlers on both sides collected the wickets after rain. He had, at last, seen Hammond bat and it was not insignificant that Hammond had seen *him* bat. But for the next month he struggled to find form and health. He realized he had returned too soon, and the demands of day-to-day cricket were over-taxing. Against Warwickshire he collapsed at the wicket and was helped off the field. It was a sad and dejected young man who caught the train to Leeds from Birmingham on Friday afternoon 14 June, 1935. Instead of travelling to London to play against Middlesex at Lord's, he was going back home to Fulneck to have a complete rest. At the same time, Denis Compton, two years his junior, was scoring stacks of runs for North Middlesex, including a century against the Indian Gymkhana while Hammond was passing the 32,000 mark in first-class cricket. The Yorkshire Committee minutes for 19 June 1935 noted that a medical report had shown nothing seriously wrong but urged the need for rest. On 6 July the Committee recorded that 'he be constantly looked after, only play on occasions and be paid £3 a week when not playing'.

Following out these precepts, the Committee did not select Hutton regularly until the very end of July, when he made three consecutive noughts, bowled or lbw to Larwood, slower than in his 1932–33 days, and to the Essex fast bowling pair, Holcombe Read and Maurice Nichols. He had the doubtful distinction of participating in Yorkshire's dismissals by Essex for 31 and 99. By mid-August he looked back sadly upon a period of two months in which he had scored a total of 73 runs for an average of 10.43. It was a time when he needed and got the support of family, friends, the Yorkshire authorities and his fellow professionals. Among these was Patsy Hendren, at the end of his own great career, who gave him so much advice and encouragement before the return Middlesex match that he made a century and Yorkshire won by an innings. Carew wrote perceptively in *The Times*: 'obviously a man born to bat and to play strokes that are perfect in technique to which he adds a patience and temperament which are almost too mature for so young a batsman. All his cricket needs is a sense of daring and imagination'. A few days later he made 92 against MCC in the Scarborough Festival. This time *The Times* remarked that he applied himself with the passionate concentration of a scientist dissecting a beetle. In his last two games he made half as many runs as all season and ended on a high note. Yorkshire were champions once again and he was told he would be in the Yorkshire party to go to

Jamaica at the end of the year. The press which had flattered him with its attentions in 1934 had had little to say at the end of the 1935 season though *The Cricketer* suggested in the Winter Annual that either he or Washbrook should go to Australia in 1936–37, as representative of the talent of the younger generation. Again *The Times* critic was less than effusive and did not include his name, in an end of season summary, in a list of potential England players.

Shortly after the 1935 season ended Hutton was at a dance with the rest of the Yorkshire side. Frank Dennis, who had played ninety matches for the county between 1928 and 1933, brought along his young sister, Dorothy, wearing her first long dress. Lady Hutton recalled the first meeting of herself and Leonard: 'Two shy young-sters, a little out of our depth, non-drinkers in an adult world'. They would meet again at Scarborough in the following year. At this stage, Leonard was much more excited at the prospect of going to the West Indies, but his delight had to be contained through four winter months till the party set sail from Avonmouth at the end of January. He consoled himself by resuming his golf, playing the various Yorkshire courses and partnering Sutcliffe in the foursome. Nor did he neglect his trade. He would be seen cycling home to Fulneck in his overalls from a day's work with Verity's, his employers.

This was the first time a Yorkshire side had toured abroad and only once before had an English county done so, when Kent went to America in 1903. In later years, when cricket touring had taken him all over the world and he had travelled and retravelled over Australia three times, Hutton still recalled that first overseas 'vision of splendid palm trees, banana trees, coconut trees, humming birds, heat-blistered buildings and wickets baked by the tropical sun'. The tour introduced him to the social requirements of the game abroad with a reception at Government House and a dinner given by the Jamaica Cricket Federation. He made 107 against Cornwall at Montego Bay and played in the three first-class matches against Jamaica, Yorkshire winning one and two being drawn. He had a best score of 59 and an average of 41 but not a lot could be read into figures which put Verity ahead of him and Sutcliffe at the bottom of the list. One experience to be savoured was the batting of George Headley, then at the height of his career; the memory of him would lead Hutton to act with a courteous gesture when the elder statesman was called out of retire-ment in Jamaica seventeen years later. And the presence as manager of George Hirst, who had first toured abroad in 1897, allowed Hutton to get to know even better the man to whom he owed so much as a coach.

Back in the mercies of an English summer, Hutton, between 2 May and 11 July 1936, travelled up and down the length of England and on sixteen occasions there were journeys either by rail, involving changes, or by road through town after town. The days began and ended in hotels and several of them were spent looking out of pavilions on grounds covered in rain. Whoever composed the Yorkshire fixture list that year must have had a fiendish imagination as players were dispatched from London to Hull and back to Oxford; from Stourbridge to Swansea and north to Sheffield; from Cambridge to Leeds and back to Birmingham; from London to Chesterfield and down to Westcliff. A friend sent Hutton a suitcase for his twentieth birthday, writing, 'You must be pretty tired at times, moving so much from one place to another but I suppose you will be getting used to it all by now.'

This was the daily rigour of county cricket, unrelenting in its demands on those who played it. He needed all his enthusiasm as the weeks went by in May and June with 15 against Oxford, a 'pair' at Worcester, single figures against Glamorgan, Kent, Lancashire, the Indians, Hampshire and Somerset. It was proving difficult to live with expectations when all Yorkshire, let alone Pudsey, had such high ones; difficult to tolerate the press when *The Times* critic wrote of his batting, 'the young Hutton grew prematurely old, perhaps he was born that way'; difficult to smile when he lost a skyer in the shadows to get hit in the face and fear for his damaged nose; difficult to cope even with the kindness of Sutcliffe who dropped to No. 5 to let him open with Mitchell against Kent and try, but without success, to break a desperate sequence.

Yet it had not begun so badly. He had started with a half-century at Lord's against MCC, though Carew in *The Times* harked back to his comments of two years earlier and accused Hutton of being 'over zealous in his hiding of those attacking strokes of which he was the fortunate possessor'. He had made 83 out of a partnership of 247 for the fourth wicket with Leyland against Essex – 'Defence was his watchword and valuable it was', approved *The Times*, at last. And there were compensations in seeing Verity take 15 wickets against Kent and his skipper, Sellers, get a double-century against Cambridge University, and in playing against his future England colleague, Denis Compton, for the first time. Hutton, in his own quiet way, took pleasure in the success of his friends and, once he got to know his opponents, warmed to the camaraderie of cricketers as a whole.

It was before the Headingley crowd against Surrey in the first week of July that the clouds lifted and the runs came. He opened with

Sutcliffe as substitute for the injured Mitchell and they put on 250 for
the first wicket. Hutton stayed and put on a further 191 with Leyland
for the third. That Saturday evening, as the crowds made way for
him and Leyland, each with a century, he returned to the pavilion 154
not out in Yorkshire's score of 413 for 2. On the Monday he added a
further 9 to complete an innings of seven hours. He had been patient,
watchful, correct, against bowlers of the calibre of Alf Gover, but
Carew in *The Times* felt the bowlers remained on top: 'it is difficult to
write of Hutton – the bowler for long intervals was allowed to feel he
was the bowler'.

A few days later on 11 July 1936, the Yorkshire Committee met and
Leonard Hutton, just turned twenty, became the youngest capped
Yorkshire player in modern times. He would become entitled to a
basic fee, £11 a match instead of £8, with an extra £4 when playing
away and a one pound win-bonus. He had made a single century in
each of the three seasons he had appeared for the 1st XI and he had
averaged around 30. He had shown promise rather than performance
as a bowler but confessed to being surprised at the big successes which
he had had. He had been exceptionally good in the field with some
sharp catches to his credit. His performances overall had been solid
rather than spectacular. But what must have weighed in his favour
was his mastery of technique and his qualities of concentration. Much
would be expected of him in the future, but something of the tension
had been relieved with the award of the cap. The apprenticeship was
over: henceforth he would be a journeyman. One day, like Hobbs and
Hammond, he would become the master craftsman.

There remained a dozen matches in Yorkshire's 1936 programme.
One of them was Yorkshire v. Nottinghamshire for Larwood's
benefit. Hutton's sympathies, as a youngster, had lain with Larwood
in the controversies of 1932–33 and he was ruefully glad for the
bowler when he bowled with something of his old pace to dismiss
both himself and Sutcliffe for four and nine respectively. The Trent
Bridge crowd showed their appreciation by contributing over £2000
to Larwood's benefit, a Nottinghamshire record. In the Roses match
at Old Trafford, ruined by rain, Hutton took 4 wickets for 49 in a
sustained spell of bowling, a performance which he bettered in
Yorkshire's final match against MCC when he had a match record of 8
wickets for 77. As he also made 58 in the match, he again ended a
season well for the holiday crowd at Scarborough. To some extent,
Yorkshire supporters in 1936 had had to take his form on trust. Apart
from the Essex and Surrey matches he had reserved his better
performances for Yorkshire on tour.

The anonymous writer of the report on Yorkshire for 1936 in the Winter Annual of *The Cricketer* summed up Hutton as 'something of an enigma'. For someone of his great natural ability 'there was still a reluctance to make full use of the strokes at his command. His negative attitude is not in the best interests of himself or of his county' and he had yet to fulfil the expectations Sutcliffe had of him. Praise, by contrast, was bestowed on his fielding and his bowling. 'He may well develop into a leg-break and googly bowler of the front rank'. Far nearer the mark, as events were to prove, had been the comments of Gerald Pawle a couple of years earlier. Hutton the batsman would excel; Hutton the bowler would atrophy through disuse.

With the first-class season behind him, he was able to enjoy a few late-summer games organized by the Gentlemen of Craven in various areas of the country. As autumn came he played golf, taking part in the annual match between cricket and golf professionals and winning the Gibson Cup, competed for by Yorkshire cricketers. He had not been picked to go to Australia, nor had he expected to be. In an article in *The Cricketer* noting the names of batsmen unlucky not to be selected, the editor, P. F. Warner, had not mentioned him. Australians would have to wait ten years to see him bat, and – it is a sobering thought – they might never have done so, for he might have been lost to cricket for good. An uncle had emigrated to the United States and set up a heating business near Boston. Since his own son had gone to Yale and embarked on a law career, the uncle hoped his nephew might emigrate and come into the business. But by 1936 Hutton had his county cap and there was no turning back. Nor would he have wished there to be. He was launched on a career which had its own status in the 1930s. The professional cricketer, as Kilburn observed, 'held a high ranking in sport' and in the sombre economic climate of the time county cricket attracted surprisingly large public support. Its performers were offered modest security (so long as they were good enough) and the more intangible rewards of glamour and publicity.

Yet it needs to be emphasized that the winning of his county cap made all the difference to Hutton. He had taken the first rung on the ladder which would enable him to leave far behind the uncapped county professional whose future – summer and winter alike – was an uncertain one. In social and economic terms, the capped professional cricketer of the 1930s was among the aristocrats of working-class society and there were players such as Sutcliffe (besides Hobbs and Hammond) whose independence of attitude, social ease, business acumen and cricketing talent would enable them to move into a middle-class milieu. Hutton would, in due course, join their ranks.

3

England Debut

1937–39

'This was a cricketer, an artist, with more than Hammond's strokes – much more.'

Neville Cardus, *Manchester Guardian*, 1939

As the season of 1937 began, Hutton had put behind him any idea of going to the United States to join his uncle, though working with wood in the winter months continued to make its appeal. Perhaps linseed oil on wood had even more appeal as he arrived at Lord's for the season's curtain raiser, Yorkshire v. MCC. Yorkshire found themselves set 406 to win and he batted virtually throughout the innings. When he was bowled by Walter Robins, soon to become England captain, he had made 161 and there remained only one wicket to fall. Yorkshire lost a grand match by 25 runs, and it was a fitting prelude to Hutton's first representative appearances at Lord's three weeks later as part of the celebrations of MCC's 150th anniversary. For the North against the South he made a century and for the Rest of England v. the MCC Australian XI of 1936–37 a half-century, though in each instance he was on the losing side. The cricket, but not the temperature, was worthy of the occasion and Cardus called it a martyrdom to watch in such petrifying weather. The cream of English cricket talent of the late 1930s was on display – the elegance of Joe Hardstaff, the technique of Hammond, the guile of Verity, the pace of Farnes, the determination of Wyatt, the potential of Compton, and the courage of Eddie Paynter, all of whom made runs or took wickets.

The enthusiasm of the Yorkshire press for Hutton's performances may be taken as read – Kilburn would always advocate his cause – but distinguished critics from elsewhere joined in. Cardus, despite his discomfort, wrote in the *Manchester Guardian* that 'a grave interference with destiny will occur if Hutton does not develop into one of the finest batsmen in the record of the game'. The broadcaster, Howard Marshall, declared 'he does his job and that is a sound enough recommendation for any man'. Once again, *The Times* was apt to damn him with faint praise: 'There is a technical question mark somewhere. Is there a possibility that young cricketers are over-coached?' *The Cricketer* described him as rigorously plodding towards an England cap.

The 'plodder' returned to the county circuit, made centuries against Worcestershire and Kent and presently faced a momentous week. On Sunday 20 June the family at Fulneck gathered nervously around the wireless in the evening. The calm, impersonal tone of the newsreader read out the England XI to play in the first Test against New Zealand and the name of L. Hutton (Yorkshire) was announced. On Monday a letter from Sir Pelham Warner (who had just been knighted) arrived inviting him to play, forbidding him to write for the press, requiring him to stay at the Great Central Hotel, offering him £20, paying his third-class rail fare and asking him to telegraph his acceptance.

From that moment onwards, the week would have no respite for Hutton and be among the most memorable of his life. He had a taste of what to expect as telegrams began to pour in at his home. He made his way to Bramall Lane past crowds streaming down Shoreham Street and John Street as though a Cup Tie was to take place on Sheffield United's ground. The match between Yorkshire, the champions almost of right, and Derbyshire, the actual reigning champions, had caught the local imagination and had something of a 'Derby' atmosphere about it. Saturday had seen 18,000 spectators and, even on a working Monday, the crowds were not a great deal less. A procession of telegraph messengers bore more telegrams to the pavilion and it was a relief for him to escape from the bustle and attention, go out with Sutcliffe and resume where they had left off at 182 on Saturday night. Soon, Hutton's 88 became a century and both were together at lunch. Shortly afterwards, Sutcliffe went, but Hutton carried on relentlessly, effortlessly to a second century and eventually to 271 not out when Yorkshire declared at 525 for 4. To the Yorkshire reporter,

Thomas Moult, writing in the *Morning Post*, he had displayed a fearlessness against speed, footwork against spin, and a cover drive than which 'few things were more lovely in present-day batmanship'.

Sutcliffe, in the pavilion, and not the least apologetic for his extravagant projections of two years earlier, murmured, 'He will be England's opening bat for the next 20 years'. Indeed, the papers on Tuesday morning harked back to Sutcliffe's book of two years ago and the *Daily Express* extended the 20 years to 25, adding that he would go to Australia four times and 'break every individual batting record for England in Test cricket'. This was the sort of pressure under which he was living as the first Test approached later in the week. Tuesday was a comparatively calm day for him as he fielded during Derbyshire's second innings and watched someone else make a century.

On Wednesday 23 June, as every Yorkshireman and most of England knew, Len Hutton was 21, an adult in law and master of his own affairs. One cartoonist depicted him with 'the key of the door' opening the England dressing room. There were more telegrams and then a hasty goodbye to his family as he drove out of Pudsey with Sutcliffe, skirting the edge of Leeds, and out on the eastern road past Castleford, Selby, Howden and along the north side of the Humber to Hull. Yorkshire won the toss and with compelling purpose Sutcliffe and Hutton moved into another century partnership and Hutton completed his third successive century. They came in to tea with the score at 315 and a birthday cake with 21 candles on the table. The cake remained uncut while the business of making runs was still to be considered. Sutcliffe suggested to Hutton they might 'go for 556' – to beat the record partnership of 555 between Sutcliffe and Holmes in 1932, about which there had always been some doubt – an unrecorded no-ball was conveniently 'found' when the scorers had calculated only 554, an equalizing of the earlier record. But Hutton was bowled by the first ball after tea, for 153. Yorkshire batted on to reach their second 500 in three days. Hutton had time to change before the cake was cut and toasts drunk at the end of the day's play.

On Thursday and Friday Leicestershire fought back and earned a draw. Hutton spent a day and a half in the field before catching an early afternoon train on the Friday to London and joining his England colleagues at the Great Central Hotel. At 11.30 next day Hutton and James Parks – the fledgling and the old pro both making their debut – went out to open the England innings against New Zealand. Half an hour later, bowled by the pace of John Cowie for nought, Hutton walked dejectedly back again. The week of high drama had ended and he was best left to his own soliloquy. The second innings on the Monday would bring his first run in Test cricket, but no more. He had begun his second-class, first-class and Test careers each with a duck.

On the eve of the Test – and what happened to him in the match itself is entirely unimportant in the context of his later Test career – Kilburn in the *Yorkshire Post* shrewdly summed up his achievements:

> Hutton in his 'teens was not a great batsman, or rather he was only a great batsman for his years, yet such was the acclamation offered him that his pedestal was already built, and there was inevitably a certain amount of disappointment when it was found that he could not stand securely upon it.
>
> He was accused of dullness, accounted strokeless because his totals were laboriously built. Here there was misconception; Hutton was never strokeless, and he had only the dullness of repetition. He appeared strokeless because, being but a boy in a world of men, he could not take command.

But the discipline had been worthwhile, patience had been rewarded and what Kilburn called the 'soulless shell of technique' had given way to batting which had broken the fetters, and a creativeness which could be accounted great. The *Observer* declared that not only should he play in the second Test but also in the third 'even if he had bagged a brace'. As for the man himself, he had survived the glare of publicity and the portents of greatness with a modesty which did him credit and a personal phlegmatism as compelling as his batsmanship. Opening a bazaar at the young people's day at the Moravian Church in Fulneck, he paid tribute to the steadying influence of his Moravian upbringing 'which helped me to keep cheerful in times of adversity as well as days of success'. Not every young man, even in the 1930s when one supposes a stricter code of morality and obligation prevailed than in the 1980s, would have been able to tell an audience of his own generation that 'the country has a right to expect good service from young people in the churches as well as on the cricket field' and to assume the responsibilities which earlier generations had done. Occasions such as this and his attendance at sportsmen's services, in which he would read the lesson and occasionally say a few words from the pulpit, were becoming another part of his public life.

Meanwhile, he put the Test Match behind him with a century against Essex which tempted the *Daily Express* columnist, William Pollock, into a limerick:

> There was a young player called Hutton
> Who for runs was a terrible glutton;
> He failed in the Test
> But today was a pest
> To all of the bowlers they put on.

Against the New Zealand bowlers in Yorkshire's match a fortnight later he scored a century in conditions punctuated by rain. Then at Old Trafford, in the second Test, he scored the century that had been foretold on his behalf for so long by so many. It was, said *The Times*, 'a good enough innings'. He opened with Charles Barnett, they put on a century for the first wicket and E. H. D. Sewell, nearing the end of a long career as a journalist, commented: 'I like the look of our opening pair. We want no more reshuffle. Duck or a hundred partnership, in the name of common sense let us stick to this partnership until it lets us down badly.'

Not everyone agreed with Sewell. There was some mild advocacy for Sutcliffe (last an England player in 1935) to return to the side on the grounds that Hutton batted better when his mentor was at the other end, that Sutcliffe himself was still good enough and that a stable partnership would ensue. Kilburn looked at it another way. Hutton had learnt so much from his master that in his own person 'autumn and spring were wonderfully blended and blossom and fruit had become indistinguishable'. Sir Leonard's own view, in retrospect, was that he was sometimes glad to get away from Sutcliffe: 'I was terrified of him. He was a formidable influence.' In the event Sutcliffe was not brought back but the Hutton-Barnett partnership would last only for four matches. It would never be Hutton's luck to establish an alliance as entrenched as that of Hobbs and Sutcliffe until he was joined by Washbrook in 1946; in the eight Test matches in which he played before the war he had six different partners.

Just before the third Test, Hutton reminded the cricket world that he was a bowler as well. After taking four Leicestershire first innings wickets for 25 runs in 9 overs, he was brought into the attack again in Leicestershire's second innings when Leicestershire, with 8 wickets in hand, needed to bat for 100 minutes to save the match. On a wicket with some dust, he turned the ball enough to beat the bat and took 6 wickets for 76, bowling 36 continuous overs to give Yorkshire victory in the last over of extra time. In the third Test, at The Oval, he scored only 12 in a three-day match reduced to two by rain. England's collapse to 36 for 3 was a tribute to a New Zealand side who had seemed all summer rather better than their results suggested.

Then he travelled north overnight to play against Glamorgan at Scarborough. There he renewed his acquaintanceship with Dorothy Dennis. Dorothy came from Wykeham, a village near Scarborough. She had won a scholarship to the Girls' High School and came from a family where books were important (her father would buy them at auctions) and where cricket mattered. From now onwards she and Leonard would meet from time to time: not very often because they worked and lived in different places. Roland Wilkinson, his schoolfriend at Littlemoor, was now a bus driver and he recalled Leonard putting Dorothy on the bus from Pudsey to Leeds: 'Look after her, Roland.' Some fifty years later, Lady Hutton confessed that she saw little enough of him but she knew he 'was worth waiting for'.

After Scarborough came more travelling and retracing his steps back to The Oval for a match crucial to the 1937 Championship in which Yorkshire had been pursued for the title all summer by Middlesex. He became the seventh Yorkshireman ever to score 2000 runs in a season purely for the county. The confidence gained by so much run-making led him to bat in the Scarborough Festival later in a way appropriate to the occasion – and perhaps conscious that Dorothy was watching! For H. D. G. Leveson Gower's XI against the MCC 1936–37 Australian side he and Sutcliffe put on their ninth century partnership of the season and Hutton was able to use the bowling of his county colleague Verity, opposing him, as an opportunity to gain more experience. Finally came the match in which Middlesex, the runners-up, challenged Yorkshire, the champions, to a four-day match at The Oval. In spite of Lord Hawke's disapproval, as setting a precedent besides being linked to a wager between the two captains, the match went ahead and raised over £700 for charity. Hutton scored his tenth century of the summer and won particular praise from the former England captain, Charles Fry, for the way he dealt with leg-break bowlers. He was 'one of the best of the younger generation seen for many a day', a view confirmed by his inclusion in *Wisden*'s Five Cricketers of the Year – all the other four chosen were long-established players much older than he.

Hutton began the season of 1938 where he had left off the year before and he felt assured and confident. He scored centuries against both Universities, making 180 at Cambridge, the highest score ever by a Yorkshire player against the University. Curiously the bowler who gave him most trouble was his county colleague, Yardley, the University captain. His 93 not out against Essex was, said *Wisden*, 'magnificent and without a bad stroke'. He batted right through the innings, making the winning hit with fifteen minutes to spare before a dash from Ilford to Paddington to catch the evening train to Gloucester. On the same train were the Gloucestershire side, their opponents of the next day, who had just lost to Middlesex at Lord's with even less time to spare and had caught the train still in their white flannels. The Middlesex-Gloucestershire encounter had seen a stand of 304 between Edrich and Compton, a promise of what would happen so often in the future.

A third century, against Sussex, displayed that astonishing maturity which had been his from the start, agreed several critics. It was followed by rather a lifeless Test trial played in bitter weather. Hutton and a new partner, Edrich, put on a century for the first wicket for England v. The Rest. Immediately after, the Roses match took place at Bradford and Hutton was introduced to the former Yorkshire and England cricketer, Bobby Peel, who had been a contemporary of W. G. Grace and had appeared in twenty Test matches in the 1880s and 1890s. The two men, sixty years apart in age, chatted on the pavilion balcony and Peel gave him advice on the role of an opening batsman: 'Wait for a loose ball. Once you think about getting quick runs you are finished.' Hutton was honoured and grateful though, in a sense, Peel was preaching to the converted. Hutton's interpretation of what was expected of a No. 1 was thoroughly understood by himself, if not always by the press. No one could have accused him of taking risks or throwing caution to the winds.

So to Trent Bridge, the Australians, and an England side captained by Hammond, now an amateur. Edrich and Compton appeared together in a Test for the first time, and Paynter and Stan McCabe both scored double-centuries. There were, indeed, seven separate centuries in the match and Hutton and Barnett set the tone by scoring one each in an opening partnership of 219, the highest for England against Australia in England. Hutton, said *Wisden*, 'was very sure of himself . . . He summed up the length of every delivery to a nicety and three fieldsmen close to the bat did not have the least chance to snap up'. He offered, wrote *The Times* critic, 'a prim and proper answer to every question the Australians set him'. Cardus in the *Manchester Guardian* called it an innings 'intelligent, as old as the hills and technically correct'. Perhaps what distinguished Hutton in 1938 from the year before, successful as it had been, was the quality of self-confidence, not only as a cricketer but as a person able, he said, 'to enjoy the good fellowship and the fun' of Test cricket. He was, of course, no longer the 'new boy' and five fresh faces would appear in the England side in 1938.

The second Test, as had the first, ended in a draw. It was a match played during a brief period of beguiling calm in the troubled European political scene. On the Saturday the largest crowd ever to come to Lord's led the authorities to reduce the playing area slightly so that spectators might sit on the ground. The newspapers carried pictures of the British and Italian fleets lying together in Valletta harbour, Malta. One caption read, 'Peace and strength blend in harmony: the friendliness of two great nations'. The running of Sidney Wooderson and the tennis of 'Bunny' Austin caught the public imagination and Hammond chose the occasion to score 240 in an innings which, said *The Times*, 'can seldom have been surpassed'. It was Hammond's finest hour. Never again in the atmosphere of stern, competitive cricket would he exercise such an unrelenting dominance and display such captivating elegance.

Hutton scored only 4 and 5 and took what consolation he could in watching Hammond from the pavilion. They had yet to have a great partnership together but there was no one from whom Hutton was more ready to learn. 'Hammond taught by simply showing', Hutton would declare. At least he had watched batting fit for a king and been presented to King George VI who had visited the match. One day he would meet heads of state and statesmen and women as a business-man. This first meeting with royalty, achieved because of his cricket, remained 'a moving experience'.

There followed a spell of nearly two months in which he could do scarcely more than look back on the memories of the early part of the season. He did little against the Australians at Sheffield in a match attended by 35,000 spectators, and sat in the pavilion at Old Trafford for the third Test while it rained so persistently that the match never began. He made a half-century in the first defeat of the Players by the Gentlemen since 1914 and broke a finger at Lord's on a wicket so dangerous that he, Paul Gibb and Leyland were all unable to bat or forced to retire in the second innings. This was the supreme disappointment for, on the next day, the England side for the Headingley Test was to be announced and 'I was on the verge of playing in a Test match at Leeds and batting there with my people looking on'. Not for another nine years would that happen and he would then make a century. For the moment his world had collapsed around him and he was the desolate observer of a Bradman century, an

England side which did not really bat at Test level after No. 6, and an England defeat.

He was fit by the fifth Test, though extremely out of practice. He had missed seven county matches through the injury to his finger and had made about a hundred runs in all since mid-June. Although the Ashes were not at stake – still firmly in Australian hands – there was the possibility of drawing the series and, in any case, it would be the last occasion for four years when English crowds could expect to see an Australian Test side. With Europe (in Winston Churchill's words) 'confronted with a programme of aggression, unfolding stage by stage' many wondered, indeed, whether there would be an Australian visit in 1942. The real enthusiasts had set up camp the night before outside The Oval and by 6 a.m. there were long queues at each entrance. Although thousands poured in the moment the gates were opened, the all-night vigil had not been necessary and the ground was never full. It was, after all, the first day of the English football season.

Bradman, loser of three tosses running, lost again and Hutton and Edrich opened the England innings, Barnett rather surprisingly having been replaced. Yorkshire had five representatives in the side and there would be a Yorkshireman at the wicket the entire innings. Edrich was lbw at 29 and Leyland joined Hutton. Both gave a stumping chance and both were there at the end of the day. Leyland, in the last of his forty-one Test appearances, went on to make 187 and Hutton would eventually be dismissed for 364. He and Leyland established an England second-wicket record of 382 which still (1988) stands. England declared at 903 for 7 and dismissed the Australians for 201 and 123. Both Bradman and Jack Fingleton were injured, Australia batted with nine men, and England won by an innings and 579 runs – the greatest margin ever between the two countries. Such are the well known statistics.

Hutton's innings fulfilled all the attributes of skill, concentration and endurance so often credited to him, and he reached the pinnacle of endeavour. If the press were lost for words, they hid the fact successfully enough in column upon column of reporting. Some day, wrote one reporter, 'Hutton will tell the full story of his Oval innings and give a slight idea of the mental and physical strain it imposed'. Eleven years later he did so in his *Cricket is My Life*, which provides a narrative account of the innings but gives relatively few indications – beyond mentioning sleepless nights – of its impact upon him. Much later, in his *Fifty Years in Cricket*, he looked back more thoughtfully to the events of the Oval Test in 1938: 'As my innings developed, it was obvious that something out of the ordinary was in the offing', and he paid especial tribute to the way in which Verity had nursed him through the various intervals:

> The very kindly and wise Verity made it his duty to stay with me while I nibbled at a sandwich and sipped tea. We both knew that the most likely way I could lose my wicket was by sheer fatigue or by a lapse of concentration. His quiet, natural dignity was an immense source of strength to me throughout those long hours.

On the Sunday, when Hutton was 160 not out, Verity took him down to Bognor Regis to have lunch with a friend and – by way of a change – play cricket on the beach. On the Monday, tension around The Oval increased as the great wall of the innings was industriously built, and individual Anglo-Australian records began to be passed – Hammond's 240 at Lord's earlier in the season and Reginald Foster's 287 at Sydney in 1903. Yet, throughout the day, observers noted, he displayed an almost uncanny calmness and assurance.

Once he had reached his 300 on the Monday evening an appeal against the light was upheld. Hutton was enticed up to the commentary box by Howard Marshall and (for a fee of three guineas) commented on how peaceful The Oval looked without the spectators. 'I am looking forward to a good night's rest so that tomorrow I may be able to carry on with the good work. But you know it only takes one ball to get the best batsman out.' The next morning the *Daily Mail* cast him in the role of the clean-limbed young Englishman: 'a healthy and charming young man. And as modest and unself-conscious a product of England's greatest summer game as ever one could hope to meet'.

He had not slept well and he approached the Tuesday, as he recalled, not so much as someone chasing a record for its own sake but in the enormous recognition of what was expected of him by his well-wishers. 'I felt I had gone too far by then to let everyone down.' More than anything, telegrams – at one point arriving at the rate of one a minute – had shown him how much the public had identified itself with his innings. That which gave him greatest pleasure had come from the eighty-nine-year-old mother of Foster, whose record he had eclipsed.

So the anguish of pursuing the last 35 runs began. The Australians gave nothing away with both Leslie Fleetwood-Smith and Bill O'Reilly keeping a good length and the whole side fielding with a keenness that belied the 600 or so runs which had already been made. O'Reilly had scarcely bowled a bad ball all match and Bradman's fielding had been magnificent. After an hour Hutton was 321 not out. When he was 331 he missed a no-ball and some minutes passed before he hit the four which took him past Bradman's record. Bradman, who had been fielding close to the bat, 'beat everyone in the race to shake my hand and could not have been more generous in his praise'. As the players crowded round and the celebration drinks came out, Hutton raised his cap to the crowd on either side of the ground. Minutes later he left behind Hammond's 336 against New Zealand and then Bobby Abel's 357 in 1899, the highest score made at The Oval. At half past two he was caught by Lindsay Hassett off O'Reilly for 364, having batted for 13 hours 20 minutes. By contrast with the player of today whom custom expects to walk back to the pavilion savouring the applause he has earned, Hutton ran the last part of the way back. He had been at the wicket while 770 runs were scored and it had been an endurance test matched perhaps only by that of James Aylward who batted for Hambledon against All-England in 1777 from Wednesday afternoon till Friday evening. More seriously, he had pushed Adolf Hitler and Neville Chamberlain, the great names of contemporary political history, to the back pages. The Oval had temporarily displaced Munich. Hutton's jocular remark to Dorothy that he was being more talked about than Mrs Simpson had more than a grain of truth. Not since the Abdication crisis involving Edward VIII had the thoughts of millions throughout the British Empire been so centred on one person. 'The Empire holds its breath', said the Movietone News commentator as the target was approached. Assumptions such as these may be tested on the evidence of the papers of the day, and two examples given of what may be thought of as the 'imperial' approach to Hutton's achievement. The *Leeds Mercury* wrote:

> Foreign commentators sometimes laugh at our devotion to a game when there are so many harassing world affairs that call for England's attention. It is a fair reply that the spirit of Drake lives among us. We can win our game and still have time to defeat the Spanish Armada or whatever has taken its place today. England is not weakened but stimulated by his superb demonstration. Young England will emulate his steadiness in the cricket field and in those other fields where the spirit of cricket has stiffened British sinew and resolve.

And the opportunity was too good for Cardus to miss in the *Manchester Guardian*:

> As the ground became resonant with the cheering, the thought occurred to me that it was being heard far and wide all over the Empire. People

walking down Collins Street in Melbourne would hear it and it would roar and echo in Kandy, Calcutta, Allahabad and Penang; they would hear it in the Cocos Islands and join in, and on liners patiently going their ways on the seven seas, they would hear it too and drink Hutton's health.

Even the American *Time* magazine featured his performance. In England, as the *Daily Express* put it, 'clerks and managers in the offices, master and man in the factories, shared in the celebrations'.

Among the spectators at The Oval was the poet Edmund Blunden, whose 'good luck' it was to be there. He saw Hutton's innings as a textbook on the art of batting, 'his body and his bat were as truly one as love itself'. Cricket, at Anglo-Australian level, was no 'sweet, sentimental eclogue' but raised by a 'thousand tongues of fame and rumour' to the level of an international crisis. The youthful Hutton repelled thirteen hours of temptation to play an innings 'patient, serious yet charming'. Here was the articulate voice of someone in the crowd, not the cricket writer hastily composing his piece for a demanding editor but the biographer of Leigh Hunt and Shelley, a composer of verse who worshipped cricketers with unfettered adoration.

In Yorkshire, the *Evening Post* opened a shilling fund for him. In Pudsey his father was at work building a telephone exchange at Laisterdyke and people in nearby houses had kept him in touch with the score. His mother, and the whole of Pudsey, never turned their wirelesses off. Dorothy was working at the time at Marshall & Snelgrove's in Bond Street, Leeds. She saw the score mounting in the newspaper placards in the *Yorkshire Post* office as she passed by. On the Tuesday afternoon, when she left work for home, the press crowded the staff entrance and pursued her to her aunt's home where she stayed. The next day the manager decided she should leave by the normal shop entrance to avoid continuing press attention. Complete strangers shook each other by the hand, the Mayor of Pudsey sent him a telegram every 50 runs and the parish church rang a peal of 364 changes, one of the ringers being a brother of the earlier Pudsey and Yorkshire cricketer, Major Booth. Someone counted thirty-two boys and twenty-four girls out playing cricket till dusk in the street in Fulneck in which Hutton lived. Reporters packed the single street which is Fulneck knocking at the doors of any members of the Hutton family whom they could find. His sister-in-law, Mary, recalled being asked endless questions and she remembered his mother saying, 'If it happens again I hope he's married by then.' A few miles from Fulneck, at Harewood House, the Princess Royal, daughter of King George V, had been 'thrilled at Hutton's wonderful innings' and wrote as much in a letter to Sir Pelham Warner: 'How I wish I had been at The Oval. However it was most exciting listening to the wireless and one felt one knew what was going on.'

One turns to the technical judgement upon the innings. Cardus, writing in *The Field*, commented:

> Though he scores slowly, his innings was always interesting to the connoisseur. He has a lovely forward style, quick and elegant footwork and he lends the bloom of wristwork to his strokes.

Wilfred Rhodes, in the *Yorkshire Post*, declared:

> When stamina is blended with artistry, his present ability and his tremendous promise can well be realized. He is already one of the greatest batsmen the world has ever seen.

And R. E. S. Wyatt, in the *Daily Mail*, called it:

> One of the most astonishing feats of endurance and prolonged concentration ever known in the history of the game.

The Times placed it in context:

> When once the reason for a time-limitless match is recognized, it must be said that no one could have played his part more adequately. Throughout his innings, while making it his main object to remain at the wicket, he took every opportunity which he considered safe to score runs.

This was a different critic, Major Richard Vincent, who was primarily a golfing man and a rugby enthusiast but typical of a generation of sports writers in *The Times* who turned their hands to most sports. Neither in Carew nor in Vincent did *The Times* have men to measure up to the stylishness and dedication of Cardus, the innovations of R. C. Robertson-Glasgow, or, for that matter the professionalism of Kilburn writing for the *Yorkshire Post*.

That the Test was 'timeless', as Vincent observed, is essential to an understanding of Hutton's innings – twice as long as Bradman's in 1930. Hutton has written that he 'never felt the need to defend' his scoring rate nor was he under orders from Hammond 'to stay until 1000 runs were on the board'. He was merely carrying out the policy of batting as long as he could in a match which was intended to be played to a finish. The former Australian captain, Bill Woodfull, asked what were the effects of snow on the wicket and wondered if Australia would bat before the summer was over. The groundsman, after all, had declared the pitch would last till Christmas. William Pollock noted that at 688 the fourth new ball was taken 'and at 10/– a ball, bang had gone a couple of quid . . . well not exactly bang, the scoring rate was so slow'. The lack of urgency which a timeless Test created would be demonstrated once more, at Durban a few months later.

Finally, one may look at the impact upon Hutton. 'I was famous overnight, and I wondered what had hit me,' he recalled. 'The first thing I remember was getting a call from Billy Butlin asking me to go down to Skegness and judge a bathing-beauty contest. They offered to send a Rolls-Royce for me.' An Australian businessman living in England, Arthur Whitelaw, gave him a very substantial present of £1000, as he had done to Bradman eight years earlier. The *Leeds Mercury* stood back from the vortex of statistics to consider the penalties of fame. 'The great record has not been earned without cost and the boy from Pudsey has learnt that, while it has brought him greater fame than he ever dreamt of, it has also brought him a considerable amount of anxiety.' It went on to speak of 'an entirely unwarranted and completely vulgar intrusion on his private affairs'. Yet by the standards of the 1980s this was minimal. There were a few brief references to a possible romance and the name of the Dennis family was mentioned, though not Dorothy specifically. As we have seen, she had her share of press harassment at work. The press also made romantic journalism out of his mother weeping tears of joy over the wash-tub as she heard the news.

As to the £1000, his father was quoted as saying, 'Len was always a thrifty lad. He'll not waste it.' Overall, Hutton received nothing but kindness from the press, who saw him as quiet and modest. Success had not gone to his head and fellow players remembered that he had a word for everyone back in the dressing room. Later he joined the broadcasters again, parrying a question from Bill Oldfield, 'What is it like to achieve greatness?' with the reply, 'It was very tiring and hard work'. In the evening he and Hammond spoke on the Empire Programme and then he was taken to Radio Olympia for a television interview. Many years later he would write that 'to become a record-breaking celebrity at an age when I was just qualified to vote' was possibly the 'second worst happening' in his career: the worst being his wartime injury (see Chapter 4). From August 1938, he would always live with fame and with '364'. He would probably never make as many runs again in an innings (would he have wanted to?) or bat for so long, but henceforth there were always the public expectations. It was as if Sutcliffe's dictum – endlessly seen in print – was now set down in tablets of stone proclaiming that stardom was his for ever.

No way was this more marked than in what we may call the 'Bradman phenomenon'. Wilfred Rhodes had once said to Hutton that he had bowled against Grace, Victor Trumper and Ranjitsinhji and Hobbs, 'but Bradman was the greatest'. Immediately after his 364, Hutton would read such comments in the national press as 'England finds her Bradman' and 'We have a batsman whom we can set against the great Bradman himself'. The argument was offered that Hutton had done more than anyone else to diminish the inferority complex from which English cricket suffered in relation to Bradman. 'In spite of the brief mastery of him by the bowlers in 1932–33, there had been no one, until now, whom one could speak of as a batsman in the same breath', wrote Kilburn in the *Yorkshire Post*. Now, it was agreed, all this had changed and Hutton could pack his bags to go to Australia in 1940–41 with the Australians fearful. Hutton himself held Bradman in similar awe, as indeed he did Hobbs: 'I could not bring myself to think I was in their class.' He recalled his own disappointment when he had first seen Bradman against Yorkshire in 1930 and the great man was out for a single. From now onwards, Hutton felt that he had to perform well so as not to let down the youngsters who would watch him, let alone the adults who pinned on him their hopes for English success. Hutton's 'obligations' to youth may be expressed in another way. Up and down the land small boys who had not previously been 'Huttons' when they batted, promptly became so; 'Hammonds' were out of fashion. And converts were won. There is a tale of a lad who turned down his father's offer to go to watch the Australians in a game just before the fifth Test. A few days later, on the family summer holiday, he preferred the wireless commentary from The Oval in the hotel lounge to sandcastles on the beach. Youth, of course, could identify. Hutton, slight, even frail, looked little more than a boy. There lay part of the appeal matched to the magic of statistics, the magnitude of endurance and the mastery of technique.

Two months earlier Hammond had played an innings which had been superlative in conception and perfect in execution. It had been an image to take away and savour for a lifetime, artistry encapsulated in an afternoon but essentially an experience for those who were actually there. Hutton's 'long weekend' caught the imagination of the country as a whole and gave as much pleasure (more?) to those who listened and read about it as to those who saw. 'Did you hear?' makes better table-talk than 'Did you see?' The 'Joneses', of course, saw; and their neighbours could not keep up with them. Everyone heard and, because everyone heard, Hutton had to live with their recollections. Fame was not so much the spur as the saddle.

From the drama of The Oval, from broadcasts, from press interviews and from an appearance on the new medium of television, Hutton returned to the Yorkshire scene. A few days later he made a century for Yorkshire against MCC in the Scarborough Festival, and guided his country colleague, Frank Smailes, to the 'double'. Smailes, promoted in the order, needed a further 23 runs, and his achievement was the first by a Yorkshireman since 1926. The prospects of Hutton ever so doing were fast receding. He had taken only 20 wickets in 1938 and 28 the year before. The better he batted, the less Yorkshire would need him as an all-rounder, though the County Report at the end of the year still saw him in the future 'bearing an increasingly greater proportion of the attack', and 1939 would give some credence to the argument. It was as well that the season was over. Hutton had been acutely conscious of being expected to make another 364 every time he went to the wicket or, at the very least, a century. 'I was by no means unaware of the unique position I had gained in cricket, or ungrateful for the way the great, generous-spirited cricketing public had shown their appreciation', but he was 'ready for a new world and a change of scene which MCC's tour to South Africa would provide'.

First of all, however, there was the dinner in October organized by the mayor and town council of Pudsey. The Albert Hall was decorated with '364' picked out in lights and there were over 300 guests including the Lord Mayor of Leeds, Sir Granville Gibson, MP for Pudsey and Otley, the Yorkshire side, George Hirst, John Tunnicliffe and, of course, his own family in places of honour. Hutton spent the day before gardening and thinking about the speech he would have to make in front of a large audience and the Movietone cameras, something which he would have to do frequently fourteen years later when he became captain of England. Near him at the dinner, giving moral support, sat Dorothy Dennis to whom he had just become engaged, though the news had not been made public. To the toast of 'Our Guest', Leonard Hutton, Esq., as the menu styled him, replied, and by all accounts acquitted himself well.

In the days before air travel made the great Atlantic liners obsolete, there used to leave every Thursday from Southampton at 4 o'clock a Union Castle ship in a mauve livery, bound for Cape Town. Such a vessel, the *Athlone Castle*, bore the MCC team to South Africa in

October, under the captaincy of Hammond making his third trip to the country where he would live for the last dozen years of his life. Hutton and Edrich were initially seen as MCC's opening pair, and they had partnerships of 262 against Griqualand West and 207 against Natal, Hutton making a century on each occasion. There was a set-back when he was hit on the head by a ball from Eric Davies, the Transvaal pace-bowler, which not only knocked him unconscious but also bowled him. Dorothy who sometimes felt the *Yorkshire Post* office window was her best source of information about her fiancé, read about his injury as she made her way home from work. Her worries were allayed first by a telephone call, then a letter from him in hospital. Hammond decided he should miss the first Test and his Yorkshire colleague, Gibb, opened instead, making 93 and 106. In the second Test Hutton was bowled on the last day of the year for 17, but began the New Year with a double-century at Port Elizabeth against Eastern Province, a match in which players and spectators were engulfed in smuts and smoke from a bush fire. Runs came his way in most games though his 31 in the third Test was modest by comparison with Paynter's double-century and Hammond's century. Immediately afterwards MCC went to play two matches against Rhodesia at Bulawayo and at Salisbury. Neither ground had yet gone over to turf, while that at Bulawayo had no grass at all. White sand was used to dry the outfield, giving the impression of snow. At Salisbury the clay which formed the base of the matting wicket was dried by lighted petrol, amidst sheets of flame and black smoke. Added to such hazards, the tour was providing arduous in terms of long train journeys across the southern continent, but at least they were accomplished in reasonable comfort. Thirty years earlier P. F. Warner's MCC side had played XV of Rhodesia at Bulawayo. Some of the Rhodesian side had travelled from Salisbury in a cart pulled by oxen for four days and nights and across a river 100 yards wide.

Hutton was the mainstay of England's innings in the fourth Test at Johannesburg, batting for three and a half hours for 92 runs against effective bowling on a damp wicket and in a game eventually spoilt by rain. The final Test at Durban was intended to be as 'timeless' as the game at The Oval six months earlier. It was played on a wicket which Robertson-Glasgow, the former Somerset bowler writing for the *Morning Post*, described as 'so far outstripping perfection as to be of little use to the bowler'. The game became one of endurance producing the highest aggregate of runs, 1981, in any first-class match.

Two people enjoyed it: the South African wicket-keeper, Ronnie

Grieveson, who batted for the first time in a Test, got himself an average of 57, stumped Hammond twice, relished the occasion, and wanted it to go on and on; the other was Edrich who, after a string of failures at Test level, made a double-century and vindicated Hammond's judgment of him as a player of genuine Test class. No one was more delighted than Hutton at his colleague's success. He himself contributed 38 and 55, modest scores compared with a double-century, five centuries and eight other scores over 60. In the end England were 42 runs short, with five wickets left, of their target of 696. The match, begun on 3 March, had to be abandoned on 14 March to allow the MCC party to catch the boat-train. The possibility of returning to England by flying-boat was discussed by the authorities and rejected. Instead MCC caught the 8.05 p.m. from Durban to Cape Town. The night which they spent in the train Hitler spent in the ancient royal palace at Prague: Czechoslovakia had fallen. The following morning, as they boarded the *Athlone Castle*, newspapers carried reports of the speech of the British prime minister, Chamberlain. Boat drill on the ship was taken very seriously.

By his own standards Hutton had not made the runs in these Tests which he might have anticipated, but there were plenty of others who did so. He had prospered in the provincial matches and Louis Duffus, the South African journalist, wrote that he batted 'with eager enterprise and daring recklessness to the surprise of spectators'. It paid off, for his aggregate of 1168 runs was the highest on the tour. Duffus regarded Hutton as 'potentially the most dangerous player in the side' and *Wisden* declared that he always looked the most accomplished player. This was high praise, indeed, in the company of the pre-war Hammond and again a reminder to Hutton of what was expected of him. *Wisden*, of course, was not 'instant' journalism and its reflective judgements must have been of great cheer to him when it appeared in April 1940, a small consolation for the first-class season on which neither he nor anyone else would be embarking.

The Yorkshire report on 1939 in the same *Wisden* made equally pleasant reading: 'Hutton gave further evidence of being one of the world's greatest batsmen. He became attractive to watch and he developed strength when forcing the ball away in front of the wicket.' Some might have cavilled at the verb 'became' but Hutton's own professionalism had always put technical mastery first. Robertson-Glasgow, writing instead of the Editor, in *Wisden*'s Notes on the Season, saw 1939 as a year in which the freedom of strokeplay was more often to be found and accounted it as one of the bonuses of the summer. Hutton and a dozen others had contributed to that.

What then was Hutton's contribution to that last season before the war? For Yorkshire alone he scored 2316 runs, with ten centuries and an average of 59.38. Two more centuries came in the Tests against the West Indies, in which he had an average of 96.00 and, in the overall first-class averages for the year his 62.67 was 0.89 behind that of Hammond who was top. His aggregate of 2883 runs was more than 400 higher than that of anyone else. It was late May before he ran into form with a century against a Cambridge University side weakened by examinations and it was promptly followed by another against Warwickshire on 1 June. Three months later, to the day, he would put away his bat for nearly four years, and he would look back on those summer months of 1939 as 'the end of an epoch' in his professional career.

Against Hampshire, he and Sutcliffe had their last great partnership, putting on 315. Hutton made 280 not out, his highest score for Yorkshire. The runs (only 84 behind the Oval score) came in just over six hours and included 36 boundaries, and the defeat of Hampshire was brought about by a spell of nine overs in the second innings in which he took 4 for 40. He batted throughout the innings against Glamorgan for another century. The Yorkshire side had been winning match after match, several by an innings, and Hutton's success had been matched by huge scores by Sutcliffe – still quite capable of opening for England, said a few persistent observers – and the bowling of Bowes, Ellis Robinson and Verity. Such victories, often in two days, gave the side a day off from time to time so that Hutton approached the first Test not jaded by day after day of cricket. These breaks were welcome to a team constantly feted by invitations to theatres, parties and golf courses. It is difficult at this distance of time to realize how much the Yorkshire cricketing public in the 1930s idolized in a very personal way a successful county side.

The West Indies team contained some fine players in Jeffrey Stollmeyer, Learie Constantine and 'Manny' Martindale, together with Headley who scored a century in each innings of the first Test, but they were up against a very strong England side and were thoroughly outplayed. Hutton and Compton put on 248 in just over two hours for the fourth wicket in that game, Hutton making 196, his first Test century at Lord's. *Wisden* called the match 'memorable for the batting of the two youngsters' and one is reminded that Hutton, in his sixth season of first-class cricket had only just turned twenty-three when the match began. Compton was two years younger and the attention of the press and public was very much focused on him in the way it had been on Hutton in the previous two years. Compton in

1939 had displaced him as the 'wonder-boy'. In the popular imagination, Compton would seem the more glamorous figure, whose batting – even his running between wickets – had an element of risk and whose football for Arsenal kept him in the public eye all the year round. Sir Pelham Warner called him 'the best stroke player in the land'. All this took a little of the pressure off Hutton, though Sir Leonard was reluctant to concede the point. Certainly, Yorkshire had no eyes for anyone but Hutton and the gate receipts at the various grounds in the county rose considerably when he played.

The Lord's Test was played in conditions so cold and dark at one point that Tom Webster's cartoon in the *Daily Mail*, calling it 'Winter Sports', seemed to symbolize the cold fears in people's minds while the claps of thunder around the ground hinted at the more ominous sounds which would soon fill the London skies. The England captain, Hammond, appealed over the loudspeakers for men to volunteer for national service, and hoardings on the Grandstand and Mound Stand asked, 'National Service – are you playing?' That very month the very first conscription in peacetime had begun with the registration of militiamen. Cardus must have had more than cricket in mind when he wrote in the *Manchester Guardian* that the cricket of Hutton and Compton, 'these two young men, was not only sumptuous in itself but gave a thrilling promise of the part they will play in more searching engagements of the near future'. It was not only Compton who distracted public attention from Hutton. Back in Yorkshire, local enthusiasts noted a young player called James Smurthwaite who made his debut for the county at Sheffield during the Test and took 5 wickets for 7 in 24 balls to dismiss Derbyshire for 20, though Smailes's all-ten wickets in Derbyshire's second innings stole some of Smurthwaite's thunder.

Between the first and second Tests Hutton made substantial scores in almost every county match, coming within an ace of two centuries in the game against Surrey and scoring 177 against Sussex at Scarborough in conditions so strange that the players and spectators seemed to become detached as a thick mist came in from the sea, allowing the players to see each other but blocking out the spectators. 'Only when a boundary shot hit the fence did the crowd know we were playing and we were re-assured of their presence by their applause', Hutton remarked. The thunder which had threatened the first Test ruined the second as if symbolizing the gathering in intensity of the political storms. Once again, Hammond appealed for volunteers, 'addressing the right stuff', remarked Constantine, 'for only the lion-hearted remained to watch in the appalling conditions'.

Almost as if taking a great farewell to his own Yorkshire supporters, Hutton made centuries at Bradford and Leeds. Cardus wrote that he played at Headingley 'one of the greatest innings I have ever seen in my 30 years as a student of the game,' as he compiled 105 out of the 147 runs which Yorkshire needed to beat Lancashire. 'The Lancashire bowlers used their arts to get him out. Dazzling fielding sought to keep him away from the bowling. He went his masterful and conquering way without the slightest trouble. This was a cricketer, an artist, with more than Hammond's strokes – much more.' John Bapty in the *Yorkshire Evening Post* called his Headingley century one 'which would never be forgotten by those who were fortunate enough to see it, but not, perhaps, just for its technique and artistry.' The heavens opened as Yorkshire, or more particularly, Hutton scrambled the final runs to beat Lancashire in torrential rain.

England and Yorkshire went through the motions of finishing the 1939 season. Players and crowds assembling for the third Test at The Oval saw barrage balloons in the sky, an anti-aircraft gun on a tractor, the drone of aircraft and plenty of men in uniform. The cricketers themselves, as if determined to leave memories to be cherished, made it as interesting a game as they could in the three days allotted. Hammond passed Bradman's number of centuries in Test cricket, Constantine batted with the exuberance which had made him such an attractive personality in Lancashire League cricket, and Hutton scored 73 and 165 not out. *Wisden* contrasted his batting to his innings on the same ground a year earlier: 'He never neglected a scoring chance and his off-driving off the back foot was superb.' The final act in Test cricket between the wars was played by Hutton and Hammond, two of its greatest performers who set up a new third-wicket record of 264.

Four days later, most of the West Indies team were on board ship sailing from Greenock to Montreal, their remaining fixtures cancelled. Hutton went south to play against Hampshire at Bournemouth and against Sussex at Hove. The second match was for Jim Parks's benefit and for his sake the players felt they should see it through to the end. George Cox made 198, Hutton 103 and Yardley 108, but Hutton's own poignant recollection was of Verity's 7 for 9 in 36 balls to dismiss Sussex for 33 and give Yorkshire a nine-wicket win. County cricket matches usually end with cursory farewells and a quick drink between men anxious to get away to the next encounter or snatch a few brief hours at home. The final game of a season with dusk falling soon after the last over, a whiff of autumn in the air and no play for some months, may prolong the departures. Close of play at Hove, at half past two on Friday 1 September 1939 had a disquieting and sombre sense of finality about it. In Europe, German troops were marching through Poland and German aeroplanes bombing Warsaw and Cracow. Members and friends crowded into the picture-lined Long Room to say goodbye to the Sussex and Yorkshire players. Hutton was not the only one who wondered if we would 'ever play cricket again'. He felt very serious and he looked very pale. Presently the Yorkshire party boarded a charabanc. They included Sutcliffe, who a few days earlier had made his 50,000th run for Yorkshire and had stood down in this last game, and who would play no more for Yorkshire in Championship matches; Verity who would die of wounds received when leading his men on a July night in Sicily four years later; and Bowes, who would languish for three years in a POW camp.

So these men, united in the bond of cricket and friendship, each nursing his own fears for the future of themselves and their families, set off from Hove for home. As they approached London they were met by carloads of people hastily leaving the city, usually with children being taken to some place of safety. They spent a short night at Leicester, not even bothering to unpack their overnight kit. Next morning they travelled northwards through blacked-out towns, along with holiday-makers anxious to be back in their own homes when (no longer *if*) war broke out. By mid-day they were home themselves.

An article in *The Cricketer* of July 1939 asked, 'Why is Yorkshire supreme?' Evaluating the strength of this side which had won the Championship for the fifth time in seven seasons, it said, 'It was the strongest, most efficient and the best example of what an XI can be.' This was achieved by captaincy, team spirit, batting in depth, accurate bowling and tight fielding. One might add that there had been a unity of spirit, a sharing of success and a recognition of respect for each other which was the hallmark of this side. Hutton would never experience the same thing in any team ever again. The averages for 1939, the last season this side played together, have a certain symbolism: Hutton, the successful 'pupil', top; Sutcliffe, his 'teacher', second; Leyland, Barber and Mitchell – the rocks on which so many Yorkshire innings were built – third, fourth and fifth; Yardley, the future captain, sixth; Sellers, the current captain and without a peer at county level, seventh; and Turner, dependable, perhaps undervalued, eighth. First and second in the bowling averages were Bowes and Verity. These were the men who dropped off the charabanc one by one as it drove through Yorkshire on the morning of Saturday 2 September, 1939. When it reached City Square, Leeds, it was empty and one of the finest county teams of all time was no more.

Hutton and his parents sat in their home the next day and heard the prime minister's fateful announcement. His wedding to Dorothy Mary Dennis, planned for October, was hurriedly brought forward and they were married in Wykeham parish church near Scarborough on 16 September. It was a small occasion attended chiefly by both families, but important enough to attract the newsreel cameras from Movietown and Pathé. The outbreak of the war had created a fear of the unknown and people were reluctant to leave their homes. Hutton had some difficulties in persuading even his own parents to travel the few miles to Wykeham. 'Coupons' had not yet brought the austerity clothing of later war years, and Dorothy wore a white wedding dress. People leaving the church could be seen carrying their gas-masks. There was a reception at Brompton Hall and the couple left for a motoring honeymoon.

Leonard and Dorothy Hutton began married life at Kingsmead, 29 Woodhall Park Grove in Pudsey, a new semi-detached house in which they would live until 1955. Thanks to the £1,000 Leonard had got the previous year, they were able to avoid a mortgage. In domestic terms, the young couple had a good 'start'. A bonus of £30 from the County to each player for winning the Championship came in October and in the past year Hutton had gained an additional income from advertising when, acting on the advice of Bill Bowes, he had lent his name to Slazenger's products. He had also begun to acquire that understanding of the stock market which would serve him well in years to come. Fellow-cricketers remembered him studying the economy of South Africa during the 1938–39 tour. The Huttons would never be rich but they would be careful and they would husband their resources sensibly. The domestic security of the marriage would soon be challenged, like that of thousands of other young couples, by separation and Leonard would go off to the Forces – just when, like many a man in other walks of life, he had become established in his chosen career.

For Hutton the essential difference between him and countless other men was the status he held in the public eye. He had ended a season which the Yorkshire County Report called 'one long triumph' and he was accepted as one of the major batsmen of his or any generation. In six seasons he had scored 11,658 runs in first-class cricket and had met the most optimistic demands of his supporters. Sutcliffe had declared that he had only made his 50,000 runs for Hutton to eclipse them one day. Sutcliffe's own career, because of the first world war, had not even begun when he was Hutton's age in 1939 but good health would allow him to play for longer. Hutton would eventually score over

40,000 runs in about 200 fewer innings than Sutcliffe. In Test cricket, despite all he had already achieved, by far the greater demand upon him, both as batsman and captain, lay ahead. Only as a bowler, despite the predictions, had he accomplished far more than would be asked of him after the war. By 1939 he had taken two-thirds of the wickets which would ever come his way. Sir Pelham Warner wrote that his skill rivalled that of the greatest masters. 'He has every stroke conceivable and he moves with beautifully smooth celerity while the power with which he plays off the back foot is a joy to watch.' Had Hutton, for whatever reason, played no more first-class cricket after 1939, he would still have been accounted 'great' in cricket's panorama.

4

Interrupted Years

1939–45

'His driving represented batsmanship of his own standard,
and there is no higher.'

J. M. Kilburn, Yorkshire Post, 1945

By the spring of 1940 many of the Yorkshire side which had played at
Hove were in the Forces, and one Yorkshire cricketer of earlier years,
Macaulay, had become one of the first casualties of the war. Hutton at
once volunteered and was called up to serve in the Army Physical
Training Corps. After initial training he was promoted to be a
sergeant-instructor. His fears that their might be no more cricket for
years proved groundless for the game flourished to a surprising
degree. In contrast to the view taken in 1914 that it was unpatriotic to
play, cricket was offered to the public as entertainment and as a way of
helping war charities, and to the players as relaxation. In Sir Pelham
Warner's view, 'If Goebbels had been able to broadcast that the war
had stopped cricket at Lord's, it would have been valuable propaganda
for the Germans.'

The different ways in which the two wars were conducted also
contributed to the change of attitude. Men in the first world war were
for the most part in trenches in Europe or serving at sea. In the second,
there was no occupation of Europe between the Dunkirk retreat in
1940 and the invasion of Italy in 1943. Large numbers of troops were
being mobilized in Britain, and the RAF throughout the war operated

from stations in the British Isles. Operational pilots and their crews might play cricket in the intervals between night raids on Germany. Wartime cricket was stimulated by the foundation of two clubs, the British Empire XI and London Counties. Both of these sides played a large number of matches for charity predominantly in the south of England. Cricket in the North and Midlands was sustained by the Leagues which, as in the first world war, 'recruited' professionals and amateurs from the first-class counties and offered most of the best cricket in the country. The averages for the Bradford League in 1940 show Hutton of Yorkshire and Pudsey St Lawrence top of the batting and Bowes of Yorkshire and Saltaire top of the bowling. 'It was a great day for Pudsey St Lawrence when Hutton turned out for his old club and scored 133', recorded *Wisden*, though he played only twice and the place at the top of the averages properly belonged to Paynter of Lancashire and Keighley.

A formidable array of great names appeared in the League, including Hutton, Barber, Mitchell, Arthur Wood, Yardley and Bowes from the Yorkshire side alone, together with Constantine, the veteran of the Lancashire League, who had joined Windhill in 1940. In the Midlands, the Birmingham League averages were topped by two Warwickshire players, Wyatt of Moseley and Eric Hollies of Old Hill. Hutton's return to the Pudsey scene was brief enough in 1940 but Pudsey, as we shall see, would play an important part in his physical rehabilitation after injury.

None of the first-class counties arranged more than a handful of matches in 1940 and Yorkshire, as such, played only one. Hutton played at Headingley and at Sheffield for Sutcliffe's XI in aid of the Red Cross. The old distinctions of amateur and professional with their separate dressing rooms seemed outmoded and blurred as Captain Sutcliffe and Second-Lieutenant Verity (the professionals) found themselves on the opposing side to the Yorkshire amateurs Aircraftman Gibb and Private Yardley. Somewhere between them in service rank was Sergeant-Instructor L. Hutton, who scored 56 and 30 in the two games and who secured the wicket of Constantine when the Yorkshire XI played the Bradford League. The Bradford League XI could have drawn upon more than half the Yorkshire side but, for the purposes of this match, it was composed of its best players exclusive of Yorkshiremen. Constantine's century came in under an hour and Sutcliffe's for Yorkshire was not far behind. These three matches, attracting crowds of over 6000 on each occasion, raised over £500 for the Red Cross and – perhaps as important – were immensely good for the morale of players and public alike in the year of Dunkirk and the Battle of Britain.

Robertson-Glasgow, in his review of the season in *Wisden*, made the interesting, even satirical, observation that the financial fortunes of some of the first-class counties had actually gained through the absence of fixtures but the retention of subscriptions. It was, of course, scarcely the point and he yearned as much as anyone else for the proper resumption of the game. Looking to the summer of 1941, he hoped for 'more, much more and soon, but first a task falls to be completed. *Delendus est hostis.*' One may assume that a fair proportion of the readers of *Wisden* could have translated the Latin tag. The decline in the teaching both of Latin and of cricket in our national education system lay in the distant future. The depressive personality which was 'Crusoe' Robertson-Glasgow would find little comfort for himself in the post-war world when it came.

One afternoon in March 1941, while on the last day of a Physical Training course in York preparing to be a commando for what would be the raid in Dieppe in 1942, Hutton fell in attempting a 'fly spring' in the gymnasium when the mat slipped from under him. The X-ray showed a fracture of his left forearm and a dislocation of the ulna at the base of his wrist. What appeared at first to be a temporary setback, both to his army career and to his cricket prospects for the summer, turned out to be very much more serious. Within a few days the army authorities had transferred him to Wakefield and he was placed in the hands of Mr Reginald Broomhead, a Leeds surgeon, who was afterwards made a life member of Yorkshire County Cricket Club for making it possible for Hutton to play cricket again.

Instead of playing, Hutton made his first incursions into journalism, the *Pudsey and Stanningley News* of 9 May, 1941 publishing an 'exclusive article by the renowned record-breaking batsman' on Pudsey St Lawrence's League match against Lightcliffe. The aspiring journalist concluded his piece:

> For the few Pudsey people who followed the fortunes of their team their journey was, indeed, worthwhile. Not only did they see a grand victory but they spent several serene hours – broken at intervals by a demonstration of our efficiency in the air from Spitfires on manoeuvres.

By midsummer Hutton had returned to his unit and was able to take part in a match at Sheffield in which he scored a century and played with Reg Simpson, a future England colleague, though the match was followed by 'a long, sleepless night in the barracks with considerable pain'. During the season, the Sports Committee of the Army and the RAF staged a four-match tournament at different grounds throughout the country. All four contests drew huge crowds, raised a considerable amount for charities and included sides composed almost entirely of first-class cricketers. Hutton played in the second one at Harrogate in August. After the RAF were dismissed for 144, he and Sutcliffe put on 78 for the Army's first wicket, Hutton making 58 and, with Leyland to follow, the Army won by eight wickets. Play continued and the chief feature of the remainder of the game was the wicket-keeping of Gibb who secured five wickets. A fortnight later Hutton played for Sir Pelham Warner's XI at Lord's against the RAF. His 19 was the top score for Warner's XI, who won a very low-scoring match by 26 runs. He was again in great pain and did not bat in the second innings, nor for twenty months would he bat again.

Another operation followed, involving a bone graft from his right leg to his left arm and then came the drawn-out anguish of awaiting its results. He recognized that there were others in hospital whose injuries were worse than his and whose recovery had been taking much longer. He recalled a sixty-year-old merchant seaman who had sailed through mine-infested waters, and a motor-cyclist injured in an accident. 'Time went on, often dragging and drab, but lightened by the warmth and kindness of the friends who were around me and the friends who visited me.' Dorothy, doing voluntary work with the WVS, visited when she could and another visitor was Sir Stanley Jackson.

Stanley paid Hutton several visits and he would talk about the great names of Yorkshire and England cricket at the turn of the century. He was a former captain of England, president of MCC and Governor of Bengal. He was also the current Yorkshire president and had first played for the county in 1890. Professional cricketers of Hutton's generation, in the normal course of events, had little to do with public figures, such as Lord Hawke and Jackson, who led cricket from the top. In getting to know Jackson, Hutton learnt much he might never have known about the folklore and traditions of the game. Other frequent visitors included Bert Foster, president of the Bradford League, and Sidney Grimshaw, a Leeds stockbroker. Perhaps to aid the patient's recovery and with an eye to business, Grimshaw remarked, 'Time to forget shocks and scares and to think about stocks and shares.'

When there were no visitors (most of the time, as any patient knows) there were books. Hutton drew upon the hospital library, tackling Goldsmith's *Vicar of Wakefield* and Boswell's *Life of Johnson*. Both might be thought heavy material for a games player laid low but

Hutton found a pleasure in Boswell's *Life of Johnson* which he retained over the years. His own sons would receive copies as gifts and he would explore Dr Johnson's Fleet Street haunts during his days in journalism there twenty years later.

Towards the end of 1941 he underwent a third operation, this time with a bone graft from his left leg to his arm, since the previous grafting had been unsuccessful. He had gone from hope to despair as successive graftings had failed and he had had many weeks of almost total immobility. Nevertheless, his surgeon allowed Sir Stanley Jackson to tell the Yorkshire members at the Annual General Meeting early in 1942 that there was every hope that he 'would make a good recovery'. Finally, the summer brought his discharge from the army, weeks of massage and therapy, and his return to civilian life with a left arm almost two inches shorter than his right. The need to readjust his batting technique would be a major priority when he played again. For the first time since he had been old enough to hold a bat he would have a summer totally without cricket. The nearest he came to the game in 1942 was when he staged a match between an XI in his name and George Duckworth's at Pudsey in aid of the Red Cross.

Civilian employment with the Ministry of Pensions was considered but he accepted instead a temporary civilian appointment with the Royal Engineers. During the war property was requistioned and it was the responsibility of the Royal Engineers to maintain it. Hutton, unable to drive a car and with one arm virtually out of action, travelled round the Leeds area by bus and tram inspecting properties and measuring them up where repair work was needed.

Gradually strength returned and it was with great delight that he dared to hold his infant son, Richard, born on 6 September 1942. From baby-carrying he advanced to carrying golf clubs in the following spring. He had been approached by several Bradford League clubs but his loyalties were to Pudsey St Lawrence and he accepted their offer to become a professional and to assume the captaincy. So it was that Hutton, of Yorkshire and England, with 11,000 first-class runs behind him, returned to the club where his cricket had begun and led it to victory in the away match at Bankfoot on 24 April, 1943. 'The duck I made was nothing compared with the grand fact that I was playing again.' Unfortunately, a sprained ligament when bowling made him miss the Priestley Cup match on Easter Monday though he was back for the next League one. It was like old times again, making his way to Tofts Road, though this time from Woodhall Park Grove instead of from Fulneck and with Dorothy bringing Richard in his pram.

Bradford League cricket is demanding enough at any time and it was especially so during the war when, for example, over seventy county players appeared in 1943, including fourteen who had played at Test level. Hutton, once a week, was getting something of the practice he needed and confidence he sought with which to return to his professional career when the war ended. But success as a batsman was not matched by success as a captain and when Pudsey, playing in Division 'B', lost three Saturdays running, to Spen Victoria, Queensbury and Baildon Green, there was much discontent among Committee members. To the crowds who watched he was very much the local hero and one young Baildon Green supporter recalled changing loyalties when Pudsey came on 29 May to their little ground on the Moor just outside Bradford. He hoped both for Hutton's personal success and Baildon's triumph. Cardus, as a small boy, had prayed at Old Trafford: 'Please God, make Victor Trumper score a century out of an Australian total of 120.' The small boy at Baildon got half his wish – Baildon won – and after the match he asked for Hutton's autograph. He was told he would have to earn it by carrying his bag and half a mile later he was rewarded for his efforts. Hutton had other things on his mind, for Pudsey with a score of 170 had looked safe when half the Baildon side were out for under a hundred but the seventh wicket pair, taking advantage of their own very small ground, had hit out successfully and Pudsey had lost yet again.

A member of the Pudsey side recalled the wrath of Joe Hart, the president, in the bus going home. 'Sack the lot', he was heard to mutter, though by the following Tuesday, when the weekly selection meeting took place at the Commercial Hotel, his mood had changed. Despite victory in the Priestley Cup match against Lightcliffe, Hutton became more and more disenchanted with the captaincy, especially as it meant attending selection meetings which went on till midnight and which he saw as an excuse for Hart and his friends to drink after hours. There wasn't a row but there was certainly some clash of personalities and Hutton saw no reason why he should make his way home late at night without transport just to suit Hart. By early June he had had enough and he resigned. Nothing appeared in the *Pudsey and Stanningley News* beyond the team list for the match against Bowling Old Lane on 12 June which read: 'H. Gill (capt), L. Hutton . . .'

There were those among the younger men on the fringes of club affairs who thought that Hart had made it difficult for Hutton to continue in office; that it appealed to his sense of authority to treat in an arbitrary fashion a man who had been Pudsey's honoured guest five years earlier. There would be movements to reduce his influence. Yet he had the saving grace of a burning ambition for Pudsey – to get back into Division A and to win the Priestley Cup. For Hart, no player was greater than those goals.

Meanwhile, Hutton settled down to the business of scoring runs and taking wickets. Against Bankfoot he made 105. By July, Pudsey had reached the quarter-final of the Cup against East Bierley, and he made a half-century sharing in a partnership of 106 with his brother, George, and helping the club to victory. In the return League match against Baildon Green he took 5 for 26 and made 41. Then, after success in the semi-final, came the Cup Final on 21 August at Park Avenue, Bradford. Leonard and George came together after an over and put on a century partnership before both were out, Leonard for 64 and George for 40. The collection round the ground brought £16 4s for Leonard's half-century of which, by wartime agreement, half went to the Red Cross and half to the player. Then, at 113 for 3, the rain came down and the match was not resumed until 24 September. Pudsey's score of 149 (no one else made double figures) scarcely seemed a winning total but, as the *Pudsey and Stanningley News* reported, 'The Brighouse innings was a very steady procession and at no time did the batsman appear likely to make any productive stand'. Brighouse were dismissed for 65, Hutton taking 3 wickets for 22 in 8 overs.

Later in the evening at the Royal Hotel, as the local paper continued, 'Mr Hart presided over an exuberant company and the cup was filled with champagne. The Mayor could not remember another occasion in all his mayoralty when he had felt so proud.' Speech after speech followed and Leonard Hutton in his remarks stressed the importance of coaching young players and promised to continue the coaching programme he had begun that summer. If there was some bitterness at not being the captain, he did not show it and he shared in the general jubilation, he and Dorothy later going to the dance in the Liberal Club. It was an occasion worth getting a baby-sitter for, to look after young Richard who had recently had his first birthday.

The coaching to which Hutton had referred had been something he had established that summer on two evenings a week. The absence of men on war service meant that Pudsey and other clubs often selected youngsters and two, in particular, had taken part in the Cup Final and benefited from Hutton's coaching: Roland Parker and Jim Thompson were both teenagers who would become Yorkshire Colts and successive captains of Pudsey St Lawrence. A year later, some prophets were seeing Thompson as another Hutton who would 'forget all about accountancy after the war and become a star batsman' (suggested the *Yorkshire Post*). This was not to be. Thompson would be a star within Bradford League terms in the 1950s and a local accountant and company director. As for Hutton, his first full season in wartime Bradford League cricket found him third in the averages, after Cox of Sussex and Paynter of Lancashire, and fifth in the bowling with 43 wickets at a cost of 8.97.

He was, of course, still far away from Lord's, the southern centre of wartime cricket where during 1943 an England XI played the West Indies; Sir Pelham Warner's XI took on the Royal Australian Air Force; the Army met the RAF before a crowd of 22,000 and – most sensational of all at the height of the war – England opposed the Dominions in a two-day match in which the ground was packed and England won by eight runs. All these games owed almost everything to the indefatigable organization of Warner, deputy secretary of MCC for the duration. The leading players of England, Australian and West Indies cricket were brought together with some of those, scarcely more than schoolboys, such as Trevor Bailey, who would make their mark after 1945. But among the Wyatts and Edrichs, the Constantines and the Martindales, the Millers and the Hassetts, there was no Hutton.

He was not forgotten. The *Sydney Morning Herald* proposed an Empire team to tour Australia the moment the war ended. Herbert Collins, a former Australian captain, was asked to select a possible side and he picked five Englishman, Hammond, Edrich, Compton, Doug Wright and Hutton. Only the death of Hutton's friend Verity, which was confirmed in September 1943, marred a summer in which both his own return to top-class cricket and the defeat of Germany began to be realistic prospects. Even the setting up of MCC Select Committee for Post-War Cricket – together with the Beveridge Plan and the Butler proposals – suggested that politicians in every sense were preparing for a saner world where cricket, as a leisure industry and pursuit, would take its place with changes in social welfare and in education.

The 1944 season began with Pudsey in Diyision A and on four successive Saturdays Hutton played for them in the League, but he missed the Whit weekend matches against Lidget Green and Bingley because he was given leave to play in two matches at Lord's, his first return to 'the big-time' for five years. On Whit Saturday, with the gates closed leaving thousands outside, the Rest of the World played Australia. Hutton of England opened with Charles Dempster of New Zealand. He was, said *The Times*, 'the real Hutton of elegant and brilliant stroke-play' despite the bandage on his left arm and the obvious use which he was making of his right one. It was the sort of occasion which, forty years later, would be seen so often in the best of the one-day competitions. The Rest declared (no limited overs in those days) at half past three with a total of 280 (Hutton 34) and, as *The Times* put it, 'So the last pair were in, with the spectators' eyes swivelling from the clock to the pitch and five runs wanted in five minutes. It was done and what a grand finish.' Five runs in one minute would be more the style of the one-day game in the 1980s!

The crowds returned on Whit Monday to see an England XI, with four past, present or future England captains, defeat the Australians by six wickets. The England batting order read: Barnett, Hutton, Edrich, Hammond, Ames, Robins, Allen, Bailey, Mallett, Evans, Wright. None of the Australians had played in a Test match, yet they did not do so badly in making 243. The more discerning critics viewed their performance with some alarm. If an Australian side of unknowns could run a virtual England Test XI fairly close, what did the future hold when the war was over? The *Daily Telegraph*, not yet enjoying the style of E. W. Swanton, echoed the same thought and felt that several of the Australians batted 'like real Test men' (hardly a Swanton-like phrase). Hutton made 84 batting, said *The Times*, in a way which would not have been allowed in a Roses match at Headingley or Old Trafford but which was just right for Whit Monday at Lord's in wartime. He met the bowling with sure defence and used every means of scoring. His reappearance after his injuries was, thought Robertson-Glasgow, one of the better prospects for peacetime cricket. If we played Australia again in 1946, he speculated, Hutton would be still only thirty and (save for Compton) the youngest established England batsman. England would, indeed, play Australia in 1946, lose by an innings twice and use half of the men who had played that Whit weekend at Lord's while the Australians would only 'retain' Keith Miller. Bradman would re-emerge and make 187 and 234.

This is to anticipate events. Hutton would play no other representative cricket at Lord's in 1944 and we must return to the hard realities of Pudsey St Lawrence. On the Saturday after the Whitsun matches he helped them to victory against Eccleshill in the first round of the Cup and later in June there was a tense League match against Saltaire. He opened with the eighteen-year-old Thompson. His own contribution was to make 34 and to guide the youngster towards a score of 76 against the pace of the Derbyshire and England bowler, Bill Copson. It was this game which led the *Pudsey and Stanningley News* to extol the achievements of three Pudsey men on the same day – four wickets, taken by Herbert Sutcliffe for Pudsey Britannia, Hutton's innings and Thompson's promise. Pudsey St Lawrence finished the season fourth in Division A and they had reached the semi-final of the Cup. Hutton came second top of the Bradford League averages with figures of 56.36.

A tale survives of the match against Windhill. Pudsey needed four to win and Hutton needed four for his 50. He was batting with his brother George to whom he indicated that he would get the four and they would go halves on the collection for Leonard which would follow. Ellis Achong, the bowler and a West Indian Test cricketer, overheard the remark, resented the assumption of victory, and promptly bowled a ball which went for four byes, leaving Leonard stranded on 46 not out.

The collection would have been a nice bonus to the weekly income he was now drawing as a representative for Thomas Owen and Company, the paper manufacturers. Through the good offices of William Harrison, the chairman and a cricket devotee, Hutton would find employment with the firm, when not playing cricket, for some years to come.

On 3 September, five years to the day since war had broken out, he took part in the Hedley Verity Memorial Match at Roundhay Park, Leeds. The players wore black armlets and a bed would be endowed in Verity's memory at the Leeds General Infirmary. The weather spoilt what would have been a distinguished tribute to a distinguished cricketer. The Yorkshire XI made 129 for two (Hutton 82) before the rain came down. The XI captained by Hammond did not bat. Three days later, a sort of Scarborough Festival was attempted in which Yorkshire were to play the RAF, led by Hammond, but the rain persisted and not a ball was bowled.

The war in Europe ended on 8 May 1945. The sense of relief was tempered by the continuing conflict in the Far East, where victory over Japan was not officially celebrated until 2 September – six years, less one day, from the outbreak of war. The interval between these two events spanned a cricket season and the decision was taken jointly by MCC and the Inter-Services Sports Committee to make a partial resumption of first-class cricket. What happened, in effect, was a curious amalgam of wartime and normal peace activities. In the context of wartime cricket the British Empire XI and the London Counties side each played a full season while, in the North and Midlands, the Leagues enjoyed, for one more summer, the prestige of Test and county cricketers playing for them. All three Services fulfilled individual programmes, among them being the Desert Air Force, and the Central Mediterranean Force who played in Italy until August. In the context of peace, many of the first-class counties played a few matches, though scarcely any of them of three-day duration. The Royal Australian Air Force and the Australian Imperial Force merged into the Australian Services, playing a programme of some fifty matches, including five Victory matches designated as 'England v. Australia'. As Norman Preston, editor of *Wisden* wrote, 'When VE Day came, arrangements grew like a snowball'.

Within eleven days of peace, the first Victory match was staged at Lord's. Spectators were admitted anywhere in the ground for one shilling and advised to bring their own refreshments. On paper the England XI was vastly more experienced than an Australian side whose only Test player was Hassett, but the Australians made the best of the conditions and won on the third last ball. Hutton had opened with Washbrook, the beginning of a partnership which would serve England over the next four years. 'There was immense glee among the Australians in the crowd when the menace of Hutton vanished with one run on the board', wrote *The Times*, and it was a great uplift to the bowler, Robert Williams, just back from four years as a POW, and who would dismiss Hutton four times in the series. Another ex-POW fast bowler also had some success elsewhere that day – Bowes, in his first game for four years, took 8 for 9 against Giggleswick School. He would play once more for England, against India in 1946, but no place would be found for Williams at Test level in post-war first-class cricket in Australia.

England won the second match in mid-June on the bomb-scarred Bramall Lane ground, owing a great deal to a fine century by Hammond. Hutton made top score (46) in England's second innings, surviving a blow from Miller bowling short at great speed. He was hit on his vulnerable left forearm, looked sickly pale and then recuperated. He also ran out Douglas Carmody – another ex-POW – with a return from cover to the wicket which was 'sheer brilliance'. These contests were tough and, in Hutton's own view, 'the best way to get back into practice' besides being an opportunity to forge old friendships and encounter new foes – not least Miller. At once, Hutton had an 'uneasy suspicion that here was an adversary of the future to be reckoned with'.

From now onwards he became almost as busy as in a normal first-class season. There was a two-day Roses match with Lancashire, in which he made top score in each innings, followed by a Yorkshire match against the Australian Services at Bradford in which he alone

LEN HUTTON

batted with any comfort against Williams who took 5 for 41. These
Yorkshire matches were occasions he had longed for, even more than
the 'England' contests of the summer, and he was content with
the press judgments on him: 'calm and assured yet missing no chance
of scoring'. His 82 against the Australian bowlers was followed in the
third Victory match at Lord's by 104 and 69 – 'every over looking
more like the Hutton of 1938'. His responsibilities were increased in
that Hammond retired with the lumbago which would end his career
in a year or so and the England selectors – hitherto rather unfairly
being criticized for playing older men – had gambled with youth and
selected three 1944 schoolboys. Two of these, John Dewes and
Donald Carr, would both briefly play at Test level but the burden was
Hutton's, with some support from Edrich, and he batted for a
substantial part of both England's innings in a vain endeavour to stave
off defeat. Ten days later came a century for Yorkshire against the
Australian Services to give him 366 runs off their bowlers in four
innings. He was as much carrying the Yorkshire batting as England's:
any doubts of his fitness for the future were publicly dispelled. He
alone knew the private pain of holding a bat and his courage was
increasing the arthritis which would grip him relentlessly in his old
age.

Young men under thirty do not contemplate the ills of veterans and
he enjoyed his summer of 1945. In the third of the 'Internationals',
again at Lord's, his batting, said *Wisden*, changed the character of the
match and was measured not so much but its 35 runs as by its sheer
quality. The series ended at Old Trafford with England's first victory
against Australia there since 1905. Old Trafford lived up to its
reputation as thousands turned up in pouring rain for the second day,
but they were rewarded by play starting only an hour late. England,
set 141 at a run a minute on the last day against Williams and Miller,
won comfortably enough through Hutton and Edrich. Dozens of
buses labelled 'Cricket Ground' bespoke the mood of peace, but two
unrelated incidents serve as reminders that the temper of war still
prevailed. Thousands of miles away from the game, E. W. Swanton,
walking out of his Japanese prisoner of war camp as a free man, came
upon a wireless set in a Thai village. He tuned in and picked up the
commentary from Old Trafford. The other incident was at Old
Trafford itself, where the pavilion was being repainted by German
prisoners of war. Paid at the rate of three-farthings an hour (£0.003 per
hour), they can scarcely have become converts to the game.

Side by side with Hutton's appearances in his natural role as
England's opener, were his dozen games for Pudsey, including a

century against Brighouse. He had been absent from the Priestley Cup
Final on August Bank Holiday, which Pudsey narrowly lost but the
Committee insisted on his playing in a League match at the end of
August against Lidget Green thus making it impossible for him to play
for England against the Dominions. It can scarcely be held to the
Committee's credit that they had denied him participating in the
showpiece of the season, a game which Sir Pelham Warner described
as fulfilling 'every known axiom as to how cricket should be played'.
It was, fittingly, the swan-song of wartime cricket. Just after, came
the news of Japan's surrender. Up north, Hutton took part in a
Scarborough Festival as near to the real thing as made no difference.
Yorkshire played the RAF – Washbrook, Edrich (DFC) and Wyatt, no
mean airmen – and Leveson Gower's XI played first the New
Zealanders then the Australians. Hutton collected 376 in the three
games, 'never in any trouble', said *Wisden*. His 188 against the New
Zealanders was a massive innings containing 21 boundaries. Kilburn
was able to tell his *Yorkshire Post* readers that 'his driving, his forcing
back-foot shots, his hooking and his late-cutting represented batsmanship of his own standard, and there is no higher'.

The game against Lidget Green proved to be Hutton's last for
Pudsey. Two matches remained but, as we have seen, his commit-
ments lay elsewhere. With the players he had had a harmonious
relationship and they had benefited from his contribution and his
example. With officialdom, relations had been rather more strained.
One or two committee members – the legacy of Hart – felt it their role
to 'cut down to size' a very distinguished cricketer who had always
retained a modesty of approach. The concessions in 1945 to allow him
to play at England level had been made with great reluctance. It may
be thought that the Committee's attitude was that of small-minded
men not prepared to take a broader view of the needs of English
post-war cricket or, indeed, of a professional player wishing to keep in
touch with the game at a high level. Yet there is something to be said
for their opinion. They were paying Hutton about £100 a season as
their own professional, money which the club found difficult to raise,
and they regarded Bradford League cricket as a tough enough exercise
in itself. Furthermore, their own sights, as Hart had demonstrated so
focibly two years earlier, were set, legitimately enough, on League
and Cup. One may see both points of view. Sir Leonard felt that
players, rather than Committee members, saw his personal dilemma
in 1945. It would be with Pudsey cricketers of the 1940s, such as
Roland Parker, his brother, Geoffrey, and Jim Thompson, that he
would retain a friendship over the years and it would be with a later

generation of committee men, such as Keith Moss, that he would feel welcomed when he visited the clubhouse in Pudsey from his home in the south of England.

For the moment, he was all set for the proper resumption of cricket in 1946 and felt 'Test match conscious'. The war had taken six years of men's working lives, but at least he belonged to the generation of those who had – whether in sport, in the professions or business – 'qualified' before the war. They were a little more fortunate than those who had to begin their training in 1946 in their mid-twenties. Hutton, in 1946, was the master craftsman ready to resume his trade. Among the apprentices, not yet journeymen, would be Alec Bedser and Godfrey Evans.

5

'Cricket is my Life'

1946–49

'He had played a splendid and flawless innings, as near
perfection as the most hypercritical could expect.'
John Hughes, *The Times*, 1949

Cricket at Fenner's in Hutton's day, played in front of the distinctive
pavilion with its elegant wrought iron veranda and its classical
balustraded balcony, had a timelessness about it. Panels bearing the
names of successive Cambridge XIs against Oxford lined the inside
with the unique addition of the 1878 side which beat the Australians.
Undergraduates in scholar's or commoner's gowns found a moment
between tutorials to watch a college friend perform or lingered longer
to see a county batsman, perhaps Hutton, make some runs. The
nearby Gothic spire of the Roman Catholic church challenged the
monopoly of the Anglican towers and spires adorning the nearby
colleges. It was a setting which appealed to Hutton, and he envied the
opportunities which the ancient English universities gave to young
men and women for study and for sport. Some of those who played
for Cambridge University against Yorkshire in 1946 in the county's
first official match since 1939 were no longer quite so young. They
had far more in common with a county side than usual, for the
majority of both teams had served in the war.

For Hutton the resumption of his craft began with that match –
cricket day in and day out to meet the expectations of the public. He

65

would set off dressed as if for the office in a double-breasted suit, pocket handkerchief discreetly showing, soft collar and tie, carrying a raincoat and wearing a trilby. Sutcliffe had set standards for the Yorkshire professional, on and off the field, and Hutton to the end of his career diligently followed them. On this first Yorkshire Southern tour for seven years he made 10 against the University in a match which Yorkshire won easily and of which the most striking feature had been the bowling of Arthur Booth who had last played for Yorkshire in 1931. Now, re-appearing 15 years later, he took 5 for 16. He went on to top both the Yorkshire and the national bowling averages and was seen as the left-arm slow bowler to replace Verity, but 1946 proved to be his brief moment of glory. With the emergence of John Wardle and his personal lack of fitness, he only made four more appearances for the county.

Despite Kilburn's view that the Yorkshire side bore no comparison with that of 1939, the county went on to win the championship again in 1946, owing most to the bowlers and to Hutton's batting. His average of 50 put him far in front of anyone else and on several occasions he held the innings together. Among significant performances were 99 not out against Glamorgan, 101 against Surrey and 171 not out against Northamptonshire. The common denominator in all these innings was the faultlessness with which he batted and the old qualities of endurance and concentration were as entrenched as ever.

The Indians were the tourists and against them, for Yorkshire, he made 183 not out. Kilburn saw it as an innings in which Hutton 'was everything a great batsman should be, missing no opportunity yet flirting with no temptation'. His arm injury restricted his wrist movements, however, and a full-circle turn was therefore impossible, and although for the rest of his career he would seldom hook the ball, in this particular innings he managed to hook the fast bowler, Shute Banerjee. That innings apart, the Indians got off lightly; Hutton averaged only 30.75 against them in three Test matches.

Cricket was once gain his livelihood and the match against the Indians earned him £11/10s – £1/10s more than Yorkshire had paid him for playing against Cambridge. The Committee paid him £13 for each county match at home and £20 for each one away and there was a £2 bonus for a win. He was selected for the MCC tour of Australia and the Committee gave him leave of absence from two matches to have a few days with his family, voting him £20 in lieu of the £40 he would actually have earned by playing against Sussex and Hampshire. The time was spent playing cricket in the garden (and doing most of the bowling) with Richard, whose fourth birthday party he would miss by four days. In between cricket there was packing to be done and, with a special allowance of clothing 'coupons' and some of his own (wartime rationing was still in force), he got together six pairs of flannels, six cricket shirts, four pairs of boots, four lounge-suits and one dress-suit.

To go to Australia was to fulfil the ambition of a professional cricketer's career and Hutton, at thirty, might in normal circumstances have fulfilled it some years earlier. In financial terms, it would earn him £550 together with expenses and bonuses. His pleasure at the prospect was tempered by sadness at saying his farewells to the family and making his way quietly and unobtrusively, with Jim Kilburn, travelling for the *Yorkshire Post*, to catch the 12.45 from Leeds Central Station to King's Cross. It was left to Dorothy to explain to Richard that his father would not be home for Christmas. John, born in May, was far too little to begin to understand. Dorothy would have to run the little household through the coming months. Lady Hutton recalled graphically that bitter winter of austerity: 'no car, trudging through the snow to the shops with the children, keeping a scrapbook of the tour'. It was his third overseas cricket tour though the first on which he had embarked as a married man with the conflict of divided loyalties between family and career. In later years, when the children were older, Dorothy would be able to join him briefly. The real burden, as Richard Hutton told me, fell on his mother. The boys came to take their father's absence as a matter of course.

Under the captaincy of Hammond the side left Southampton on the last day of August in RMS *Stirling Castle*. The ship had not been converted from its second world war role as a transport vessel and only the captain enjoyed really comfortable quarters. Hutton shared a cabin with the Lancashire bowler, Richard Pollard. In far sparser conditions were the many women and children crowded together in dormitories who were going out to Australia as wives or fiancées of men whom they scarcely knew and whom they had met in a brief wartime romance. The cricketers at least had the security of a known environment to which to return. The women were venturing into an unknown future. One girl, who had become engaged after a week's acquaintance before her fiancé became a POW, would arrive in Australia and change her mind.

The ship was stocked with frozen food from Australia. Menus which gourmets on desert islands dreamed of were set before those who had got used to spam, snoek and reconstituted egg. Hutton, who still retained the spare figure he had had for years, benefited from the variety and the amount of food without acquiring unnecessary extra weight. Players felt a little guilty as they thought of their families and friends back home, and on arriving in Perth there was a rush to send food parcels back to England. The Australian view of English conditions was probably unnecessarily grim and the cricketers and journalists, as emigrés from a 'starving homeland', were feted and welcomed. Hutton wrote to Dorothy of the 'kind-heartedness in everything that happened to us' from which he would soon want to exclude the effectiveness of the Australian batting and the ferocity of the Australian bowlers. That the tour was a goodwill mission was emphasized by the politicians and administrators on both sides and it marked the restoration of Anglo-Australian encounters as the hegemony of the game. Hammond also took the view that his team deserved to enjoy themselves after the frustrations and deprivations of war. Yet behind this benevolent thought there is no evidence that the side gave anything but its best. To later accusations that the social side played too large a part, the manager, Rupert Howard would reply that he had never known a 'more careful-living set of players'; neither had the much-travelled journalist, Bruce Harris.

The farmers of Northam in Western Australia were the first to see Hutton bat 'down under' with a half-century that served as batting practice, and they rewarded him and his colleagues with a barbecue and a barn dance in the evening. At Perth his golf served him better than his cricket, he and Compton beating their opponents by 5 and 4. He survived the boredom of the three-day train journey across the Nullarbor Plain to make 164 in front of the iron-smelters of Port Pirie. Between then and the first Test in Brisbane five weeks later, he gave all the great centres of Australian cricket an indication of his art with 136 at Adelaide, 151 not out and 71 at Melbourne, 97 at Sydney and 42 at Brisbane. The Melbourne innings led Woodfull, the former Australian captain, to write, 'Like the great Sutcliffe, he is a real student of the game, suiting his style and pace to the occasion'. The 97 at Sydney ended in a run-out; there was one over left and he and Gibb attempted an impossible single off the first ball to give him the bowling. Compensation came when the former Australian Test batsman Charles Macartney came into the dressing room with his congratulations.

The reporter in the *Brisbane Telegraph*, on the strength of his 42, called him 'the greatest batsman in the world', while a Yorkshire lady, long-resident in Australia, wrote home to her uncle, 'Let me tell you that Len Hutton is being made an idol in Australia. The comments the broadcasters make about him make my eyes nearly pop out. I have never heard anyone so highly spoken of before.'

Several matches were affected by rain but MCC, by and large, had got the best of the encounters with the State sides as they came to the first Test at Brisbane, a game which has its own place in cricket history. Had Bradman been given out from an appeal by John Ikin for a slip catch (a controversial decision which engendered much debate) he might have decided to retire from playing; had he done so, the course of Anglo-Australian cricket in the immediate post-war period might have taken a different shape; had there not been storms and hurricanes of titanic proportions, England might not have been so devastatingly beaten. In the immediate context of the match Hutton's contributions of 7 and 0 (first ball) have no positive significance. In a broader sense, he was learning that the mastery of Miller's pace and accuracy was essential to himself and to England's fortunes.

Brisbane was left behind with a margin of defeat comparable to that inflicted on Australia in 1938. Soon after the game ended at 5 o'clock, Hammond set off by car for Sydney. His passengers were Hutton and Washbrook, who chatted to each other. Their captain, in silence, drove the 900 miles through the night with only stops for petrol and requests to have his cigarette lit. The skipper was brooding on his own personal problems, for the Australian press was full of his impending divorce and Hutton thought that Hammond 'found their comments most hurtful'. The burden of captaincy, as Hutton would learn in due course, was sufficient without the public enquiries into one's private life which Hammond had to endure.

Hutton's very brief dialogue with Miller was resumed at Sydney in the second Test. Within minutes, he was struck on his damaged left arm though it would be the off-break bowler, Ian Johnson, who dismissed him with his third ball in Test cricket. Hutton's 39 in two hours was the flavour of the England first innings – dogged, grim and defensive. Bradman and Barnes replied with 234 each: the signal that Australia were establishing an overall supremacy in the series. In another England defeat by an innings, in this six-day Test match, 24 minutes may be salvaged from the wreckage. When Australia declared at 659 for 8 on the fifth day, half an hour before lunch, Hutton went out to play an innings that won the cheers of the crowd and the plaudits of the press both, perhaps, clutching at English straws since a one-sided series was neither entertaining nor news. Hutton's 37 runs encapsulated all his talents. Against a closely set field, he found the open spaces, dispatching Miller for boundaries as if he were knocking off a mere handful to win the match. On the stroke of lunch he was out hit wicket, the thumb of his batting glove slipping off and becoming entangled with his bat: 'I lost my grip on the bat and it clipped the

LEN HUTTON

wicket.' Even the Australian fielders were sorry to see him go. Three former Australian captains made their comments: Woodfull, while full of admiration, felt it was 'more in the nature of an exhibition than the anticipated fighting knock from a member of a team striving to avoid defeat'. Victor Richardson noticed 'all the glories of batting and every known shot produced with elegance'. Collins said 'it was an innings he would always remember'. Hutton's county captain, Sellers, reporting for the *Yorkshire Evening Post*, called it the greatest display of batting he had ever seen Hutton give, and it was left to Kilburn, always ready with the polished phrase, to add to his own form of rapturous approval:

> Everyone of us was beneath a spell borne on wings of enchantment, high above figures into the cloudlands of great moments. Hutton scattered light, loveliness, and brave beauty across the sunlit Sydney ground and took cricket to the pinnacles of artistry.

Hutton himself cherished a letter from an elderly Australian who had seen all the 'greats' of the twentieth century. He called his innings: 'a delight to the connoisseur of batsmanship which brought back visions of the peerless Trumper. My friends and I can pay you no greater compliment.'

His innings inspired an Edrich century and a Compton half-century and England's 355 was an honourable total. Had Hutton made a century as well the match might have been saved. The following two Tests were drawn and England made over 300 in all four innings. But for an errant batting glove, England might have come to the fifth Test all square. It is an interesting speculation but the hard facts remain. England's 300s were matched by Australia's 400s and 500s. There was a differential in batting which could only have been reconciled by a stronger English tail, a Hammond of pre-war vintage and a Hutton whose highly respectable average of 50.33 in the third and fourth Tests was made to match the almost indecent figure of 140.66 achieved by his opposite number, Arthur Morris, in the same two matches.

Christmas Day far from home was bitter-sweet. Hutton, whose thoughts were with the small family back in Pudsey, spent a quiet day in Sydney before setting off by train on Boxing Day for Canberra where he met the Governor-General, the Duke of Gloucester, and entertained him with a century before the rain came down. Rain, so often needed in Australia, had pursued the cricketers during the tour with a suspicion of partisanship.

Neither Hutton nor, for that matter, Washbrook, Compton and

70

'Cricket is my Life'

Edrich, believed they had much with which to reproach themselves in
the third and fourth Tests at Melbourne and Adelaide. Hutton and
Washbrook, by having three consecutive opening partnerships of
over 100, equalled what Hobbs and Sutcliffe had done in 1924–25. At
Melbourne Hutton displayed that imperturbability which marked so
much of his career by resisting a battery of short-pitched balls from
Miller and Ray Lindwall for three hours to contribute to England
saving the match. Swanton considered that he established a moral
superiority over the Australian bowlers which was not reflected in the
England scoreboard. Not every journalist agreed. Some who had
lauded Hutton a few weeks earlier had their doubts after the
Melbourne Test. Woodfull thought he was not 'the tower of strength'
he had been, and Kilburn reported to his Yorkshire readers that he
seemed 'unconvincing against the speed of Miller and Lindwall'.
Sellers wrote, 'He will get over this difficult period' and it was left to
the third Yorkshireman reporting the tour, Bill Bowes, to have a
word with Hutton as they walked over the Torrens river to the
Adelaide Oval during the fourth Test match. 'Tha knows what
they're saying, Len. That tha's afear'd of 'em.' Hutton halted in his
stride, looked Bowes full in the face and said nothing. His 94 runs in
the first innings was technically sound while his 76 in the second
contained a blistering array of strokes off anything Lindwall and
Miller could offer. The comment of Sutcliffe in a letter to the
Australian press was widely quoted: 'I expected Hutton on Australian
wickets to get near his 364.' As with his remarks in 1935, his words
were meant well but Hutton could have done without them.

The Adelaide crowds had a splendid ten days: four half-centuries
from Hutton in the State and Test matches; 188 from Hammond
(which proved to be his last century in first-class cricket) against South
Australia; a century in each innings in the Test from both Compton
and Morris, and another from Miller. Bowlers toiled in the heat, and
one of them must have been thinking his own thoughts on past
endeavours. Voce, making his third trip to Australia, took 4 for 125
against South Australia on the same ground where fourteen years
earlier the bodyline bowling crisis had erupted. His presence on the
tour, aged thirty-seven, highlighted the core of England's problem:
fast bowlers combining youth and talent did not exist. There were no
counterparts to Miller and Lindwall.

MCC came to Sydney for the last leg of the tour. Hutton, despite
being hit on the chin and needing stitches, led a spirited pursuit of a
target of 339 in four hours set by New South Wales. He and Compton
scored 85 in just over half an hour and only rain frustrated their

attempts. The fifth Test produced much the most interesting cricket of the series. England's bowlers, especially Wright, strove hard but the Australians emerged victors by five wickets. Hutton batted throughout the first day for 122, his first Test century in Australia. Swanton felt that his innings was not vintage and 'far removed from what we expect of him . . . After some wild swings he displayed batsmanship which would not have disgraced the great Hobbs and then he became pedestrian and closed up altogether'. At least at the end of the day he was still there, a day in which the Australian bowlers bowled from two to three bouncers an over and the *Sydney Morning Herald* conceded that a high percentage of them were directed at Hutton and trusted that 'sober-minded onlookers' would regret their frequency.

It rained all the next day, and on Sunday Hutton felt unwell with a sore throat. On Monday his temperature, registering 103°, matched that of the Australian summer, and he was dispatched to hospital with tonsillitis. For him, the tour was over. The New Zealand crowds, who would shortly see Hammond's last Test innings, would have to wait a few more years to see Hutton. In his first tour of Australia he had not enjoyed the best of health on several occasions, yet he had done well enough to top the averages in both the Tests and all first-class matches. He had withstood bravely a pace attack which was significantly faster than anything that England could offer, and he had unflinchingly faced the risks of injury to his weakened left arm. He had done all he could for a side which was the weaker in leadership – Bradman far outclassed Hammond as a strategist – and in all departments save wicket-keeping. Norman Preston in an ironic sentence in *Wisden* summarized the superiority of the Australians: 'they were in a dilemma as to which bowlers they should leave out.' Something else needs to be added in terms of a man who would captain England in Australia in eight years' time. Hutton liked the Australians and they liked him. His appeal was not one of pawky humour but rather one of sincerity, genuine endeavour and great courage – for this he won the respect of players and he himself made no secret of the fact that going to Australia was the pinnacle of his ambition. There was nothing patronizing about him: instead, a matter-of-fact simplicity which the average Australian took at its face value.

With some of the journalists, he flew home to England, becoming the first professional cricketer to return from an Australian tour by air. From clear skies he looked down on the vastness and barrenness of the Australian outback and wondered at the loneliness of people's lives there compared with the bustling thousands who had filled the great bowls of Melbourne and Sydney. Over Singapore he had time to ponder upon cricket and upon life itself as the plane, with a mechanical defect, circled for three hours using up fuel before daring to land. In Malta, he saw the devastation caused by the war. Finally came London, Heathrow, King's Cross, Leeds and Pudsey. The Hutton family was united but the home-coming was soon saddened by the death of his father to whom he had always been close and who had done so much to encourage his cricket when he was young.

Less than two months later, the 1947 England season began. With centuries against both Universities, Glamorgan and Sussex, and major contributions of 95 and 86 in the Roses match, he came to the first Test against South Africa full of runs. All this was achieved despite continued poor health and some after-effects from an operation for the removal of his tonsils. He missed some games in May but nevertheless had seemed, at one point, as if he would make one thousand runs in a month. In the first three Test matches in which his county colleague, Yardley, was the England captain, he played a modest part and there were the inevitable critics who suggested he should no longer open for England.

He met no such criticism at Headingley in the fourth Test, the first which he had played before his own Yorkshire crowd. John Arlott watched the spectators as they recognized the demands made upon him on a bad wicket and their tolerance of his dogged defence in a way no other crowd would have done. When his century came, they cheered their man 'like an Emperor'. To *The Times* critic, 'he was always playing to the pitch of the ball and utterly certain in his footwork'. A further 83 in the fifth Test was a reminder of his concentration, an innings said *The Times* which 'might well have lasted to eternity', though Arlott felt it one of 'labour rather than glory'. By the end of the summer, he began to feel fit again and his capacity for a long innings was demonstrated in fine fashion in the closing three matches of Yorkshire's programme. He scored 681 runs for an average of 170. Seven thousand people at Southend saw him make 197 and 104 against Essex. He shared in a partnership of 273 with Yardley against Hampshire at Bournemouth and finished with 270 not out – the highest score of the season.

Yorkshire, by their own standards, had a poor season, finishing eighth, and the infrequency of Hutton's appearances had something to do with this, together with the absence from the scene of those stalwarts of the 1930s, Leyland and Barber. The county were experimenting and twenty-six men made an appearance for the 1st XI. The most distinguished of the newcomers would prove to be Wardle.

The summer of 1947 belonged to Compton and Edrich who scored massively at both Test and county level and both of whose aggregates broke the 40-year-old record of 3518 runs by the Surrey player, Tom Hayward. Robertson-Glasgow, in a special feature article in *Wisden*, called Compton the man of genius and Edrich the man of talent. Hutton, without an iota of jealousy in his make-up, was content for it to be so. As a professional cricketer, and a Yorkshire one at that, he had a living to earn and high standards to set, but some of the pressure on him as a batsman at Test level was temporarily removed by their performances and some of the limelight cast in other directions.

In the winter MCC were due to tour the Caribbean. The president of the West Indies Board of Control, Robert Nunes, had asked Sir Pelham Warner to use his influence to get a side sent out as soon as possible after the war; Nunes indicated that the West Indies would not be very strong and Warner, sometimes rather gullible, took him at face value. Hutton would normally have been an early choice for the side but after playing continuously for sixteen months he needed a rest, confessing to Bowes, 'I don't enjoy the game as I used to.' Accordingly he told MCC that he did not wish to be selected, and at the same time the Yorkshire Committee instructed Nash, the secretary, 'to write to MCC asking that Hutton should not be invited to tour'. One is reminded again that the professional cricketer of those days was very much the servant of his Committee in terms of rewards and sanctions. At the same meeting the Yorkshire Committee voted to pay Hutton for a match he missed against the Gentlemen of Ireland; but his request a year or two later to play in a benefit game for Pollard, his cabin-mate on the 1946–47 tour to Australia, was turned down, while permission was given to write some articles.

Gubby Allen, who had captained England in the 1930s, was brought back to lead the new tour. With Compton, Edrich and Bedser also rested with the 1948 Australians in mind, his only colleagues of proven Test ability were Evans, Hardstaff, Ikin and Kenneth Cranston. Injuries on board ship and in the early matches compounded the weakness of the side and the climax of these disasters was reached when there were only seven MCC players in the field against Trinidad – three were off injured, and the captain, himself suffering from both eye and leg trouble, was away telephoning MCC about the crisis. The upshot of his conversation was a phone call to Hutton on 7 February, inviting him to fly out. Compton had been Allen's first preference but he was not fully recovered from a knee operation. Hutton discussed the invitation with Dorothy, with his winter employer, William Harrison, and with the Yorkshire Committee. Dorothy raised no objections, Harrison strongly supported his going and the Yorkshire secretary indicated that the Committee would leave the decision to him. The concern on their part that Hutton was not fit enough, was balanced by the view that a few weeks' sunshine would do him some good. At first Hutton's instinct was to refuse, until reassured by the Committee of their support.

After a busy weekend of injections and some practice in the indoor shed at Headingley, he left Leeds on the coldest day of the winter, five days after the phone call. His plane was even held up for him at Heathrow. Transatlantic air travel, forty years ago, was still something of a novelty and not the swift journey of later years. Hutton flew to Lisbon, then to Dakar in West Africa for the short Atlantic crossing to Brazil. The final stop was Georgetown on the humid mainland of British Guiana. The trip had taken four days during all of which England had been playing the second Test in Trinidad and saving a match in which 'Billy' Griffith made his maiden century in first-class cricket. Hutton, meanwhile, got some practice in the open air and greeted his colleagues on their arrival. Exactly seven days after leaving London, he scored 138, batting throughout the entire day and, wrote Norman Preston, 'dwarfing everything else in the match'. The psychological value of his innings was enormous. He and Jack Robertson put on 100 for the first wicket, the first century partnership of the tour. MCC were able to set British Guiana a challenge (albeit a stiff one) after Hutton made 62 in the second innings. In the Test he scored 31, alone of the England players mastering a difficult wicket. He and Robertson gave England a start of 59 but, as *The Times* correspondent wrote, 'once Hutton was gone, the innings turned into a procession', and England lost by seven wickets. By now the England players recognized the massive batting strength of a West Indies side which included Frank Worrell, Everton Weekes and Clive Walcott – though for all three their greatest achievements lay in the future.

From British Guiana MCC travelled to Jamaica, where Hutton had played a dozen years earlier. His century at Melbourne Park once again helped MCC to have the best of a colony match and was the prelude to contributions of 56 and 60 in the final Test at Sabina Park – not enough to save England from a second defeat but a fine personal example of superb scoring strokes. Swanton felt that the England side came up against 'an accuracy of length and direction and a zest in the field' with which only Hutton had the experience to deal. In his six weeks in the Caribbean he had managed to score almost as many runs as anyone else in the party and his average of 64.22 led the list by far. From Jamaica he flew home via Nassau and New York, where a magnificent ham in his luggage was excused customs duty when he was described to the Americans – for the first, but not the last, time – as the 'Babe Ruth of English cricket'. Tanned and fit, he was ready for the 1948 Australians.

Once a cricketer is firmly established as a Test player, his county has to accept that he will appear in a substantially reduced number of matches – as true in the days when the county championship was the only competition as in our own times. Before the second world war, Yorkshire had such a strong reserve strength that the absence of three or four players seemed to make little difference to their championship prospects. In the years just after, success by their own high standards was not so assured. Yorkshire in 1948 rose from eighth to fourth, with both Yardley and Hutton absent from more than half the games. What Hutton's absence meant was demonstrated by his figures: he scored over 1500 runs, by far the highest aggregate, and averaged 92.05. Eight times he made a century for the county, among the more spectacular occasions being a 176 not out against Sussex – 'a joy and an education to watch', wrote his colleague, Wardle – and 133 against Middlesex at Lord's. He was left stranded on 99 not out against Leicestershire when the county were set 267 to win in three hours, batting throughout the innings until running out of partners with Yorkshire 66 runs short. Of his overall form for Yorkshire, there could be no doubt. As Kilburn reflected in his *History of Yorkshire CCC*, 'the disparity of achievement in 1948 between Hutton and the other batsmen was a source of some misgiving to Yorkshire followers'.

By midsummer he had played against the visiting Australians five times, including two Test Matches. His 74 in the first Test calls for some comment. The Australians had far eclipsed England in the match, leading by well over 300 in the first innings. An England fight-back led by Hutton and Compton seemed to be denying them victory. They were, as Arlott put it, 'threatened by two great batsmen batting at their greatest'. Miller bowled a bouncer to Hutton, then another, then another. Hutton was struck on the shoulder and a Trent Bridge crowd which remembered that Larwood could not bowl against the Australians on their ground in 1934, reacted with boos and protests. For a moment – just a moment – there was tension in the air, and the day's play ended with Miller, the fighter pilot who had faced sterner enemies than a Nottinghamshire crowd, grinning and walking into the pavilion. He had not vanquished Hutton, though that would come early next day – in the dusk of a gloomy morning just before the umpires took the players off.

From the moment of their arrival the Australians showed themselves to be a formidable combination. They won a very large number of matches by the margin of an innings and beat England in the first two Tests by eight wickets and 409 runs respectively. In the desperate search for an equation which would bring success, in the belief that Hutton had played below his true stature and perhaps in the knowledge that he would benefit from a rest, the selectors – without any formal statement – omitted him from the third Test. The Australians feared Hutton the most and they had relentlessly pursued a policy of seeking to shake his confidence. To an extent, they had succeeded – not as much towards Hutton himself as in creating a climate where other batsmen felt that, if he were in trouble, where stood they? He was replaced by the worthy George Emmett who had established himself in the Gloucestershire side after some years. It proved to be Emmett's only Test: fine player of fast bowling as he was, he could not cope with Lindwall. The point needs to be made that nowhere in England might any batsman have found bowling of the pace of Miller or Lindwall against whom to practice. Emmett's ability to play county fast bowlers was only a relative thing.

Hutton's omission caused something of a sensation. *The Cricketer*, still under the editorship of Sir Pelham Warner, usually regarded itself as a supporter of the selectors but this time joined issue with the decision. *The Times* called it a temporary passing and related it to Hutton's concern at being hit on his damaged arm by the pace of Australian bowling. Hutton's telephone never stopped ringing: 'Of course, I had nothing to say.' It was something of a relief to get away, go to the land of his ancestors and play for Yorkshire against Scotland at Paisley. There was a distinct Scottish ring to 'Hutton caught McLaren bowled Laidlaw', and his old county captain, Sellers – in Yardley's absence – gave him a bowl! Scotland saved the day against Yorkshire, as did England against Australia.

Those who have a curiosity as to how a biographer gathers his ideas may find a passing interest in this tale. Rain having stopped play at Lord's one day in 1987, I went into the MCC library and made some notes on the Test matches of 1948. The moment came for a cup of tea and by chance I joined Sir Leonard in the Long Room. We talked about his omission from the third Test. 'I never asked Yardley about it,' he said. 'I'm dining with him on Sunday: won't mention it.'

Immediately after the third Test Hutton returned to the centre of things as captain of the Players against the Gentlemen at Lord's in the match to mark the centenary of the birth of Grace. Yardley led the Gentlemen. Before the match the president of MCC, Lord Cornwallis, took both captains aside and asked them 'to restore the fixture to its rightful place in the cricket calendar'. Hutton did this best in his first experience of leadership in a representative game, achieving a win for his side with a few moments left, and making 59 and 132 not out. *The Times* gave him fulsome praise. He had batted in a way 'which can seldom have been excelled by the most illustrious in this match of such immense memories'. He and Compton represented respectively classic formalism and the genius of informality, and Hutton had 'led the side with efficiency'. It was, of course, too soon for anyone to see him as an England captain and, unlike the example of Hammond, no rumours were circulating that he might one day turn amateur. When they did, Hutton refuted them.

Three weeks later, Scotland played Ireland at Glasgow and their opponents were Mahoneys and Hools, not Yorkshiremen. Hutton was back in his firmament in every sense, for England were playing the fourth Test at Headingley. As he went out to bat, the cheers of the crowd were both a spur and a reminder of a faith and affection that had never faded, wrote Arlott. Those cheers also told Hutton what was expected of him. For all the warmth and goodwill, it was a lonely road he trod to the wicket. With scores of 81 and 57, in Swanton's view, 'he rehabilitated himself completely'. He and Washbrook achieved century opening partnerships in each innings and set a new record by doing so for the second time in Test matches. The match, of course, belonged to the Australians, who were set 404 on the last day and achieved their target. Until that fifth day, England had been 'in the game' and given as good as they got. Hutton was called upon to bowl and, in Cardus's words, delivered 'five innocent, amiable full pitches from which Bradman and Morris flicked five fours with lazy strokes over the grassy outfield'. It was something to which the Yorkshire crowd did not take kindly. They had not come to see Hutton, the batsman, become bowling fodder for the Australians.

Whatever vengeance the Australians might have contemplated for The Oval, 1938, was duly extracted at The Oval, 1948. Bradman played his last Test innings and was bowled by Hollies fractionally short of a Test match batting average of 100. Hutton alone saved the England first innings from utter ignominy. Play began on a wicket saturated by a week's rain and great mounds of sawdust made their appearance. The England innings lasted two hours and ten minutes. There were five ducks and everyone made a single-figure score save Hutton, who was last out for 30. He had batted, wrote Cardus, 'in splendid isolation, an innings of noble loneliness withstanding one of the finest pieces of fast bowling of our times'. 'It was Hutton', wrote *Wisden*, 'in his customary, stylish, masterful manner.' His dismissal – and in Arlott's view he had looked entirely unruffled throughout – typified the greatness of this Australian side. A sound leg glance was caught by Don Tallon, moving three yards to his left and making a catch which was possibly beyond the achievement of any other contemporary wicket-keeper except Evans.

When England batted a second time, Hutton, though not for the entire innings, played the same role. Alex Bannister, who would get to know him so well a few years later, wrote that he alone offered 'a gallant resistance to the inevitable conclusion'. The Oval crowd warmed to him even more than they had done ten years earlier. Then he had set up statistical ramparts. Now he stood, the one solid bastion in the English defence. The English, good in defeat, offered generous plaudits to the Australians. They had won handsomely and magnificently said *The Times* and 'they had in Bradman the greatest cricketer of the present age to rank with Trumper, Ranji and Hobbs'. With Bradman now gone, there was no one in the world to challenge Hutton's supremacy.

Hutton in 1948 had faced one of his sternest seasons. The Australian fast bowlers were at the peak of their form and he had had to readjust his reflexes to a pace not comparable with anything else he had ever met. Added to which there was the ever-nagging thought of his arm to which a further injury might put paid to his cricket for ever. The Australians regarded an attack on him at his weakest point as a legitimate weapon against the batsman they most feared. To reduce him to the ranks of mundane batsmanship was to render the whole of England's batting sterile. To remove him from the arena altogether was to create a sense of total triumph, and this they had achieved when the selectors omitted him. All this made him an anxious man, concerned to adjust his batting to his own physical circumstances and conscious of the responsibilites he bore. How far he triumphed over adversity may be measured by his performances after he returned to the England side. Part of the credit must go to his partner Washbrook: their century partnerships at Leeds were joint exercises in technique, concentration and courage. His season ended with a pleasant Southern tour, the Scarborough Festival and a final look at the Australians. By now it was mid-September and time for a little golf and family life before embarking with MCC for South Africa.

From a dismal start on the first day of the tour at Cape Town, marked by poor fielding, indifferent bowling and a Western Province total of 386 for 4, MCC could only get better. The story is best begun on the second day. The new England captain, George Mann, led from the front with a century and MCC were launched on a tour in which they would suffer no defeats, win the Test series and bring unprecedented crowds to see them wherever they went. They were a happy party, as much a team off the field as on, commented the journalist, R. J. Hayter, and they gave English cricket a much-needed fillip after the experiences of the preceding summer.

In all this Hutton played a not inconsiderable part, revealing in match after match a brilliant display of stroke-making which was the hallmark of his cricket as the 1940s came to an end. He, Washbrook and Simpson were the three opening batsmen and all of them finished with a tour average of over 50. With substantial contributions coming from Compton and Jack Crapp, Hutton had no need to feel the burden of total responsibility for an MCC or England total. Instead, in Hayter's view, he 'strode from triumph to triumph'. When England came to the first Test just before Christmas, he had already scored three centuries. In the Test itself, he and Washbrook gave England a solid start to which he contributed 83. John Arlott, one of seven journalists accompanying the party, wrote that he coped with the very considerable pace of Cuan McCarthy and produced cover drives in which he 'threw his bat at the ball with the joy of a boy and the elegance of a fencing-master'. The match itself was memorable because four results were possible with three balls left. England won off the last ball after Cliff Gladwin and Bedser had scrambled a leg-bye.

The second Test at Johannesburg was played on the new ground at Ellis Park in conditions greatly favouring batsmen and before the largest crowd ever to watch a match in South Africa. Hutton and Washbrook put on 359 for England's first wicket, of which Hutton made 158, still (1990) the record England first-wicket partnership against all countries. It was a day of shimmering heat which, wrote Swanton, 'even the locals found tedious'. By tea each had made a century and Arlott spotted them both relaxing affably with no sense of strain. After tea the two, in Swanton's words, 'reaped the fruits of their utter subjection of Nourse's seven bowlers and they struck at the ball without a seeming thought of either safety or the bettering of statistical milestones'. Despite requiring South Africa to follow on, England failed to force a victory. There was a certain irony in the draw, for Eric Rowan, who saved South Africa with 156 not out, knew he had already been omitted from the next Test starting two days later at Cape Town.

1 LH, aged five, 1921.

2 The Street, Fulneck.

3 'Fascinated by wood and timber', 1931 (*Evening Standard Collection BBC Hulton Picture Library*).

4 Edmund, George,
Reginald and LH,
Pudsey, 1933
(*Telegraph & Argus*).

5 Yorkshire, 1934
(*Albert Wilkes &
Son*).

6 With Sutcliffe at
Hove, 1937
(*Sussex Daily News*).

7 The Oval Test, 1938: Saturday, opening the innings with Edrich (*Central Press Photos Ltd*).

8 Sunday, on the sands at Bognor with Verity.

9 Monday, leaving his hotel with Hardstaff (*BBC Hulton Picture Library*).

10 Receiving congratulations from Hardstaff and Bradman
after passing Bradman's record (*Central Press Photos Ltd*).

11 Charity match at Headingley, 1940: arriving with his wife
(*Mail Newspapers PLC*).

12 Verity, Smailes, Sutcliffe, Leyland, LH (*R. J. Du Bois*).

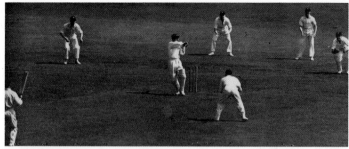

13 The Rest *v.* Australia at Lord's, 1944 (*Sport & General*).

14 Yorkshire *v.* Australians at Bradford, 1948.

15 England *v.* Australia at Headingley, 1948 (*Sport & General*).

16 Yorkshire *v.*
Middlesex at Lord's
1951 (*Sport & General*).

17 Surrey applaud LH's
century of centuries at
the Oval, 1951
(*Central Press Photos Ltd*).

18 The Bedser–Hutton
trap: England *v.* South
Africa at Old Trafford,
1951
(*Central Press Photos Ltd*).

19 With his wife and John on the day he became England captain, 1952 (*Photopress*).

20 The captain waits his turn, *c.* 1952 (*Douglas Glass*).

21 The side which won the Ashes at the Oval, 1953 (*Central Press Photos Ltd*).

Newlands, Cape Town, on the first day of the New Year, was a scene of colourful splendour with the massive backcloth of Table Mountain skirting its entire length, its colours changing in shadow and shade as the sun reached and passed its northern zenith. It was a peaceful setting before which a holiday crowd watched from under the massive oak trees or the nearby pines. But the year was 1949 and the Nationalist Party had begun to assume its grip on South African politics and to pursue the policy of apartheid which would bedevil both the country and its cricket. Not even the wicket itself was immune from the undercurrents of change. Instead of the former somnolent Newlands turf, there was a pitch with the chicanery of bounce and spin. For Hutton deception stood in wait. First he beguiled the crowd and sapped their partisanship with his batting, then he slipped, fell and was run out with slow-motion ease. To his 41, ending in mishap, he added in the second innings 87 'charming and masterly runs'. So adjudged Swanton who allowed himself the extravagance of saying that Hutton was 'surely hitting the ball through the covers as well as any cricketer had ever done'. The match itself, which began with expectancy and promise, ended lamely with South Africa failing to accept an admittedly stiff target.

MCC set off northwards to the Transvaal and Rhodesia, the Rhodesians, not for the first time, having a visiting MCC side in the wet season. Their disappointment at curtailed play gave the weary England travellers a little rest in a tour of much travelling before returning to Ellis Park, Johannesburg, for the fourth Test where an effort had been made to produce a more balanced wicket. Hutton's century held together an innings which was in danger of collapse against Athol Rowan's off-breaks – sometimes a Hutton weakness, but not on this occasion. He had played, said John Hughes, writing for *The Times*, 'a splendid and flawless innings, as near perfection as the most hypercritical could expect'. The game itself was drawn. Arlott criticized the failure of the South Africans to accept a challenge.

The second victory for England came in the fifth Test in circumstances as dramatic as their earlier one in the first Test. Under the rules as they stood – before the days of twenty overs in the last hour – one minute remained for play and England needed ten in three balls; they were safely secured by Crapp. Narrow as the two victories in the series had been, England's success was deserved. The side had attacked, with Hutton setting an example, when so often South Africa had defended. Nevertheless, it had been a series of great friendliness. Arlott detected not the slightest suggestion of even the mildest strife. Contentment within the party conveyed itself to the crowds and

MCC were popular visitors. Hutton, never one to play to the public, detected a familiar accent in the crowd while fielding on the boundary. When a wicket fell, he turned round, exclaimed, 'A Yorkshire lass', and got into conversation. He was told she had bowled to him in Roundhay Park, Leeds, as a schoolgirl. Suddenly Pudsey became important. Sad as were the farewells on a tour of particular enjoyment, the voyage home beckoned.

In cold and cheerless weather Yorkshire played the New Zealanders at the end of April, Hutton's 167 being the predominant feature. Over four months later, at the beginning of September, he made a century for the North against the South at the Scarborough Festival. The two occasions stand as symbols of his performances throughout 1949. In match after match he featured substantially to the tune of more than 3000 runs and 12 centuries. And, since cricket of all games is the great leveller, there was one match against Worcestershire when he was dismissed twice by Reg Perks for nought.

At Old Trafford he became only the second Yorkshireman to score a double-century in a Roses match, the prelude to centuries in the first Test and against Northamptonshire and Middlesex. Against Sussex he scored two centuries in the same match for the second time in his career, and by scoring a further 80 against the same county a week later, he achieved an aggregate of 1294 runs for June, breaking the previous record of 1281 runs in any month established by Hammond in August 1936. He had already reached 1000 runs earlier in the season than any other Yorkshireman had ever done. With only four Tests instead of five and with fewer rests, Hutton played in a larger number of matches for Yorkshire than usual, helping the county to return to the top of the Championship (shared with Middlesex) and to win more than half of their games. When the circumstances dictated, he batted with the dedicated defence of which he was so capable, but if quick runs were wanted to bring about a Yorkshire win, he would respond. He was essentially a cricketer for whom the needs of the side came first. The selfish pursuit of personal targets was never a factor of his approach to cricket, though when in form some of his partners noticed that he tried to get most of the bowling.

His highest score of the season was made at Wellingborough against Northamptonshire where Yorkshire played for the first time on the grounds of Wellingborough School. Inspired, perhaps, by W. G. Grace's front doorstep which had found its way to the school to become the pavilion step, he made 269 not out. Kilburn in his *History* remarked that:

The match epitomized the season's character. The batting was dominated by Hutton and the bowling was quite inadequate on anything but bowlers' wickets. His performance was remarkable even by his own standards. His was the most precious of Yorkshire wickets.

Almost immediately afterwards came another double-century in the fourth Test at The Oval. Freddie Brown, the new Northampton-shire captain, had bowled unavailingly against him in the earlier game. Now, as the new England captain as well – brought back to Test cricket because he had led Northamptonshire so successfully – he must have been glad to have had Hutton on the same side. Hayter, who saw so much of Hutton's batting over the years, called it an innings which 'could not be faulted in any way' and felt the Oval crowd were watching a display of power, grace and certainty which few could have ever seen before. The final days of the summer brought him two centuries and four half-centuries in the three matches of the Scarborough Festival.

It had been a season for the statisticians, and to their records he and Simpson had added the highest first-wicket partnership against New Zealand and he and Edrich the highest for any wicket against New Zealand, while his 206 was the highest by an England player in England against New Zealand. In all first-class cricket his aggregate of 3429 runs was fourth, behind those of Compton, Edrich and Hayward.

After the season was over came a two-day game at Maltby between his XI and Sellers' which realized £190 as the opening round of his own benefit account for the coming year. A few days later the Centenary Dinner of the Roses match was held in the Grand Hotel, Sheffield, to which eighty-seven survivors of the contest came. Hutton, by his double-century at Old Trafford, had made the centenary year memorable. Now he had earned a winter at home for the first time for four years. His main preoccupation would be to establish a sports business in Bridge Street, Bradford, near St George's Hall, of which he and Dorothy were co-directors. It was the first indication that he would not play cricket for many more years and of the need to provide for the future. The business got off to a sound start, thanks to the advice of his brother Edmund, secretary of the Bradford and Bingley Building Society, to the hours put into it by Dorothy and to his own willingness to deal personally with customers' requests. One small customer recalled being allowed to talk cricket to the great man without having to buy something and to part with a precious sixpence.

On the evidence of the season of 1949 Hutton was at the height of his powers. At the age of thirty-three he was the utterly mature cricketer with over 70 Test innings, 25,000 first-class runs and exactly 85 centuries behind him. For both England and Yorkshire he had averaged over 50. From Bath (where his average would be 3.00!) to Bulawayo – and on 56 other first-class grounds besides – they had seen him bat. In an article in the *Wisden* of 1950, Vivian Jenkins, the sports commentator and Welsh rugby international, called him 'a man fit to wear the mantle of England opener handed down from Shrewsbury, through Grace and MacLaren to Hobbs and Hayward and who in his person and his craft personified dignity and elegance'.

The editor of *Wisden* also singled him out for special attention in his own 'Notes', and in another paragraph opened the debate on who would be the next captain of England. Age was catching up on the current amateurs, Mann and Brown, and there were no obvious replacements. The assumption still remained that an amateur would be appointed and neither the names of Hutton, who had led Yorkshire occasionally and had captained the Players, nor of Compton, who had also sometimes captained the Players, were mentioned. Albeit, attitudes to professionals were changing. 1949 saw the election of the first honorary Life Members of MCC from the ranks of retired professionals. Hutton himself had suggested the idea to Allen on the MCC tour of the West Indies and it had won the approval of the Committee. Hutton, as a player, was of course not eligible. From the roll of Yorkshire cricketers, the honour went to Bowes, Hirst, Leyland, Rhodes and Sutcliffe.

When one sets aside the statistics of 1949 and distances oneself from the public image, one comes back to the private person of Leonard Hutton. Cricket remained something to which he was dedicated and committed. He would one day say it was not a game he played for fun – a remark often thrown back at him and whose utterance he half-regretted in conversation with me. 'Of course I enjoyed it, but at the level I played you had to be stern in your approach,' he commented. And it was essentially a business enterprise in which his particular talents were put to their best use. He thought about his role much as an actor contemplates the part he may play on stage and brought the same sense of preparation to his own performances. 'Think as you walk out to bat,' he would tell an inexperienced partner. Off-stage he infinitely preferred the domesticity of home and family to the irksomeness of travel, the odour of dressing rooms, the monotony of hotels and the clinking of glasses. He was never unaware of what was expected of him and the public image he had to present. Thomas Moult, the journalist and poet, helped him in 1949 to assemble his first book of memoirs. Cricket, Hutton wrote, had displayed to him humanity, goodness, sternness and sentiment. Perhaps the words were more recognizably those of the poet than the cricketer but the title of the book itself, *Cricket is My Life*, was indisputably his own aphorism.

6

Senior Professional

1950–51

'Hutton alone maintained the reputation of English batsmanship. He would have been outstanding in any age or
generation.'

A. G. Moyes, *Sydney Morning Herald*, 1951

A picture in the *Yorkshire Evening Post* on Saturday 15 July, 1950
caught the mood of the moment – a spectator shaking Hutton's hand
as he walked into the Headingley pavilion in blazer and flannels, a
young lady poised with her camera, another with her autograph book,
schoolboys in shorts, a smiling police sergeant. Behind them was a
crowd of some 30,000 who had come on a cloudy St Swithin's Day to
pay their tribute, in cash and good will, to Hutton in his benefit match.
Eighty-four-year-old John Levitt, a retired miner, had left his home at
5 o'clock in the morning to be the first person through the turnstiles at
the Kirkstall Lane end. Gordon Blyth, a railway clerk in London and a
Middlesex supporter, had travelled up overnight to see his favourite
cricketer. Middlesex's Gubby Allen had come out of retirement to
lead the county and it was he who tossed up with Hutton, using a 1788
spade ace guinea provided by a Yorkshire supporter.

The morning paper, the *Yorkshire Post*, carried an Open Letter to
Hutton written by J. M. Kilburn in which he spoke of the pleasure
which he had given to so many:

Without your cricket the world would have been a poorer place, for you

86

have created beauty, you have sought and touched perfection in your chosen sphere.

You have taken people outside themselves, given them a glimpse of artistry, however dimly understood, to lighten the gloom of frustration and warm the hearth of memory. We are better men for having seen you stand upon your back foot and flash the ball through the covers, because, so watching, we have sipped the wine of wonderment, which is man's privilege above the beasts.

The match itself was badly affected by rain. Disappointing as this was in cricketing and social terms, collections throughout the summer, together with insurance for loss of play, gave Hutton the outstanding benefit of £9,713, up to that point by far the highest ever received by a Yorkshire player, and free of income tax. The Committee, in accordance with their normal practice, retained two-thirds of the sum and invested it for him in gilt-edged securities. He did not get the capital back until 1972. To protect a professional's benefit money must sometimes have been wise and it would have been difficult for individual exceptions to have been made. Twenty years earlier the Warwickshire cricketer Jack Parsons, who had returned to professional cricket after commissioned service in the Indian Army, very much resented his Committee investing on his behalf the entire £881 which was the net profit of his benefit in 1926. Hutton, too, thought he could have invested his money to better advantage, and strongly resented the paternalism of the Committee. Parsons' benefit had been the second highest in Warwickshire's history. Hutton's, with little inflation in the intervening years, was ten times as much and represented a very substantial sum.

By and large, the professionals of Hutton's generation never became rich through their cricket. In the immediate post-war years as a capped Yorkshire player Hutton earned about £600 in a domestic season and during the winter months the County paid him £3 a week. He would also qualify for a share in the end of season talent money and occasional bonuses. One year, the Committee voted him a bonus of £20 and, in the same meeting, voted £25 to an amateur as a wedding present. At first glance, the figures seem incongruous – a season's efforts worth less than a wedding present – until one remembers that amateurs were finding it hard to be able to afford to play first-class cricket for nothing but their expenses. From other directions, Hutton derived an additional income. From time to time, the Yorkshire Committee record in their minutes permission for him to publish an article. The story is told that when he returned from the tour in South

Africa in 1949, for which he was paid £450, Thomas Moult greeted him with the finished manuscript of *Cricket is My Life*. Hutton's first question was, 'How much will we make?' – a reasonable question from an author, echoing the dictum of Samuel Johnson, his own literary hero, that 'no man but a blockhead ever wrote, except for money'.

Advertising had come his way ever since the Oval Test in 1938 and he gave his name, as we have seen, to items of equipment such as bats and pads. During the winter of 1950–51 Slazengers worked on a new bat handle to meet his specifications. While retaining the traditional build-up of cane and the central thick rubber insert, it introduced secondary thick rubber inserts on either side, with thick cork at the top. The effect was to give greater resilience and to provide extra speed. Hutton approved the research, used the new bat and Slazengers introduced it into their range of products. Both they and he were the financial beneficiaries, Hutton being paid commission of a shilling (5p) for each bat sold. To all this has to be added the payment he received from overseas tours which marked the financial distinction between the run-of-the-mill county player and the England one. Hutton had toured three times since the war and in September 1950 he would embark on his fourth as a member of the MCC party to Australia and New Zealand. He would earn £1000 by doing so, as well as a weekly allowance of £2 on land and £1.50 at sea. Of English professional cricketers at the time only Compton fared financially as well as Hutton, and only one of them could advertise Brylcreem.

In the remaining years of Hutton's career there would be no more Championship bonuses. The Yorkshire side of the 1950s seemed unable to crystallize individual talent, and while achieving final places in the County Championship close to the top, they never managed to win. That there were players of talent measured by the highest standard is undisputed, and several of them played for England. We should notice some of those who were Hutton's colleagues, younger men than he who were in awe of the great man, and looked to him, not always successfully, for guidance as senior professional. Yardley and Harry Halliday alone from pre-war days remained, and the passing of the generations was marked by the presence of Herbert Sutcliffe's son, Billy. The Yorkshire innings, when Hutton was absent, was opened by Halliday – another product of Pudsey – and Frank Lowson, who had joined the county in 1949 and who would in a brief career of ten years play in seven Tests. By opening the batting so often with Hutton, Lowson received less attention than he might have done. As his obituarist in *Wisden* remarked, 'the crowd had come to see Ajax the

Great, not Ajax the Less'. In strong support in the middle order there was Vic Wilson, a quietly-spoken farmer from Scampston. He would become, in due course, Yorkshire's first twentieth-century professional captain. Among the bowlers were Wardle, who had carried the lion's share of Yorkshire's attack since the war, Alec Coxon, something of an all-rounder, and another young man who deserves a paragraph to himself.

Frederick Sewards Trueman, a miner's son, was taken in hand in the Yorkshire nets by Mitchell and Bowes. In Bowes' view he had three great assets: 'a love of fast bowling, a powerful physique and a smooth cartwheel action'. In 1950 speed was the main weapon in his armoury: the rest would follow. It was a speed sufficient to earn him a place for The Rest against England in the Test Trial designed to give the England batsmen some practice against really fast bowling, and the newcomer had the temerity to clean bowl Hutton.

Finally, there was Brian Close who had already played for England, the youngest man ever to do so. During the summer of 1950 he was undertaking his National Service in the Royal Signals but he would be given leave by the Army to go with MCC to Australia in the autumn. Hutton had a high opinion of him as a batsman and he would become the second Yorkshire professional to captain England. It was a happy enough, if undynamic, team under Yardley whom Hutton thought of as a kind and considerate captain, combining authority and dignity with his own talents. Yorkshire's troubles and disaffection lay in the future.

In match after match during the opening weeks of the 1950 season Hutton batted on difficult wickets affected by rain and in none of them may he be said to have failed. By the end of May, Yorkshire had won only one game and in half of their fixtures he made the top score in either or both innings. In Yorkshire's defeat by the West Indies he alone coped with any confidence against a varied attack of pace and spin. It was a pattern he maintained in the Test Trial at Bradford. After Jim Laker had taken eight Rest wickets for two, to create the lowest score (27) made by a representative side above county level, Hutton gave what *Wisden* was moved to call 'a dazzling display of batsmanship on a difficult pitch', though the comment was generally made that the bowling was indifferent and even erratic. Immediately afterwards, he hit the fastest hundred of the season in 73 minutes against Derbyshire.

By the middle of June the West Indies, with four wins behind them, were strongly established as a very formidable combination. They would be known in cricketing history as the side of the three Ws and the 'twins', but beyond those five – Weekes, Worrell, Walcott, 'Sonny' Ramadhin and Alf Valentine – there lay a bunch of extremely capable all-rounders so that, unlike most touring teams, they were scarcely affected by injuries. The first Test at Old Trafford was played on a wicket causing both lift and turn. England found Valentine particularly difficult and Hutton was hit on the index finger of his right hand so painfully that he was forced to retire. Later he resumed his innings and batted in the second innings, often taking his injured hand off the bat as he played a stroke and taking the strain with his weakened left arm. *The Times* correspondent remarked, 'an injured player is never satisfactory for there is the feeling that the opposition might unconsciously spare him. Not that Hutton required any mercy for his talent in seeing the ball and timing it could overcome any handicap, one off-drive being perfectly made as if he had four hands'. His match aggregate of 84 was a staunch display of courage and his injury was sufficient to keep him out of cricket for a fortnight. The Essex bowlers were the recipients of his return to the Yorkshire side; against them he made 156.

The Old Trafford Test proved to be England's only victory in the series. In between it and the Lord's Test the West Indies won three successive matches by an innings. They would now proceed to win three Test matches running, do the double over Yorkshire and secure a substantial number of other victories. In the Lord's Test Hutton was rather uncharacteristically stumped moving down the pitch to Valentine; he dropped out through lumbago on the morning of the third Test, while he batted at his very best both in the Yorkshire match against the West Indies and in the Oval Test. After the West Indies had made what was becoming almost their customary 500 runs in an innings, England replied on a difficult wicket with the hope of saving the follow-on and requiring the West Indies to bat in similar conditions, but the last five wickets fell for 16 and they were 10 short of their target. Hutton began the England innings just over an hour before the end of play on the Monday. He batted throughout the Tuesday and when the innings ended on the Wednesday he was left 202 not out. He had not given a chance in nearly eight hours and had made the highest score by an England player against the West Indies in England. It was an innings which, in its technical demands, called for even greater reserves of strength than had been asked of him at The Oval twelve years earlier. He alone, of the England batsmen, said *The Times*, displayed 'ease and composure', though S. C. Griffith writing in *The Cricketer* felt that he should have shown more aggression in the opening partnership with Simpson. Had he done so, England might have avoided the follow-on and saved the match. Nevertheless, he had displayed the concentration of effort and perfection of stroke play which had been the hallmark of his career for so long. Ramadhin, who had never heard of Hutton until he came to England, so he told his captain, certainly knew who he was by now.

If one discounts the war years, Hutton had now scored 4000 runs in Test cricket in six seasons – two years quicker than had Hobbs, Sutcliffe, Hammond or Bradman. He was still a comparatively young man, though a veteran in experience. Those who made comparisons with Hobbs worked out that he could still be playing for England in 1964. If the comparison be made with Sutcliffe there were seven years left for Hutton at Test match level. Sadly, both predictions would prove wrong. Injury or pain, from which he was seldom entirely free, would triumph over intent and purpose.

Shortly after the second Test against the West Indies, MCC had announced that neither Mann, who had captured MCC in South Africa, nor the current captain, Yardley, would be able to accept an invitation to lead the forthcoming tour to Australia. Immediately, the press began to discuss other possible amateurs, including Hubert Doggart, the Cambridge University captain, and Griffith, now rather more a journalist than a player. To Australians the search for an amateur, however little experienced at the highest level, seemed a strange pursuit. Mann had played only four matches for Middlesex all season, and Griffith, two for Sussex. Swanton, in the *Daily Telegraph*, denied that officaldom had a 'prejudice against the professionals' and he himself felt that one might possibly be found 'among their estimable band'. In some quarters the name of 'Tom' Dollery, the Warwickshire professional captain, of whom Hutton had a high opinion, was mentioned, as was that of Compton. Immediately after the third Test, Dollery emerged as captain of the Players at Lord's while the Gentlemen were captained by Brown. Yardley was in the side and MCC announced that it had been Yardley's wish that Brown should have an honour that had not hitherto been his.

Brown's own greatest cricketing days were over – or so it seemed – and, when he took the field as captain of the Gentlemen, he had in mind a winter trip to South Africa, business-cum-cricket. Three days later he was the new England captain, having scored 122 out of 131, bowled the most overs and taken the most wickets in the Players' first innings, and set them a target which made for an exciting finish. Swanton remarked: 'Brown's runs were the product of a style of play which is essentially that of a cricketer not under the restraints and taboos of one who plays for a living.' No one had mentioned Hutton as a possible

MCC captain, nor, indeed, had there been any reason why they should. His fellow professional, Compton, became vice-captain, ahead of the four Cambridge Blues and amateurs who were to be in the touring side. Therein lay some measure of surprise but in the appointment of Compton as opposed to himself Sir Leonard saw none: 'There was no way I could compete with him in the popularity stakes, and the debonair way he played his cricket attracted both the powers-that-be and the public.' Nevertheless, in the batting misfortunes which followed Compton on the tour lay the first hints that it might be Hutton who would one day captain England.

On 14 September, 1950 SS *Stratheden* left Tilbury with a party of sixteen cricketers and two managers. Washbrook would fly out later and two young Lancashire bowlers, Roy Tattersall and Brian Statham, be recruited in January because of injuries. For fellow Yorkshiremen, Hutton had Close and one of the joint-managers, Nash, his county secretary and a Pudsey man. To these were added twenty-eight journalists and broadcasters.

There were some distinct contrasts between this tour of Australia and the one of four years earlier. Then there had been a captain in Hammond with claims to be the greatest all-rounder in the game but whose introversion made the business of leadership difficult. Now there was, in Brown, a captain of more modest talent but whose extrovert personality made him a natural leader. Then there had been a side criticized for its age. Now there was one criticized for its youth. Then they had crossed Australia west to east by train, now they did so by air. Then the voyage out had been an austerity one, now there was comfort, even luxury. One factor remained the same, and Hutton was inescapably linked to it. England had not won a Test match against Australia since 1938 and the reliance on Hutton's batting abilities and on his cool, detached temperament were as great as ever they had been. The more the younger men would fail on the tour, the more would be expected of him. In the event his Test average would be 88, the 30-year-old Simpson's 38, the veteran Brown's 26, and no one else would reach 20.

Hutton's tour began badly. The *Stratheden* called at Colombo for fuel, MCC played Ceylon and he was hit twice on the finger which he had hurt in the previous England season. The joint swelled up and it would be at Adelaide, a month later, before he was able to make his first appearance, score a century and be gently chided by Harold Larwood in King William Street for not knowing by whom he had been accosted.

A professional cricketer unable to ply his trade through injury can find time lying heavily on his hands, especially on a tour. Hutton played some golf, batted in the nets at Perth and tried to find out what he could about Australia's mystery spin-bowler, Jack Iverson. After a dozen years not playing at all since he left school, Iverson, while serving in the Forces, had developed his own form of spinning the ball either way without a change of action. For a brief two years, 1949–51, he was a leading Australian bowler, as much feared by Brown's side as was Lindwall. Indeed, *Wisden*'s comment on the match between MCC and Victoria at Melbourne began with the statement: 'This was the first clash between the MCC batsmen and Iverson.' Hutton had jocularly tried, without avail, to get Iverson to bowl to him in the nets a day or two before the match. In the event it was Washbrook, his partner, who was bothered by the new bowler rather than Hutton and the critics felt that several others of the MCC side were equally anxious against him. The New South Wales match at Sydney, with a century from Hutton, indicated how much MCC had to depend on its trio of Hutton, Washbrook and Compton as batsmen, but the main concern was the lack of endeavour both in bowling and fielding. Compton had captained MCC against both Victoria and New South Wales and the Australian press was critical of the lack of support given to him in the field.

The first Test at Brisbane, to which MCC came with such a low public rating, has its place in cricketing history as a match totally determined by the weather and in which England, although playing much above expectations and the better side on the day, lost to Australia and to the elements. Australia batted on a good pitch and Hutton got England off to a good start by taking a sharp catch at fine leg off the fourth ball of the day. This set a personal standard for himself which he maintained throughout the tour, and he provided a demonstration in technique to many of the younger men, among whom the dropping of catches became an epidemic. Only Evans, the wicket-keeper, caught more than he, and Hutton's catching of both Hassett and Tallon in the fifth Test were oustanding examples. At the end of the first day, Australia had been dismissed for 228 and journalists in the press box were noticing that Brown had often consulted Hutton, his senior professional, rather than Compton, his vice-captain. Brown recollected that he valued Hutton's ability to think a match through. It had been England's best day in the field against Australia since 1938.

Then came the rain, as it had done four years earlier, cascading down on the corrugated iron roofs with the awesome authority of a monsoon. When cricket was resumed, after a blank Saturday, all England's advantage had been lost. On an Australian sticky wicket of unfathomable proportions, Washbrook and Simpson took England to 28 before Washbrook went. From that point onwards, 23 wickets fell for 194 runs, an average of 8.43 per batsman. England declared at 68 for 7, with Hutton 8 not out, having gone in lower down to stiffen the middle batting. Australia then declared at 32 for 7 and England were left 193 to win.

Before England began their second innings, Brown asked for the heavy roller and Dobbin, the resident horse, pulled it. The time taken in unhitching him at either end of the wicket, swinging the shafts and hitching him up again was all potential rolling-time lost and Brown insisted that it be not counted in the ten minutes which the (then) Law 10 allowed. England might have had a better chance of securing their target if the pitch had been better rolled: Dobbin's rolling days were numbered. The first six wickets fell for 30. Hutton had again gone in lower down, and he alone coped with the conditions. Australia could not assume victory so long as he was at the wicket. With Wright, he put on 45 for the last wicket, to which Wright contributed 2, and Hutton, with 62, was again left not out. Australian and English critics were unanimous in their praise. Tom Goodman, writing in the *Sydney Morning Herald* called Hutton's innings the best which he had ever played in Australia. Fingleton analysed the way in which his dead-bat technique ensured that there was no power in the ball as he played it down to his feet. He noticed the way in which Hutton defied the fielders whether set close or on the boundary and ensured that the bowling was kept away from Wright. English journalists were heard to be discussing in the bars whether the innings might not be seen as the best he had ever played in a Test match, though none of them said so in print. Swanton admired his strokeplay, John Woodcock the way he drove Lindwall, and Hayter the way, despite his physical difficulties, he hooked both Miller and Lindwall. After the tour was over, Miller in an article in *Sporting Life* was less appreciative:

> I thought Hutton's innings was over-rated by the critics who went into raptures about it. It was sparkling – spectacular if you like. But when England needed 116 to win with Wright, what did he do? He took chances. He threw the bat at Lindwall. What is more, he got away with it.

The Test at Brisbane was over but two questions remained for the authorities. Should Test match wickets in Australia be covered, and should a Test be played in Brisbane at a potentially wet time of the year? Money had been lost at the gate, the actual playing time was scarcely more than two days, and visitors from distant Queensland sheep stations disappointed. Bruce Harris, paid to watch rather than paying, took a different view – with a covered wicket he would have been denied the chance to see Hutton batting in difficult circumstances, though he was a little less enthusiastic about watching cricket a week later at Canberra when the authorities provided no lunch facilities for the press! Four years later, in 1954–55, the wickets were covered.

England came tantalizingly close to victory in the second Test at Melbourne, falling short by 28 runs. Once again, all seemed to depend on Hutton as they set off in pursuit of 179 runs in the last innings and again he batted lower down, making 40 out of England's 150. He found some difficulty in playing Johnson, when the ball dipped late in flight and turned sharply, though none with Iverson. Arthur Mailey called his mastery of Iverson 'the most consoling feature of England's batting.' Hutton had been dismissed for 12 in England's first innings, a catch at the wicket being upheld after a lone appeal. He was convinced the ball had only touched his pad and departed looking more bewildered than annoyed; Miller fielding at silly mid-on did not think he came within inches of the ball. If it were a wrong decision, and many thought so, it could be seen as a crucial one. Had Hutton made, say, another 30 in the first innings, the Test might have been won and the series remained wide open – England were still being rated as the better side. There was some parallel in his dismissal with Ikin's unsuccessful appeal for a catch against Bradman at Brisbane in 1946.

For the remainder of the tour, Hutton (with one exception) returned to his place as an opening batsman and demonstrated the rightfulness of this in a century against New South Wales at Sydney, even surviving the bringing on of drinks when he was 99. He and Simpson put on 236 for the third wicket and Hutton was particularly effective against Lindwall and Miller. It was good cricket for the statisticians and batting practice for MCC for the Test, but a few days later they lost to Australia by an innings and 13 runs, conceding the rubber and not regaining the Ashes. With figures of 6 for 27, Iverson reached the apogee of his brief career. Four times in seven overs he rapped Hutton on the pads and he secured his wicket in the second innings.

After Sydney, Brown took a holiday, Compton led MCC in Tasmania, and became the first professional captain this century to win a match on tour. Hutton, having volunteered to take charge of all the baggage, set sail for Adelaide. It was a pleasant voyage down the coast of the Pacific through the Bass Strait and into the fringes of the Great Australian Bight – names of meaning to a geographer or a sailor: to Hutton just a chance to relax as his vessel ploughed its course through blue waters under a northern sun rendered gentle by the breezes. The idyll ended at Adelaide itself where bush fires raged, mosquitoes indulged and thermometers soared. The weather was too hot even for the good citizens of Adelaide to come out and watch the state game which the MCC won comfortably enough. The players found some relief in staying at the seaside resort of Glenelg and swimming in the bay when the day's play was over. By the time the Australian Test players arrived, the temperature had dropped to a mere 90° and the fourth Test was played in slightly more equable conditions, which was just as well for Tattersall, not long out from England and making his debut at Test level.

As in the first Test, so in the fourth, a match which England lost belonged to Hutton. Morris made a double-century, James Burke a century on his Test debut, and Miller 99 – significant proportions of an Australian victory by 274 runs and England's sixth successive defeat in a Test against Australia. Hutton was the redeeming feature in England's performance. A press photograph shows him walking off the field, having carried his bat for 156 in the England innings of 272 (and for the second time in six months), head down and face drawn, the entire Australian side applauding. He became only the second English batsman to do this against Australia, the first being Abel in 1892 at Sydney. From the criticism of England's injudicious batting he earned complete exemption, wrote Hayter in his report for *Wisden*. 'The speed of Lindwall and Miller, the spin of Iverson and Johnson and the mixture of swing and spin provided by Johnston, held no terrors for him.' He made bowling look 'almost mediocre' which to others was 'lethal'. 'With all respect to the worthy victors, the Test should be remembered', wrote *The Times*, 'for the extreme virtuosity of Hutton's batting.' Brian Johnston told his radio listeners that 'his brilliance cast away the gloom of the English defeat'. Swanton, as always, took a more perceptive view. Hutton had only made one century against the Australians since the war and he had needed another 'to illustrate by figures incontradictable' his pre-eminence. Swanton considered that, tired as he must have been, he should have done more to protect the England tail – something he belatedly did in another last-wicket stand of substance with Wright. As for the figures which Swanton wanted, at this stage of the tour his Test average stood at 87.25, Brown coming next with 29.14. None of the leading batsmen in the party had given him much support.

It had not been a great match. The Australians seemed lethargic and many of the England side, Fingleton thought, looked defeatist as if 'in a hurry to get the sad show over'. To compound their misfortunes came a car injury to Brown from which he had not really recovered when he played in the fifth Test.

It was right that Hutton and Bedser, who had borne the burden of England's struggle against Australia since the war, should share in the delights of England's first post-war triumph and be each an integral part of it. Hutton, with 79 and 60 not out, and Bedser with 10 wickets for 105, were the architects of victory in the fifth Test at Melbourne as, indeed, was Brown by his sustained enthusiasm and personal example. Despite torn tendons in his shoulder from his accident, he secured 6 wickets for 81. Hutton was in at the kill, batting throughout England's final pursuit of the 95 runs to inflict the first defeat by any country on Australia in 26 Test matches, offering his bat in mock anger to some barracking, surviving a run-out and, at the end, engineering the final run with Hassett so that souvenir stumps might be appropriately claimed – a custom which economics, and perhaps good sense, ended soon after.

The Australian press welcomed England's victory; 'We were all tired of the one-way traffic,' remarked O'Reilly. It singled out Hutton as the outstanding player on either side and the ovation he received on scoring the winning run was seen to equal any which had been accorded by Australian supporters to Bradman in the past. His performances won him the sum of £1000 awarded by a Sydney firm for the best cricketer in the series and he straightaway donated it to the bonus kitty available for the whole team. Back home, the *Yorkshire Evening News* opened a fund to have his portrait painted in oils. This was undertaken by the artist Henry Carr, and later presented to him.

Hutton, as a cricketer, was always learning. Back in the dressing room after the match he was discussing how one played forward defensively to Johnson. More pertinently he had absorbed a lesson in leadership from Brown from which there was something to be tucked away if ever needed: cheerfulness in adversity, man-management on a tour, personal example, courage. Brown had all of these and on that reservoir of virtues Hutton would draw in Australia in four years' time. He also made his own contribution to the leadership, watching from first slip with a keen eye what was going on and giving Brown the benefit of his judgment.

That he was the outstanding batsman of the series was not in dispute. No one else made 500 runs, not even 400. His average was more than twice that of any other player. Normally the averages of two competing sides will give a clear indication of why one was superior. This was, of course, true for the 1950–51 series in Australia in that six Australian batsmen had an average of over 30 against only one Englishman. The Englishman was Hutton, with figures of 88.83. In the figures for the tour as a whole, he was almost equally distinguished. No one came within 200 runs of him though Compton, whose Test innings had been so wretched, had a tour batting average not far behind. He retained in full measure his attraction as a stylist and his credentials as a purist, and if he had a weakness it was against the spin bowling of Johnson rather than that of Iverson. There were fewer bouncers bowled than four years earlier – the wickets were slower-paced – but when they came he dealt with them with disdain, something which distinguished him from the Hutton of the immediate post-war years. To Swanton one of the pleasures of the tour was observing the contest between Hutton and the Australian off-side field. He, driving in an arc between point and mid-off: they – Neil Harvey, Miller, Ron Archer and Hassett – patrolling and intercepting where they could.

The Australian journalist, A. G. Moyes, in the *Sydney Morning Herald*, summed up the impact that Hutton made on Australian crowds:

> Hutton stood out among the batsmen. He could have scored faster, and yet there is always the reservation that he had to carry the team on his shoulders. Morris could be reasonably certain that Hassett or Miller or Harvey would get runs, and possibly a great many runs. Hutton could have no such assurance. HE WAS England's batting. If he failed, the side failed. But Hutton is never dull, even when scoring slowly. His technique is perfect, his batting is a matter of brain as well as physical skill. There is a fragrance about it. When he moves out to drive it is poetry. Hutton alone maintained the reputation of English batsmanship. He would have been outstanding in any age or generation.

A broader, if briefer, judgement came from Bruce Harris, in the London *Evening Standard*: 'His influence on the team and the tour was enormous. An exemplary player, sage in counsel and perfect in example to his juniors.'

There remained a Cook's tour of New Zealand, though it was James rather than Thomas who had pioneered the exploration of the islands. Cricket came to New Zealand about the same time as Thomas Cook was busy pioneering cheap excursion trips in England. The first New Zealand cricketers had something of an excursion day out themselves with a match between the Wellington Blues and the Wellington Reds in December 1842 after which all 'adjourned to the Ship Hotel to partake of a true Christmas dinner of roast beef and plum pudding'. It was also in Wellington, in the second Test against New Zealand, that Hutton's tour ended with a half-century and an England win. Like many a touring cricketer, he saw more of the country in three weeks than most New Zealanders had done but, as always, this essentially domestic man was ready to go home. The Wellington match had been played in bleak, cold weather as the southern hemisphere began its winter. Then came the long flight via Fiji (where there was a ceremonial reception for MCC at the airport), Honolulu, San Francisco, Chicago and New York to London. Because Brown had not travelled back with the party, it was Compton, as vice-captain, whom the press interviewed. He frankly admitted that the Ashes might have been won had he himself batted better. Besieged by reporters, the players were not able to greet their families immediately. 'I have seen Daddy,' shouted four-year-old John Hutton in the VIP lounge. Presently, the tour was over as men, so much in the public eye in the last few months, slipped away to their own private lives. Next morning a picture of the Hutton family at London airport with John clutching a toy car, bought by his father in San Francisco, was prominent in most newspapers.

The Times, in summing up the tour, felt that never before had a team been so entitled to be known by the name of its captain – Brown's team – but also reflected that the chief heroes of the tour were 'what may be called the old-stagers': Brown, Hutton and Bedser. The question was posed, when would youth be served? It was an unduly pessimistic view and some grand cricketers would come in the next few years, from Bailey, Close, David Sheppard, Statham and Tattersall. Just over the horizon lay others in the post-war generation such as Peter May, Colin Cowdrey, Trueman and Frank Tyson. In his summary in the Melbourne *Herald*, Fingleton showed concern from an Australian angle, arguing that the tide had turned in England's favour and that the days of Australian pre-eminence were at an end, and he wrote disparagingly of Australian wickets which discouraged strokeplay and of defensive bowling and field-placing. Finally, he asked (despite Brown), had the time not come for England to be captained by a professional cricketer?

Hutton's return to the English domestic scene in 1951 found him as much in the public eye as ever, though Compton redeemed his Test failures of the winter, approached a thousand runs in May and remained, as *Wisden* put it, 'the gay cavalier who danced down the pitch to slow bowlers'. Of the young men coming to the forefront, it would be May who would top the first-class averages and who would make a Test century on his debut. Yet it was still Hutton whom fathers took their sons to see, and to these symbols of support Hutton continued to feel he owed a special obligation – 'thirty runs at least', he would say. On the whole, those fathers and sons who braved a cold and wet early summer were only marginally rewarded by him. South Africa were the visitors and in the first Test at Trent Bridge he scored 63 and 11. In England's second innings he was severely hit over the heart by a bumper from McCarthy and was dismissed rather easily an over or two later. His departure seemed to unnerve his colleagues and England failed in their pursuit of a comparatively easy target of 186.

In between the first and second Tests Hutton scored centuries against Essex and Middlesex and the press began to agitate for his 100th century. So far, the South Africans had escaped fairly lightly at his hands, a matter put to rights when they played Yorkshire. He and Lowson put on 286 for the first wicket, Hutton making 156. The total of 579 was the highest made against them all summer. This was immediately followed by Hutton's 27 and 98 not out in the third Test at Old Trafford, the closing stages of which led to some criticism. The facts were these: England were 18 short of victory ten minutes before lunch on the last day. In the last over they were four short as the fielders came off for rain. Hutton was 91 not out. After lunch the rain stopped, Hutton secured the necessary runs and finished two short of his century. Behind the facts lay the hopes of the crowd and his colleagues that he would secure his 100th century in this Test match. Ikin, a man of generous and kindly nature, had allowed him the larger share of the bowling and then McCarthy bowled donkey-drops to Simpson who blocked them. *The Times* remarked that 'pantomime was permitted to stalk the field'. There was, indeed, all day to make the runs although the South Africans had to be in Scotland the next morning and the England team be scattered over the land.

The real threat to England's prospects lay not so much in any collusion by Hutton's partners on his behalf, as in the rain clouds over Manchester which might well have denied England victory and which bountifully fulfilled expectations after the match was over. Hayter commented: 'Records which arrive naturally are more commendable than those which are sought.' Hutton himself was not unduly concerned about getting the record which, he remarked, 'barring miracles was likely to come before the end of the season'.

He reached the target at The Oval against Surrey a week later in circumstances worthy of the occasion. A crowd of 15,000 had come on a Monday (a headmaster went to inspect the queue for truants!) and it seemed that Hutton was the least anxious man on the ground, displaying his usual mannerisms (such as touching his cap peak) but otherwise looking quite unperturbed. He became the thirteenth player to score a hundred hundreds, joining an illustrious band stretching right back to Grace. He had done it in seventeen playing seasons, something which none of the others matched. Inevitably, the prophets visualized him beating Hobbs' 197 centuries.

While batting against Surrey, he had shared in a partnership of 187 with Lowson and several critics found space to praise Lowson's batting – displaying the same calm certainty as Hutton and the same precision of timing. There were those who saw him in the Sutcliffe-Hutton tradition but his talent was not sustained at the highest level. The dignity of the occasion was scarcely matched in Yorkshire's second innings when everyone, including Hutton, hit out recklessly and raced to and from the pavilion in a vain pursuit of 43 runs in twenty minutes. Still, it was all cricket and the game is none the worse when players chase runs with feverish endeavour, fielders try to thwart them and the crowds get their money's worth. In the 1950s, such exciting spectacles were more rare than today.

With his own particular target behind him, Hutton could relax, score 194 not out against Nottinghamshire in Arthur Jepson's benefit match and, immediately afterwards, make a century in the fourth Test before his own Headingley folk. Indeed, it was Yorkshire at the wicket for an opening partnership of 99 with Lowson, making his Test debut. The press 'caught' them going out to bat with Richard Hutton in shorts and school cap in the front line of the corridor of spectators giving his father a pat on the back. There have been better Test matches: a lifeless pitch and rain on the last day created a draw in which neither side played an attacking game and the majority of the batsmen (including Hutton) lingered over their runs. Perhaps only before the *cognoscenti* of a Yorkshire crowd would such slow play have been tolerated, and Griffith persuaded himself in *The Cricketer* that they 'enjoyed every minute' of the game.

There was just a chance, at the end of an innings each, that the South Africans might win the fifth Test at The Oval and share the rubber. In the event, they lost by four wickets but there was a point, in England's final pursuit of 163 when the issue again became open. In a low-scoring match, Hutton and Lowson had put on 53 when Hutton, and then May, were dismissed by successive balls.

LEN HUTTON

The nature of Hutton's dismissal found its way into the record books. He was given out 'obstructing the field' by Umpire Dai Davies, with the agreement of his colleague Frank Chester, the doyen of first-class cricket umpires. A ball from Athol Rowan lifted, Hutton got a top edge, and ball leapt up and seemed destined to drop on to his wicket. Hutton, as he was entitled to do, endeavoured to stop it, doing so with his bat. Unfortunately, in waving his bat and touching the ball, he obstructed the wicket-keeper, Russell Endean, in his legitimate attempt to take a catch. The appeal, under the (then) Law 40, was upheld in that his obstruction was wilful and had prevented the ball from being caught. 'There was never any intention on my part to prevent the wicket-keeper taking the catch,' Hutton observed.

He had, at least, the doubtful distinction of joining Charles Absolom of Cambridge University and Thomas Straw of Worcestershire, who were similarly dismissed in the nineteenth century. Absolom, who played one Test for England in 1879, had an interesting life apart from his contribution to cricket curiosities. He lived among Red Indians for many years before becoming purser on a cargo ship and being crushed to death by sugar cane. Straw, indeed, offended again in the twentieth century in exactly the same way against the same opponents! C. B. Fry, sitting in the press box and watching through his binoculars, remarked to his neighbour that there was 'nothing unusual' in Hutton's dismissal! He was old enough to recall the other three instances. *The Cricketer* carried an article on the issues raised by Law 40 and quoting two retired first-class umpires who believed the law had been wrongly interpreted. The end of Hutton's 100th Test innings was in strange contrast to his two great innings on the same ground in other Tests.

Little of the summer remained. Hutton had been playing cricket virtually continuously since April 1950 yet his professionalism compelled him to give of his best all the time. With a century against Gloucestershire, and 78 for the Players and 91 for T. N. Pearce's XI against the South Africans at the Scarborough Festival, his season ended. Scarborough before a crowd of 10,000 on a warm autumnal day with the town band playing, the pavilion with its hanging flower baskets, and the traditional singing of 'Auld Lang Syne', was not a bad memory to carry into a winter to be spent in the shop and with the family. Richard would be taken on Saturday afternoons to watch Leeds United or Huddersfield Town. The Yorkshire Committee had written to MCC early in the season saying that Hutton 'needed a winter's rest' and it would be appreciated if he were not picked to tour

India. In later years he would visit India but not as a cricketer. He was persuaded to take part in a radio play called '*Lucky Joe*' by Kevin McGarry which was written around his own career and in which he played himself. Hutton, who would soon be making fairly regular appearances both on radio and television, felt nervous before this particular one and chain-smoked for fifteen minutes beforehand. The reviews were not particularly complimentary.

The season of 1951 ended with some criticism of contemporary cricket from several well-informed individuals. In his report to the county secretaries, the secretary of MCC, Colonel Rait Kerr, identified a list of causes which suggested 'all was not well'. These included an increasing number of drawn games, a policy by batsmen of 'security first and last', defensive tactics (the point Fingleton had made in Australia) and an assumption by some professional cricketers that somehow their livelihood did not depend on the public. Neville Cardus, in an article in *Wisden* called 'Safety First can ruin cricket', took up the theme. With his inevitable veneration of past glories and of the heroes of his Manchester youth, he challenged any modern cricketer to command the guaranteed appeal in one hour which was witnessed when Woolley or Hammond batted. 'Masterful batsmanship does not mean the ability, patience and endurance to amass runs. The art of batsmanship comprises strokes to all parts of the field.' Hutton was not exempted from his strictures: 'he is not certain in an innings of three hours not to bore us and deny his powers.' Cardus did not necessarily blame Hutton but saw him and lesser players as the victims of committees, defensive strategies, even percentages. 'The pressure of the spirit of the age hinders freedom and individuality.' Hobbs, sounded on his views, believed that there was simply a lack of the personalities in the game as he had known it. Even Hobbs' old partner, Sutcliffe, joined in the debate by writing a pamphlet: *English Cricket: What's wrong and Why?* which sold for a shilling (5p). Another of the older generation, Percy Fender, in an article in *The Cricketer*, argued that much of the trouble stemmed from the lbw law which had been changed in 1935. It encouraged seam bowling at the expense of spin-bowlers; it reduced the opportunity for unorthodox strokes and it encouraged medium-paced bowlers to bowl just outside the off stump and just short of a length to slow up the game. Hutton might not have been the personality whom Hobbs looked for but he satisfied him, he wrote, as the 'classic bat of the day' and 'virtually the only cricketer in England who could score off any bowling'. To pick up Cardus's theme, it had to be seen to be important for Hutton to do so.

Amidst these negative strictures, one finds a note of optimism sounded by E. M. Wellings in his praise of cricket in the public schools in 1951 – singling out Colin Ingleby-Mackenzie and M. J. K. Smith (a future England captain) in much that was robust, aggressive and full of promise. It would not be many years before Richard Hutton would be sent to those stables of amateur cricket.

7

England Captain

1952–53

'He did not make the mistake which mattered, that of losing a match.'

John Arlott, *Diary*, 1953

The appointment of Hutton as England captain for the first Test against India in 1952 was widely anticipated by the press. On being sounded on the subject Hutton said he would be willing to be captain as a professional but not as an amateur as Hammond had been. Hammond had coveted the status of amateur and made his friendships among the ranks of men like Beverley Lyon, the Gloucestershire captain, rather than among his fellow professionals. Hutton neither sought the social distinction nor could he afford the luxury of not being paid to play cricket. The selectors were Yardley, Brown, Wyatt and Leslie Ames, three of them former England captains and the fourth a professional with vast playing and managerial experience. All four had played cricket with or against Hutton for a generation: two of them were in a position to know him particularly well, Yardley and Brown, while Wyatt thought extremely highly of his cricket 'brain'. Wyatt had also more than a sneaking regard for the 'outsider', as he had seen himself to be in the 1930s: Sir Pelham Warner, having 'inherited' him as England captain, had at once laid plans to depose him, and Wyatt felt that Warner's natural inclinations were to prefer those from the Oxbridge, south of England stable.

The choice of Hutton as captain to succeed Brown himself was a pragmatic decision based on the desire to find the leader most likely to sustain and build upon the optimism raised by victory against Australia at Melbourne in 1951 and by the recent successful series against South Africa. Though only Brown of the selectors might be seen as coming entirely from that Oxbridge, south of England and MCC stable, nevertheless the selectors, in picking a man who could claim none of these three allegiances, had shown an independent attitude which won support from many quarters.

The editor of *Wisden*, Norman Preston, saw it as an indication that future captains of England must always be 'worth a place in the side' on their playing merit. Compton, the vice-captain in Australia in 1950–51, generously saw it as 'a triumph of common sense', Arlott believed that there was no one to challenge Hutton and he saw his appointment as part of a long-term strategy against Australia. 'An England side under Hutton will play Yorkshire-fashion and this is very near to the Australian method. Hutton will give nothing away.' Swanton commented: 'It is always a pleasure when distinction comes to a man great in his own sphere who wears his honours as modestly as Hutton.' He confessed to only one 'apprehension – the native caution said to be characteristic of the Yorkshireman' and he would be a watchful critic and observer of the new leader. In its editorial, the *Yorkshire Post* saw Hutton's appointment as a logical step in the evolution of the game. It believed that his confidence in himself as a player would ensure that captaincy did not diminish his talent, and commented with shrewdness that until his position 'had become generally accepted he would be living in an excitable atmosphere'.

Hutton's public reaction was to express his delight at being thus honoured. Dorothy called it 'the crown to everything Len has done'. The family posed for photographers at their home in Woodhall Park Grove and then went out for a picnic. Privately, Hutton wondered how he would handle southern criticism and northern enthusiasm. 'Would Lord's, the citadel of tradition, accept me?' and 'How would I cope with the pressures of my own Yorkshire folk?' As to the southern view – by which one really means MCC officialdom and the membership – Hutton was to find a particular courtesy from the treasurer, Harry Altham, and from the assistant secretary (and, by December 1952, secretary) Ronald Aird.

Nor had he anything to concern himself about in the general reaction of the members, the majority of them nameless figures who paid their subscriptions, wore their 'bacon and egg' ties, stood in the Long Room and appreciated good cricket. Part of Hutton's sensitivity was simply due to the fact that MCC was a club of which he was not a member and whose portals were barred to professional cricketers such as he. For many years, the professionals' room with hard seats and an obscure view of the playing area had been the nearest he ever got to the pavilion. It was an image which died hard with him, the more understandable in that he would actually captain MCC abroad twice without being a member of the Club. There would be an occasion in Australia in 1954 when he asked Geoffrey Howard, the manager, not to wear his own 'bacon and egg' tie at a function as the captain could not do the same. No wonder Australians found the ways of the English cricket hierarchy weird and wondrous.

The enthusiasm of his Yorkshire supporters was brought home much more immediately. The first Test was played at Headingley and Hutton led an England side on to the field from the same dressing room from which he usually followed his county captain. Yet it was Hutton, the batsman, of whom the Yorkshire crowed expected so much as if his selection as captain had to be sealed by a century. His own main concern was to create a sense of team spirit in men who had only assembled the night before and to nurse his fellow Yorkshire-man, Trueman, in his Test debut. All this was balanced, in his own mind, by the knowledge that it might be he who would have to get the runs for England if there were a collapse and by the ever-present fear of letting down his public. It was the burden of his batting responsibilities which made some commentators feel he should not have had to assume the additional one of captaincy.

Sadly, it was as a batsman and in the context of these aspirations that he 'failed' with two scores of 10. The Indians were beaten by 7 wickets, terrified of Trueman. Indeed, their second innings recorded the score as 0 for 4 wickets. As a captain, Hutton had no greater pressures than command itself bestows though sections of the press saw the match as a personal triumph for his leadership. *The Cricketer* commended his admirable skill both on and off the field, while *Wisden* noted: 'He did not falter and his astute leadership earned him many admirers and, perhaps, guided future policy' – an enigmatic remark that was possibly a pointer to the use of pace against the next Australians. Surprise was expressed in many quarters that he was appointed only for the next Test.

Alex Bannister, writing in the *Daily Mail* on the eve of the second Test, saw his captaincy as a symbol of change. Every young man joining a ground staff as a professional might see, as ultimate goals, the captaincy of county or country. The professional cricketer was 'a much-respected and skilled craftsman and his status was much raised by Hutton's appointment'. The time must come (and it would only be ten years off) when the different status of amateur and professional disappeared altogether. The young men in the England side at Leeds, Bannister noted, had very properly addressed their skipper as 'Mr Hutton'.

The skipper at Lord's dismissed India for 235, primarily by using his seam bowlers, and then contributed 150 to England's 537. After a very slow start, he reached his century in what the statistician Roy Webber called 'his normal time of four hours'. Some critics felt that his caution had a restraining influence on Simpson and May who took their lead from him, but the runs came and within a time-scale that would ensure victory. Even 184 from Vinoo Mankad, prised out of the Lancashire League by the Indian authorities, could not baulk England's prospects. Mankad had been the bowler who had most challenged Hutton in his big innings. The critics also found something with which to cavil in the slowness of England's batting on the fourth evening. Set 77 to win in 80 minutes, Hutton and his partners achieved 40 of them and finished the match off on the fifth morning. 'In our uncertain climate', wrote one, 'Hutton took a risk'. He had his defenders who argued the weather forecast was 'safe' and that the Indian spinners, who had at once rubbed the new ball in the ground, bowled extremely well. *The Times* found no fault with him. Nevertheless, as a captain he was acquiring a reputation as being on the ultra-cautious side and this judgment would stick during his years of office, though his 'caution' did not deter the selectors from appointing him captain for the rest of the series.

Weather was always the spectre at the feast in the third Test at Old Trafford which, despite constant interruptions, was completed in three days. In the course of compiling a century, Hutton passed Hobbs' aggregate of 5410 Test runs. Only Hammond and Bradman lay ahead of him. *The Times*, with an eye to the future, noted that 'for once he was dominated and overshadowed by a youthful partner – May'. On the third day, India was dismissed twice, for 58 and 82 and Trueman, used by his captain down-wind, bowled at a great pace to a field of three slips, three gulleys and two short-legs. Hutton was well served by his field, not a catch going to ground. Rain dealt an even worse blow to the fourth Test, though not before Hutton and Trueman had made their respective impacts, the one with 86 and the other with 5 for 48.

One might argue that a captain who had his opponents at 0 for 4 in one match, 5 for 6 in another and dismissed them twice in a single day in a third had had little demands made upon him, a point Hutton accepted. Without the extra pressures of a strong opposition, he was the more able to learn the craft of captaincy. He made it his policy to meet situations as they arose on the field rather than approach a match with too much detailed advanced planning. He was learning how to handle bowlers and to get their co-operation in the field-setting he believed to be in their best interest. He was beginning the exercise in man-management which would matter so much when he was a touring captain. Under him the England side of 1952 had bowled and fielded splendidly and runs had been made by the men who would be important in the 1950s and 1960s – May, Tom Graveney and Sheppard. Swanton, in the *Daily Telegraph*, gave him every credit for judging a batsman's weaknesses and for field-setting, but felt that there were still limitations in 'his appreciation of the broader scene'. 'England jogged along interminably slowly' and it was what Swanton had feared might happen. The former Surrey player, Alf Gover, still close to the game as a coach and reporter, believed that Hutton had got the balance right: 'an England team does not require discipline but nevertheless must be kept on its toes and in a happy state of mind'. Hutton, he said, was a man 'in whom players and selectors had the fullest confidence'.

After the series Hutton gave his first press conference. The questions ranged from a comparison of Trueman with Lindwall to England's prospects against Australia, and he handled them all with good humour, diplomacy and skill. The press gave him credit for the way he talked to them and he left them with his view that England cricket was much stronger than it had been for some years. If he did not want to answer a question, he posed his own one in reply – 'Have you had your holidays yet?' It was something of a politician's gimmick and – used not too often – was accepted as such.

He had two other occasions in which to display his leadership: the matches at Lord's and Scarborough in which he captained the Players against the Gentlemen. At Lord's he made a nicely judged declaration, leaving the Gentlemen to get 325 in five hours. The Gentlemen pursued their target and lost by two runs on the stroke of time. At Scarborough he made two declarations and again there was a close finish with the Gentlemen falling two short of victory but this time securing a draw. Hutton, in a Festival match which the *Yorkshire Post* called one of determination and competition, was run out by Cowdrey when 99.

Aside from these representative occasions, there were his appearances for Yorkshire. He was still the senior professional. To the needs of the county, not quite strong enough in bowling to win the

Championship, he buckled down as he always had done. No one could ever criticize him for being temperamental or displaying a reluctance to perform at his best. Cricket has always had its 'stars' to whom the great occasion calls out extra reserves of strength and who lose some of their lustre in the more pedestrian enterprises, but Hutton was never among them. For Yorkshire he made several centuries in the county championship and two against MCC at Scarborough. His Headingley followers saw 189 against Kent and 152 against Lancashire. The Lancashire match brought an opening partnership of 245 between him and Lowson while the return match against Kent at Canterbury saw a partnership of 201 between him and Sutcliffe's son, an event marking the passing of the years and not without some nostalgic memories for Hutton himself. To an extent, the side did not need his batting so much in 1952 – it was top-class bowling and Trueman's release from National Service which they craved. Yorkshire, as the County Report remarked, 'had formidable batting but Hutton once more stood in a class of his own'. Yet one is again reminded that the England captain was still a professional cricketer answerable to the Yorkshire Committee. On 19 May, just a fortnight before he became captain, the Committee had refused his request to play in a match at Arundel Castle on a Sunday for the Duke of Norfolk's XI, though a month later they allowed one to be excused from playing against Scotland.

Hutton could look back on his summer with considerable satisfaction: top of the England and Yorkshire averages, the highest aggregate in the land and, just behind Sheppard and May, third in the national averages. England alone of the Test countries was not occupied in the season of 1952–53 and it was a pointer to the busy programmes which would belong regularly to the years after his retirement that every other Test country (including the newcomer, Pakistan) was involved. For Hutton there was plenty of form to study in the papers and it was time to take off the shelves a book he had been given as a boy, Noble's *The Game's the Thing* and read again his precepts on captaincy. Monty Noble, a pre-1914 Australian captain, counselled dignity, decisiveness, application, impartiality and judgment. Hutton also contributed an article on captaincy to *The Boy's Book of Cricket* which included the advice: 'You are the boss, so be the boss but don't be bossy; take your duties seriously but do not lose your sense of humour; give encouragement as well as advice.' The combination of Noble's advice and his own would remain the guide lines on which he based his captaincy in the following three years.

An experience of a very different nature came with his part in the film, '*The Final Test*', which was made at Pinewood Studios in Buckinghamshire. As in the radio broadcast of a year earlier, he played himself, this time as England captain, and he had to say the line, 'You're as good as ever you were' to the actor Jack Warner going out to make his final appearance in a Test match. Sir Leonard recalled how difficult it was to put conviction into his words when, so far as he knew, Jack Warner had never held a bat since his days as school 3rd XI captain. He also remembered how realistically the Surrey dressing room was created in the studios, the early demands made on him by the producer (four hours earlier than an 11.30 start for a match) and the time spent on make-up and shooting.

Being captain of England increased his correspondence, and requests poured in to give autographs, opinions and talks. For the first time, he found it necessary to have part-time secretarial help. A winter at home was pleasant but it was not an idle exercise. The business in Bridge Street, Bradford, benefited from his regular attendance and the boys benefited from the presence of their father. Dorothy felt that for the second year running they had all enjoyed a normal family life. In the spring Hutton was present at two very different functions. In March he received the Sportsman of the Year Trophy for 1952 from Lord Burghley at the Savoy Hotel, and two months later he attended the bicentenary celebrations of Fulneck School at which he was the guest of honour. He brought a Yorkshire XI to play a Fulneck XI on the school's ground on the hillside behind his old home, close to the playing area where Mr Mellowes had coached him over twenty years earlier. Although he had not gone to the school himself, he had sent Richard there for a spell. In the evening he spoke at the dinner, recalling the warmth of his memories for the Moravian community and all it stood for and giving to the boys some of the advice on captaincy and leadership he had recently set down in print. It was a pleasant, nostalgic occasion.

Australia and England were led in 1953 by captains with much in common. One had succeeded the great Bradman and was learning to live with that impressive legacy; the other had succeeded to the entrenched tradition of amateur captains and had not yet come to terms with his inheritance. As captains, both Hassett and Hutton had acquired a reputation for being over-cautious and they would each bear some responsibility for a lack of colour in the Anglo-Australian cricket of the era played under their leadership and immediately after. Each was by nature unobtrusive and unassuming. Humour in the Victorian was pawky, in the Yorkshireman dry. As batsmen, both led from the front, opening the innings and finishing top in 1953 of their respective teams' averages. Each warmed to the other's personality and a series which began with Hutton making the journey from Pudsey to London to greet Hassett and his men on their arrival retained a friendliness throughout. Even the cut and thrust of sport at the very highest pinnacles is the beneficiary from such attitudes and the effect on countless players at lower levels is to the greater benefit. The reverse of such a situation makes the point. Bad manners shown at the top are all too readily copied by youngsters, especially in an age when television offers an instant display of them to millions. Hutton's behaviour as a sportsman was not the least of the legacies he bequeathed.

The Australians had come confident that they would retain the Ashes which had been theirs since 1934. Touring sides, of course, take on an identity and come with a mission, and Hassett's was no exception: to keep the pot of gold. From England's point of view, Hutton had his own share of optimism, especially if quick bowlers could be found to match the attack of Lindwall and Miller. He had a shrewd conviction that, once again, his own batting would be essential for success while hoping that Compton would return to form and fitness and that May, of the younger men, would prosper. In particular, he attached a lot of importance to how the counties fared against the Australians in the opening weeks.

The 1953 Australians were never to be the counterparts of their 1948 predecessors, but they gave English supporters cause for anxiety by winning six of their first eight games by an innings and inflicting a huge defeat on Yorkshire, in which only Hutton (in the second innings) and Yardley showed to any domestic advantage. Lindwall's dismissal of Hutton to his fifth ball in the first innings was very much first blood to Australia. This, overall, was not what Hutton had wanted, though he remained hopeful until after the first Test 'when my optimism quickly changed to pessimism'. Thus, Australia came to the first Test undefeated by any county but without the spectacular scoring record of five years earlier. They were a side which the counties could bowl out, even if only in one innings rather than two. Bedser, with near record-breaking figures of 14 for 99 bowled them out twice at Trent Bridge, but Hutton alone of the England batsmen made more than 30 in either innings despite doubts about his own fitness to play up to the last moment because of a shoulder injury from 'the hardest blow I have ever taken'. Thanks to Bedser, England set out to make 229 to win with over two days left, but a day and a session were lost to rain and they finished just over a hundred short with nine wickets in hand. Hutton, who had urged on his fellow selectors a strong batting side, had not been happy at England's dismissal in the first innings for 144, largely at the hands of Lindwall. Neville Cardus in the evening, sitting in their hotel together, was the recipient of his unhappiness.

He had another chance to observe the Australians at close quarters before the second Test in the return match against Yorkshire, making 67 and 84 and seeing the county get the better of the game, though it was not a great match. The Australians played a team picked from the bottom half of their touring party, took the occasion very casually and left a large Bramall Lane crowd disappointed by their attitude.

The second Test at Lord's was played in splendid weather before packed crowds, even on the weekdays, and with record gate receipts of £57,000. The Australians saw it as the game they had to win to obtain a hold on the series, the English public as one which would endorse the rising fortunes of England. In a match in which so much was expected of him, Hutton was plagued with fibrositis, undergoing treatment every day and, with his movement restricted, he dropped three catches in the Australian first innings. Of the pain in his neck and shoulder neither the press nor the public was made aware. Arlott noted that the crowd cheered ironically when he fielded the ball. 'No crowd in England can taunt him with justification: he has done too much for that. If he dropped fifty Test match catches in a row, our cricket would still be in debt to him.' Hutton remarked to Arlott, 'I have played in over 60 Tests and I have dropped more catches today than in all those other games put together.' The cheers had a more genuine ring at the end of the day when he was 83 not out. It had taken all his concentration and determination to put those catches behind him (giving something like a hundred runs to the opposition) and make a century which *Wisden* called 'as classical as ever'.

The first three innings of the match each produced totals around 350, and England were left with a target of 343 in an hour and a day. In the hour, they lost 3 wickets for 12, and on the final day, owing much to Willie Watson's century and Bailey's 71, they saved a match which the Australians should have won on a dusty wicket taking spin. Although England had not won, they had not lost, either. Australian critics felt their own team should have been successful and they detected a continuing note of lethargy, not entirely left behind in Sheffield a few days earlier.

The recall of Brown to the England side for the game was significant. He had succeeded Yardley as chairman of the selectors and it had been Hutton who had asked his own captain in Australia to play under him at Lord's and provide the leg-break bowling which might be needed. Both made public statements about being happy to play together. It was a mark of Hutton's gathering self-assurance as captain that he should have asked Brown, though he would concede that he felt anxious in having such a distinguished amateur England captain playing under him. John Arlott noted in his *Diary* that Hutton never consulted Brown on the field. Fingleton, from an Australian angle, felt it extremely odd that the chairman of selectors should be 'patrolling the boundary for England' at the instigation of the captain whom he might or might not choose to invite to go on being captain. No Australian parallels could remotely be conjured up.

After two Tests one may examine contemporary opinion on Hutton's captaincy. The England selectors had appointed him only for a match at a time and they confirmed his appointment for the third Test during the second. Hutton believed that they were guardedly looking around though, short of Brown recalling himself as captain, they had few options open. C. B. Fry wrote that it was quite wrong to have a man appointed as captain 'on appro – where is his prestige with his team? Where is his own confidence in himself?' The press felt that Hutton was vulnerable in both Tests in that he did not press home attacking advantages, especially in the first Test when Australia had lost an early wicket. Others found fault with the field-setting. The former Australian batsman, Sidney Barnes, writing for the *Daily Express*, called his bowling tactics in the second Test 'beyond my understanding' but still urged that his captaincy be confirmed. Journalists, of course, have to compose their piece, day by day, for sports editors seeking a story and an angle. Some 150 of them crowded in upon this particular Test series, including cricket's two knights, Sir Donald Bradman and Sir Jack Hobbs. Hobbs (J.B.) had been knighted on the eve of the Coronation. Press coverage of cricket was assuming huge public importance though, ironically, the writers in the popular press were given less space by editors than their counterparts had enjoyed before the war. Lack of space led to slickness in judgement and distracted from detailed analysis and cool appraisal. To the reporting of the press was added television coverage on a scale not previously achieved. Papers, television and radio brought a publicity to cricket which was unprecedented and hinted at the commercialism of the game which was not far distant. Cricket, at the highest level, was fast becoming big business.

One problem which had affected the selectors throughout the series was whom to choose as Hutton's partner. Don Kenyon, a highly successful county batsman, had not measured up to the greater demands of a Test match. Hutton would have liked Washbrook back, with Edrich at No. three, but his views did not prevail and Edrich opened with him. With an average of 39 at the end of the series, Edrich lay second to Hutton and superior to Hassett and in that sense he did not fail. Neither side had the batting mastery, and despite the four draws which took place this gave a certain piquancy to the series. Batting supremacy could not be assumed nor dominance predetermined. Ironically, Washbrook stood by on his home ground of Old Trafford as Hutton, still suffering from fibrositis in his shoulder, did not declare himself fit until the last moment.

The Old Trafford Test was spoilt by rain. After an innings apiece, Australia then lost 8 wickets for 35. Here Hutton, as captain, was seen at his best. A result was not possible on the last afternoon but an Australia dismissed for their lowest total ever would have distinct psychological advantages. Hutton's spinners – Wardle and Laker – got the wickets but it was his decision to deploy them. The attack based on pace had not been achieved as he had planned while Trueman remained a doubtful prospect, in a summer of wet dead wickets and his own continuing National Service obligations. By now, Australian journalists felt that something was seriously wrong with their own side and they looked for reasons: the management, the social life (an evening at *Guys and Dolls* followed by supper at the Café de Paris with seven England wickets to get at Lord's on the next day), the lack of personalities (*pace* Miller), even a failure to take the English challenge seriously. Had Australian cricket, like a government in power for too long, run out of steam?

Hutton would never have a better chance than at this point in mid-summer to clinch success for England, and it was a chance he was given by his fellow selectors who now invited him to lead the side in the remaining two Tests and who also appointed him as captain for MCC's forthcoming tour of the West Indies. He could sit more comfortably round the table with men who had shown their faith in him. Swanton realized this:

> I hardly think the veriest genius could have made a really spectacular job of the England captaincy this summer so far, considering the attack he has had to handle and the way in which certain fielding limitations have been magnified by the almost continual presence of an Australian left-hand batsman. He has coped thoroughly well with his difficulties.

His appointment was the subject of an article in the London *Sunday Times* by Fingleton who admired his bravery in accepting such responsibility at a time when some critics were falling over each other to find fault: 'if he puts Bedser on ("over-bowling him"), if he takes him off ("letting the Australians out of the net"), but most of all because he lacks the ability to win the toss'. Fingleton with a note of sardonic humour was mocking those who were over-theorizing and grasping at this and that technical argument in their race to find something with which to fault the England captain.

On the eve of the fourth Test at Headingley Hutton jokingly told the commentator Brian Johnston on television that he was going to make 365. Ten-year-old Richard, who compiled his own scorebook when watching his father, wondered if there would be enough room. He had got into the habit of driving with him to Headingley in the school holidays. 'For hours I would sit enthralled, anguishing over every ball in the fear that the apparent frailty of his play, which I failed to recognize as artistry, would let him down.'

On Thursday 23 July Richard went, instead, with his mother. His father lost the toss, pretended to look disgusted, but Hassett was not fooled. On a pitch recovering from two days of rain, Australia put England in. Then came twenty minutes more rain before Hutton and Edrich made their way to the wicket. Lindwall wasted no time on preliminaries. His first ball was the fastest he could conjure up and his second, a yorker which Hutton confessed not even to have seen, sent the middle stump flying. 30,000 Yorkshiremen and women watched in silence as Hutton returned to the pavilion. Richard, through his tears, wrote 'bowled Lindwall 0'. In seven years' time there would be a reversal of roles as Sir Leonard anxiously watched Richard make his debut at Lord's, an occasion on which there would be no need for anyone's tears.

The psychological value to the Australians of the wicket they most prized was immense and it was a vantage point from which they never looked back. When Hutton was so disastrously unsuccessful the effects on the team could be equally disastrous. The first day of the Test was one of England's worst days for years with a lack of strokeplay and aggression which Rex Alston in the BBC radio commentary box found 'pathetic to watch and to describe'. England were forced on the defensive when they went in to bat in the second innings 99 behind. The final two hours on the fifth day demanded everything of Hutton as a leader. The Australians had to get 177 in two hours – a task not beyond them if, say, Neil Harvey cut loose, and which might be compared to the 404 they had successfully chased in one day on the same ground five years earlier with four of the five batsmen then involved. The fifth, Bradman, was in the press box reporting with the same thoroughness that he had applied to his batting. Hutton, with a win desperately wanted and with the knowledge that Australia had been virtually dismissed for 35 at Old Trafford, could entertain some very slender hopes of success. He opened with Tony Lock, in whom he saw great potential and after noticing how the Australian Alan Davidson had made the ball turn. He hoped that Lock's 'attacking' qualities might snatch a victory. Instead, Lock failed to secure a length and, after three quarters of an hour, the Australians had scored 66 and were up with the clock. Only two wickets had fallen and the captain switched to defence. Bailey, with a long run, came on – still in the days before a guaranteed twenty overs in the last hour – and bowled outside the leg stump. The Australians, with wickets in hand, did not immediately give up but the target receded and England secured, rather than earned, a draw. A few Australian journalists turned on Hutton for pursuing a defensive policy; the English ones would have been critical had England lost. Negative bowling, within the law and within the context of the game in the last hour, had saved England. 'Hutton's tactics were vindicated by the issues at stake', wrote Bowes in *The Cricketer*. Hutton's own comment was: 'We were only playing the Australians at their own game.' Fingleton wrote that both captains seemed too apprehensive of defeat.

The final Test at The Oval had certain parallels with that in 1926. England had on both occasions had the worst of the post-war years and there was a public yearning for success, though one need not go so far as Sir Pelham Warner, who wrote that had England lost in 1926, then despondency would have crept over the land. Furthermore, there were competing factors in the summer of 1953 such as the mood of Coronation, the scaling of Everest, and a good Wimbledon, which diminished the autonomy of the cricket world. Nevertheless, a good many roads led to The Oval on 15 August and such was the fear of queues and congestion that the faint-hearted stayed at home. Seats could be had at 11.30.

Hutton was still hoping for his ideal of two really fast bowlers, but still he was without it. Trueman, hailed so much in the spring as the Cricket Writers' choice of Young Cricketer of the Year, was brought in (but not Statham) and public support for the choice was shown in the cheering when he came on to bowl – the England captain for the fifth time running having lost the toss. Trueman was there in Arlott's words to redeem 'the wounds Miller and Lindwall had inflicted on the body of English cricket'. It was a view shared by his captain. At the end of the first day Australia had made 275, a score much in accord with the first innings of both sides during the series and one which occasioned neither delight nor despair in the English camp. Hutton had at his disposal the best all-round attack of the summer, with Trueman, Bedser, Bailey and the spinners, Lock and Laker. Trueman marked his debut against Australia with 4 for 86, the best analysis of the innings. Hutton's catching of Harvey off Trueman was a key factor and the significance of its importance raced through his mind as he ran back from short square leg to secure it.

Hutton perilously survived one Lindwall over before bad light stopped play a few minutes early. On the Monday, The Oval was packed long before 11.30 by a crowd who felt that the day's events would determine the destiny of the Ashes. They saw a modest resumption by Hutton and Edrich, a splendid stand by Hutton and May, an indeterminate interlude by Hutton and Compton and a rearguard action by Bailey and Evans. The heroics came on the third morning when Bailey and Bedser put on 44 for the tenth wicket to give England a vital first innings lead of 31. Immediately after lunch Australia began their second innings and what happened on that August Tuesday afternoon determined the result of the match and the destiny of the Ashes. After five overs on a lifeless pitch, Hutton took off Bedser and Trueman and brought on Lock and Laker. Before the day was over these two had spun out the Australians for 162. The senior players accomplished nothing and only Archer and Davidson of the newcomers gave any currency to the innings. Hutton and Edrich set off in the closing hour in pursuit of 137 runs. In the best of fairy tales, Hutton would have stayed until they were scored. Alas! In attempting a second run, he lost his wicket just before play ended, a misjudgement reflective of the pressures of captaincy. The Australians, instead of a display of jubilation, looked on quietly as he left the wicket.

The last day began with England needing 94 to win. Sir Donald Bradman wrote of 'cricket fever gripping the Empire' and MCC sought special permission from the counties (fearful of their gates) for the BBC to televise the match all day. Television, indeed, scored its second triumph of the summer. As in the presentation of the Coronation, the public came face to face with the intimacy of an occasion in a way never before demonstrated. As one reporter put it, 'ball by ball, risk by risk, we followed the pictorial commentary and crowds in countless sitting-rooms gasped in unison with the crowds at The Oval as May hung his head like a guilty schoolboy after missing a fast ball from Miller'. 'The wind is blowing from extra cover, that is from left to right', pontificated Swanton, and 'an off-spinner is a ball that moves away from the bat, that is towards the bottom right corner of your screens'.

May, despite public scrutiny, had his share in the final onslaught on Everest but the peak was climbed by Edrich and Compton and they had done enough for post-war English cricket to deserve the honour of winning for England cricket's greatest mythical prize. At 2.53 on Wednesday 19 August the deed was done. This was a match in which the only blemish on Hutton's escutcheon was of his own making – the folly of letting himself be run out. Otherwise, he had handled his attack better than in any other of the Tests and his first-innings 82 was, as so often, England's top score.

To the world at large, and to the intruding television cameras, he presented a relaxed and dignified image in victory. With a smile he posed for photographers as a cake was cut, with a speech he greeted the thousands who swarmed on to the ground, with modesty he accepted the congratulations of his fellow selectors and the back-slapping of the Oval members. He belonged to a generation in which formal appearance still mattered. There he stood, a pleasant-faced man, characterized by the broken nose and irregular teeth, hair brushed smartly and possibly owing something to the product Compton promoted, well tailored slacks, collar and tie. He was an England captain ready to be an ambassador abroad. Part of the reason why the Establishment came to accept Hutton lay in the realization that he would never do the wrong thing. He could be trusted.

It was late in the evening before he was able to be driven northwards by a friend up the A1, through the sleeping towns and villages of England, to his home at Kingsmead, a stone's throw from where it had all begun at Pudsey St Lawrence. Nine years earlier he had not been thought good enough by some to be captain of Pudsey. Now the Mayor of Pudsey would be waiting at his doorstep in the early hours of the morning to greet the victorious captain of England, as were Dorothy, Richard and John. By now the glare of publicity was beginning to reach the Hutton boys and Richard had already been featured in several papers batting for his preparatory school, Wood Hall, near Wetherby. A few days later came a reception at the Albert Hall, Pudsey which eclipsed that of fifteen years earlier when Hutton had come back with '364'. Thousands thronged the market place for an occasion, said the Mayor, 'such as we have never had before'. Herbert Sutcliffe came up from the Isle of Wight and the local MP called it an 'historic' moment.

That was the public picture. In private Hutton was intensely conscious of the strain he had borne throughout the series. Even while batting at The Oval, the enormity of it all had struck him and for an over or so he lost concentration, thinking of the obligations of captaincy rather than the commitment to batting. Indeed, at one point it seemed worse, for he was conscious of a temporary blindness while batting. It was a matter of very serious concern when several balls passed him which he did not even see. This led to a check-up on his eyesight and nothing more than severe strain was diagnosed. A week later in that most English of settings, Worcester, he could watch the successes of others – double-centuries by Lowson and Kenyon, one of whom he had not needed in the Tests and the other who had not measured up; as for the business of captaincy, that was, in Yorkshire terms, Yardley's responsibility. Batteries recharged, he made his almost customary centuries in the Scarborough Festival. The second game, for T. N. Pearce's XI, was virtually another Test against the Australians, since each side included ten of the current Test players. It was a grand match in which, said *Wisden*, it was 'impossible to pay tribute to everyone' and played, said the *Manchester Guardian*, 'in an atmosphere of the most genuine and infectious *bonhomie*'. Hutton's contribution was 49 and 102 and Yardley set the Australians a target they just managed to achieve, thanks to a century with eleven sixes by Richie Benaud. A lingering memory was of Hutton allowing himself to be stumped off Hassett and the captains of England and Australia going off the field together.

Year after year Hutton had made runs at the Scarborough Festival, sufficient to delight the crowds but not so many that he monopolized the game. The Festival, begun in 1876, was the creation of the first Earl Londesborough, and it owed its growth to Charles Thornton and Henry Leveson Gower, both typical of that band of upper middle-class Victorians – men like Fry and Warner – who stamped their image on cricket for two generations and left a legacy which was perpetuated up until the 1960s. Cricket at Scarborough, to the amateur cricketer and his wife, was the equivalent of Henley, Wimbledon or Ascot, part of the English social scene in which the lines of demarcation were understood. An invitation to an amateur to play in the Festival meant staying in the Grand Hotel, cocktails before dinner, Leveson Gower (and later, Tom Pearce) leading the ladies downstairs to the Cricketers' Room, listening to the palm court ensemble of violin, cello and piano, dining and dancing. Next day there was lunch in the pavilion to which the amateurs brought wives. It was, Lady Hutton recalled, 'very much *their* social occasion'. Because her own home was near Scarborough, Dorothy Hutton would visit her family and friends, take the boys to the seaside and watch the last part of the day's play. Had she been a professional's wife with no local associations she would have felt a little out of things during the day, although the

Balmoral Hotel provided a focal point for the professionals and their wives for dinner. As the evening wore on everyone came together for some of the dancing.

On the field of play harmless customs were observed. Tea in china cups served on silver trays was brought out for the fielders, batsmen and umpires at the appropriate interval, the town band played during the match and play ended at 6 o'clock with everyone standing for the National Anthem. The cricket itself strove to find a balance, not always achieved, between light-heartedness and competition. Hutton, when the recipient of an orange rather than a ball from Bailey, murmured about laundry bills for his flannels. By the 1950s attitudes were slowly changing and the barriers being lowered. The touring sides, especially the Australians, had always found it difficult to adapt to the nuances of English social class and by the time Hutton was captain of England it was becoming less possible to justify distinctions, fast becoming obsolete, which would end in 1962 when all the Gentlemen became Players.

Yorkshire had seen Hutton in little more than a third of their matches during the season. When he was there he was as dependable as ever but, as the County Report declared, 'his absence was keenly felt'. For various reasons, it was one of Yorkshire's worst seasons and gone were the days when the absence of two or three players for Test matches was a chance for the reserves to prove almost as good. Yorkshire's misfortunes tempered Hutton's delight in England's success. The Committee's minutes of November 1953, recording a 'deterioration in the standard of fielding and a lack of club discipline', made no individual exceptions. Some feeling existed that the senior professional, relaxing from his other responsibilities, had not chosen to exercise a strong presence.

The summer was over and there were some months of respite before the West Indies tour. As to the England captaincy, Hutton had conducted himself with quiet dignity: no heroics, little chat, grit rather than glitter. Twenty years in the game had not been lost on him and he was shrewd in observation, if light in imagination. As Arlott wrote in his *Diary* of his captaincy against the Australians, 'he did not make the mistake which mattered, that of losing a match.' He was given unanimous credit for the way in which he – and Hassett – had conducted the series and for not outwardly allowing his responsibilities to affect his batting. Those who criticized his field-setting were countered with the argument that he often had to contend with a right-hander and a left-hander at the wicket. Those who criticized his bowling changes were matched with the view that his only real spearhead until The Oval was Bedser. Those who criticized his caution could be told that he did not command a side strong enough with which to take chances. He was by nature a man of caution and this was part and parcel of his whole philosophy as a cricketer: thrusting him into the England captaincy with scarcely any experience of leadership would not change that attitude overnight. He was perhaps lucky that his opposite number, Hassett, similarly lacked aggression. Bradman, who out-gunned Hammond, would have had a fire power much too effective for Hutton. Maybe he had been a captain without glamour, but such must be expected of a leader whose skills lay more in defence than in attack. Perhaps the most serious criticism was that he slowed the game down so that the Australians literally had fewer balls to play. The Headingley Test provided a specific instance of this in that Australia's 266 runs came from 82 overs and England's 275 from 177 overs. The Australian broadcasting commentator, Alan McGilivray, felt very strongly about it and wrote of Hutton's 'ploy to restrict his opponents' opportunity to score'. It was a policy which Sir Leonard did not deny but about which he was unrepentant.

In the issue of *Wisden* which was published in the following spring, Brown, the chairman of the selectors in 1953, wrote an article entitled 'Batsmen must be bold'. He showed his concern for the policy of defensive batting which prevailed in English cricket at both Test and county level, and he sought more emphasis upon an attacking policy based on front-foot play. 'Bowlers much prefer bowling to a batsman who is always on his back foot.' There was no specific criticism of the policies of the current England captain and, indeed, Brown cited two instances of Hutton, in his role as a batsman, displaying an aggression in Test matches, but the overall message was clear: 'batsmen must be bold' and captains had to encourage front-foot play.

Brown was not alone among those who detected the need for more aggression in cricket as it competed with other sports for public support, but let the last word on the game in 1953 come from *The Times*: 'It was to the credit of both Hutton and Hassett that no series had been played more closely in the spirit of the clubs and villages north of the Trent and south of Sydney.' Hutton, the traditionalist, was finding more and more favour with the Establishment.

What villages lay south of Sydney is another matter. 'Tell us what an English village is like?' asked my hosts in Melbourne some years ago.

8

Caribbean Conflict

1953–54

'The second most controversial tour in cricket history.'
John Hughes, *The Times*, 1954

Plum Warner had first helped to select an England side in 1905. 'You picked them in about three minutes after a pleasant lunch: MacLaren, Ranji, Fry, Jessop. . .', he reminisced. Forty-eight years later, in 1953, he was still a selector, as chairman of the MCC sub-committee choosing the side to go with Hutton to the West Indies. Despite the fact that Hutton had been captain of England for over a year, he still felt ill at ease with some of his fellow selectors and especially with Warner, the dominant figure in the selection of English teams for so long. Hutton was conscious of his presence, was reluctant to disagree with his views and sensed that he would not have been Warner's own preference as captain. Warner apart, to Hutton men who had captained England and their counties had an experience which he lacked – 'I didn't want to press my arguments'. Perhaps he was carrying sensitivity too far. He had won two series at home and his supporters far outweighed his critics.

Immediately after the fourth Test against Australia, the first ten names for the tour had been announced. In the selection of players such as Compton, Evans, Graveney, May and Bailey, it was clear a very strong side was being proposed. A signal omission was Bedser, a decision initiated by Bedser himself, so that he might rest after a long spell of continuous cricket with the tour to Australia in 1954–55 in mind. Hutton on strictly cricketing grounds did not mind Bedser's exclusion as he wanted to see the effectiveness of a younger opening attack. The tour party was completed with two fast bowlers in Statham and Alan Moss to join Trueman, together with Reg Spooner, Wardle and Ken Suttle. Hutton believed the final selection was carried out in some haste and at an inappropriate moment during the fifth Test when another matter, winning the Ashes, was more immediately pressing. The time was chosen to suit the seventy-nine-year-old Warner, present at the Test, and to save him an extra journey from his flat in South Kensington. Hutton thought Warner rather rushed events and pushed him, for example, into taking Suttle. Nevertheless, Aird, the MCC secretary, called it the strongest side to leave England since the war and Hutton agreed with him, though he had wanted Edrich. They would certainly be the fittest. Hutton instructed his men to train in the three months before they left and set an example by running in the fields near his home.

That the West Indies deserved the best that England could send was justified on several grounds. Warner, as we saw in Chapter 5, bore some small responsibility for the weakness of the MCC side which had fared so disastrously six years earlier. The 1950 West Indians had won three out of four of the Tests in England, culminating in a victory at The Oval by an innings, despite Hutton's 202 not out. Good as that 1950 side had been, they were, commented Swanton, 'probably even more formidable on their own wickets'. For the first time a few journalists in the popular press began to speak of England playing the West Indies for the 'cricket championship of the world'. The phrase had been meaningless when for seventy years England had regularly played Australia with South Africa a resolute third and the other Test countries not yet emerging as front runners. From the mid 1950s onwards it would crescendo in emphasis to a point where, in the early 1980s, the title would become almost a West Indian monopoly.

All this gave, as the journalist Hayter observed, 'a certain amount of tension before a ball had been bowled', a tension activated by political events in the West Indies. Some understanding of these is essential in any interpretation of the tour.

In the 1950s a movement for national independence gathered strength in the major territories of the West Indies. In part it was an expression of an anti-colonialism which could be found in many parts of the world after the second world war. What had happened in the Far East and would happen in Africa was being pursued actively in

Jamaica, Trinidad, Barbados and British Guiana, the islands and mainland colony where MCC would play in 1953–54. Linked to the movement for national independence was a parallel movement, inspired from Whitehall and with no grassroots support, for a West Indian Federation. Eventually, conflicts in aims would mean that individual nationalism prevailed and federation foundered on the rocks of national jealousies and self-seeking politicians. Hand in hand with these aspirations went a search for economic stability in colonies which gained little from their cash crops such as sugar, or (in the case of Trinidad) felt insufficiently rewarded by the oil royalties accruing from the European companies.

These three interacting forces of nationalism, federation and economic advancement found spokesmen such as Eric Williams, the distinguished black academic who would become Prime Minister of Trinidad, and Cheddi Jagan, of East Indian stock, the Prime Minister of British Guiana, deposed and arrested by the British authorities. Men such as these and many others represented a non-white middle-class political leadership able to secure the vast grassroots support which the idea of federation lacked. They clashed with a resident white society facing a decline in their long-standing prestige and influence. British officialdom, in the traditional persons of colonial governor and secretariat, sought to make the inevitable transition from colonialism to independence as free from conflict as possible. It was into this cauldron of hopes, grievances and fears that Hutton took his side to the West Indies.

Just before he left, he was asked to take part in a broadcast by Rex Alston who wrote in an internal BBC minute that Hutton 'would be delighted to submit himself to some sort of inquisition, though I don't think it should be solo'. Learie Constantine, always in demand by the BBC – and described in their files as a 'producer's dream' – was asked to join a panel with Hutton and the last MCC captain in the West Indies, G. O. Allen. MCC approval was sought and Aird, on behalf of the Committee, agreed providing that Hutton was not 'asked any questions which might cause difficulties in the West Indies'.

Everyone assembled at the BBC for a meal and a rehearsal though Constantine came late as he was revising for a law examination on the following morning. He had been so busy studying in the past year or two that he had declined several BBC invitations to broadcast and his appearance on this programme was a measure of its importance. He hinted at the political and social problems which would face Hutton whom Alston reminded, just before they went on the air, to say nothing which might be a source of later conflict. The programme went out under the title *Caribbean Cricket*, Hutton was paid ten guineas and Alston minuted that it had been 'a valuable occasion'. A few weeks later, Hutton was again heard in a pre-recorded programme called '*Frankly Speaking*' in which he discussed his experiences as captain with Jack Davies.

On the eve of their departure, MCC had a briefing from the secretary of state for the colonies. No one was left unaware of the current politics within the West Indies and, as the tour developed, Hutton had no doubts in his own mind that the cricketers were being used as an instrument with which to enflame the dying embers of colonial rule. As the editor of *Wisden* would later write, 'his was the most thankless task a captain had ever undertaken, subjected to the impact of deep political and racial feeling.'

MCC set off a few days before Christmas, Hutton becoming the first professional English captain to tour abroad in the twentieth century and the first captain to take his team out by air. He was therefore denied the opportunity, enjoyed by every single one of his predecessors back to George Parr, who toured Canada in 1859, of establishing a team spirit on board ship. Moments when he might have talked at leisure to young players had to be snatched during the tour itself. Hutton valued such occasions and found time for them as best he could. From a mild British winter MCC found themselves delayed by engine trouble for several hours in 28° of frost in Gander, Newfoundland, clad in their tropical suits. When they reached Bermuda they made history as the first MCC side to play there, Hutton making more history by being dismissed from the first ball of the tour. There followed a stunned silence from a crowd who realized they might never see the great man play again. Of course they were wrong: there were three matches in Bermuda, the last two rather curiously styled 'Tests' by the locals. Despite great enthusiasm in the press and the offers of much social hospitality, the actual crowd support was surprisingly low, the imminence of Christmas and the cost of transport to the ground being given as reasons.

The serious part of the tour began in Jamaica and the captain's decision to put the colony in on a perfect pitch was vindicated by an innings' victory, the first, indeed, by MCC over Jamaica. He alone had witnessed, in 1936, one of only two previous defeats of Jamaica by an overseas side when he had been in the Yorkshire party. His own contribution was to share in an opening partnership of 80 with Watson and so set the pattern for the tour: as a batsman he would lead from the front and by example. After a draw in the second match against Jamaica, England faced the first Test, just four weeks after leaving home. Yet against that disadvantage it could be argued that the West Indians, except for the Jamaican contingent and two colony matches in British Guiana, had had no first-class cricket since the visit of the Indians the previous year. Hutton, with considerable respect for the strength of the West Indian batting (despite Worrell's absence) and for the batting wicket at Sabina Park, played three fast bowlers rather than expose Laker or Wardle to a devastating onslaught in a six-day match. Neither Hutton nor Jeff Stollmeyer, his opposite number, expected a result and this rather negative view led some press correspondents to criticize each of them for time-wasting and for leg-theory tactics. Swanton called the former tactic 'sharp practice' but it would remain one employed under Hutton's captaincy both in the West Indies and in Australia a year later. Leg-theory, with its implications of bouncers and its memories of 1932–33, was not employed after the first Test although bouncers, within strict limits, were accepted by both captains as a fast bowler's occasional weapon especially on wickets which so much favoured the batsmen. Hutton had refused to agree to a formal two per over as Stollmeyer had suggested.

Despite being 247 behind on the first innings, England began the last day needing only 230 with eight wickets in hand. *The Times* saw the match 'finely balanced' but a mid-order collapse against the medium-pace of Esmond Kentish brought defeat by 140 runs – to Hutton both 'a surprise and a bitter blow' for he had felt the fourth innings target, on a small ground, was within England's capabilities. The match itself had revealed areas which would present increasing problems to the cricketers of both sides and, since they were the visitors, more especially to MCC. The crowd of 15,000, packed into Sabina Park, carried their natural exuberance to excess when they booed Stollmeyer for not enforcing the follow-on. Stollmeyer's concern for public safety (let alone his own) led him to ask for extra police to be available if the West Indies lost on the last day. In that event, the elegance of his own batting in the first innings would long since have been forgotten and in his own person he represented the approaching end of that symbol of colonialism: a white captain. The role of whites in controlling and playing in West Indian first-class cricket was nearing its end.

Linked to the crowd was the factor of umpiring. The new local hero John Holt, styled in all the papers as J. K. Holt junior, was given out lbw at 94 by Perry Burke, the umpire. The abuse, not to say potential violence, which greeted Burke's father, wife and son led him to consider retiring at the end of the match. Hutton, who rated his abilities, persuaded him to stand again in the fifth Test at Sabina Park and, to Burke's great credit, he did. Umpires who made unpopular decisions against the home team did so at their peril and, as the progress of the tour would show, they made incorrect ones simply through inexperience. Hutton wondered about the lbw against him when England were 130 without loss in their second innings.

Related to both crowds and umpires was local loyalty, seen not only in the instance of Holt but also in the massive display of public support which had brought George Headley from England. £1103 and two pence had been raised by public subscription throughout Jamaica. Headley, the batting star of West Indies cricket in the 1930s, made 53 not out in the second colony match but, as Hutton observed, 'we deliberately treated him as gently as we dared' without making it obvious. Hutton was aware of the tensions associated with Headley's presence in Jamaica. Playing for the Combined Parishes against MCC Headley had been struck by a ball from Trueman and, from that moment onwards, Trueman was a target for public wrath: 'Mr Bumper Man' to the Jamaicans. Hutton realized his error in letting Trueman bowl to Headley who had not faced top-class fast bowling for years. The selectors picked Headley for the Test, bowing to the pressure of local agitation. The *Trinidad Guardian* commented that 'even charity could find no justification for his inclusion'. Trinidad, to a Jamaican, was a foreign country and this was seen as the biased comment of the foreign press. Nationalism was far outstripping colonial cohesion.

In the Test itself Hutton displayed magnanimity, respect and possibly some native Yorkshire caution in allowing Headley to get off the mark in the first innings. His dismissal for nought would have devastated his followers and might have evoked a riot. Headley departed from the scene after the first Test, bringing to an end a career which had begun in 1929 and leaving him with an average, in 22 Tests, of 60.83. Only Bradman (99.96) and the South African Graeme Pollock (60.97) have exceeded him. As a small boy Headley had played rounders in his birthplace of Panama. It was the delay in getting his Panama passport to study dentistry in the United States which led him to stay in Jamaica and earn the nickname of 'the Black Bradman'. A great cricketer had bowed out rather sadly and rather late.

Superficially, events in Barbados were not dissimilar to those in Jamaica. MCC won the colony match and in the Test were set a second innings target of over 450 runs. In depth, distinct differences emerge. Barbados, not so politically volatile as Jamaica, provided a less tense atmosphere in which to play. The colony match was won by one wicket off the last ball, stirring stuff for the spectators but not the most encouraging prospect for a Test. Yet – and the press critics in general failed to note the point – it was the first time MCC had ever beaten Barbados. In the Test, England's attack emphasized spin rather than pace and the bowlers secured only 10 wickets altogether. Realistically, England seemed outclassed throughout and lost by 181 runs. Symptomatic of this was the slow rate of scoring and the lack of technical batting ability at the highest level after the first five. The West Indies with a lively batsman-wicketkeeper in Clifford McWatt batted down to No. 8.

Hutton, with the tour just two months old, had scored fifties in three of his first four Test innings and had displayed his usual concentration. Only when joined by Charles Palmer, making in Barbados his Test debut, had he seemed for a moment to feel all was lost and was caught hitting Ramadhin rather unnecessarily – better that it was Ramadhin, for the one bonus which emerged from the Test was the virtual end of Valentine. He and Ramadhin had plagued England in 1950 (59 out of 77 wickets in the Tests) and a further 19 out of 39 in the first two Tests in the current series. In England's second innings, Valentine had failed to take a wicket and, so far as England were concerned, the effective partnership of the 'Calypso twins' was over. Valentine would still have a few great days and another eight years in Test cricket but he would no longer harry England's batsmen. Hutton considered the decline of Valentine was the one psychological gain England had achieved as they embarked on the three remaining Tests, two-nil down in the series.

Off the field Hutton had increasingly to deal with social problems, in particular criticism in Barbados from two different sources by some ladies that his players had shown an alleged lack of courtesy. Backed by Palmer, who was manager as well as player, he publicly supported his team while privately counselling discretion and tact at all times. He had also had to get a message home to his wife that his batting at No. 8 against Barbados was because of a chill and not the threat of an operation for stones in the kidney as the press suggested. And, of course, it was not just his health with which the press were preoccupied. All the events of the tour were duly reported back to England by a flotilla of reporters. The central point at issue was whether Hutton had let down the side or the side had let down Hutton. Those who argued the former case – though not in as many words – were Crawford White in the *News Chronicle* and Swanton in the *Daily Telegraph*. To White, Hutton was imposing too much caution and restriction on strokeplayers such as Compton and Graveney, a policy 'which would kill rather than help to build this

England team'. To Swanton, as he had always feared, such cautious tactics 'must be assumed to emanate from the captain'. On the other hand, Ross Hall in the *Daily Mirror* felt that Hutton was not getting the support from the players to which he was entitled nor the 'toughness' from the manager to back him up. Inevitably, the question was asked by all the journalists and in Letters to Editors whether a professional captain really had the authority to command the very best endeavours from a side. Whatever were the rights or wrongs on the question of his leadership, his opponents were now a supremely confident side, and it is in the nature of West Indian sides to be as elated in victory as they are desolate in defeat.

To Hutton the victory at The Oval the previous August seemed light-years away as MCC made its way to the steamy and humid mainland colony of British Guiana where at least he could rest in Georgetown pavilion after being out for nought while Watson and Graveney put on 402 for the fourth wicket against the colony. British Guiana were beaten by an innings and 98 runs and, with victories against all three colonies played so far, MCC approached the third Test in a mood of determination, if scarcely optimism. Once again, the triple factors of crowds, umpiring and local loyalties were to play a part in forthcoming events. The selectors picked Robert Christiani, who had made 75 and 82 for British Guiana, and his selection slightly unbalanced the West Indian side in that an extra batsman was brought into a side which already had great batting depth, at the expense of a bowler. As in Jamaica, the local man could not be ignored. 'Our Robert *must* play', demanded the *Daily Argosy*.

More serious was the question of umpiring. Hutton objected to the standard of umpiring displayed in the colony match and his request for umpires to be flown in from Jamaica or Barbados was supported by Stollmeyer. But the local Board dared not look elsewhere and E. S. Gillette, a retired umpire, was joined by Badge Menzies, the groundsman, who was an instructor to the colony umpires' association. Throughout the Test Menzies was seen supervising the preparation, rolling and marking of the pitch quite apart from his actual umpiring duties, which, in Hutton's view, he carried out almost without error but, as was sadly shown, not to the satisfaction of the crowd. The crowd itself, fiercely partisan, politically encouraged and financially involved, took exception to the dismissal of McWatt, run out in the West Indies' first innings when going for the run which would have brought up his partnership with Holt to 100 for the eighth wicket, and made money for those who had placed bets. Menzies' decision had been academic so far short had been McWatt. There followed a bizarre scene: McWatt fled for the safety of the pavilion as bottles and other missiles poured on to the ground.

Hutton, anxious to continue play, kept Menzies and his colleague on the field and declined to take his men off. Despite pleas from British Guianan officials that it might be wiser to end play for the day, Hutton remained firm. His remark, 'I want a couple of wickets before the close of play tonight' was, remarked Compton, 'the saying of the century'. Without doubt, his coolness and nerve saved a nasty situation from getting worse. The courage he had shown, and which enabled the day's play to be completed, had been displayed earlier in the innings when he had fielded six yards in front of the bat to unnerve Walcott at the start of his innings and contributed to his being bowled by Statham for 4. Earlier, England had won the toss and Hutton's 169 was one of his finest innings, hitting against the spin of Valentine and getting the better of Ramadhin, whose dismissal of him after nearly eight hours' batting owed more to tiredness than error.

It was with a score of 435 and three West Indian wickets down for 31 that England came to the fateful fourth day and McWatt's dismissal. When he went, England were pressing hard to enforce the follow-on. Hutton secured one of the two wickets he sought before play ended on the Saturday night. Between then and Monday morning, police guarded the house of Menzies, umpire and groundsman. The governor of the colony, Sir Alfred Savage, offered Hutton the First Battalion of the Argyll and Sutherland Highlanders if needed. Again, the captain settled for a low-key approach and most sections of the crowd were ready to recognize his bravery and that of his team when England eventually won by nine wickets on the Tuesday, England's first Test victory in the West Indies since 1935.

A cable of congratulations from the secretary of MCC to Hutton on his 'personal contribution and fine example in difficult circumstances' was appropriate and well deserved. The players' view was expressed by Wardle: 'It was a Len Hutton victory. His classic batting, his skill in relieving tension, his management of the bowling, his courageous and masterly handling of an ugly situation; all these things were beyond praise.' Crawford White cabled to the *News Chronicle* 'Let one thing be hammered home: Len Hutton led England magnificently under ugly conditions'. E. M. Wellings, in the London *Evening Standard* wrote that it was time for the 'insidious campaigning' against Hutton to stop and for those who were so 'obstinately opposed to a professional captain' to give up doing a disservice to English cricket. Hutton, he said, had 'done all Jardine ever did and more in adverse circumstances. No cricket captain had ever had greater difficulty'. Hutton attributed victory to the toss, team spirit throughout the entire party, Statham's bowling and the fielding. Thirty years later Sir Leonard looked back on his innings of 169 with pride but did not see himself as a hero in the decision to play on. 'We wanted to win' was the simplistic but compelling comment.

Some of the local papers were thoroughly critical of what had happened, the Guiana *Graphic* seeing the events of the Saturday night not as a mere incident but as a 'display of lawlessness to which the masses of people are being egged on . . . What gives us anxiety is that even the field of play is not now beyond the pale of the consequences coming from the venom which the subversive political propagandists have injected into the blood of our people'. Sadly, cricket would be the ultimate loser and there would be the spectacle in the 1980s of an England party leaving Guyana (as it had become) without playing and thereafter the Test and County Cricket Board not including Guyana in the West Indies itinerary.

To approach the airstrip of Grenada, in the 1950s, was an adventure in itself. Coming in straight from the sea, past intense vegetation clinging to a strip of volcanic peaks, the British West Indian Airways plane deposited MCC beside a small shed where an official cleared their entry with a rubber stamp and pad taken from his satchel. A tortuous but beautiful drive for one and a half hours brought them to St George's, the capital, and to their first experience of a matting wicket and of the talent displayed by young cricketers, even in the more remote islands. Ian Neverson had come from St Vincent to join the Windward Islands against MCC and contributed 90 not out. Hutton, 20 years his senior, made 82. It was a brief weekend respite before the players moved on to Trinidad. Hutton had also taken the opportunity to have a long talk with May, his most promising younger player, urging him to learn from his mistakes, fight his way out of problems and see himself as a future England captain. Conscious that May was nervous about going in No. 3, he planned to put him in at No. 2 in the Trinidad colony match with the Test in mind. May scored only 0 and 4 against Trinidad and reverted to No. 3 (and 135 runs) in the Test. His concern for May and other young players, such as Graveney, led him into discussions with them about what they might expect in Australia in a year's time.

The MCC approached the Trinidad leg of the tour with some apprehension because the weekend troubles in British Guiana had reverberated in Trinidad, where several thousands of pounds' damage had been done by an arsonist to two public stands at the Queen's Park Oval. Whatever lay behind this – political agitation or some personal grievance – the buildings were repaired by the time MCC arrived. By a seven-wicket victory against Trinidad, MCC became the first touring side to defeat all four colonies. Many in the past sixty years had tried, including one intrepid MCC side in 1910–11 mustering only eleven players for the whole tour. The match itself was not without incident; the crowd resented the felling of Willie Ferguson, a local man, by a ball from Trueman. Ferguson's subsequent selection for the Test once again emphasized the policy of local influence on selection though, in fairness, he was a bowler who prospered on his own matting wicket.

The Oval at Port of Spain is one of the most beautiful cricket grounds in the world. Like Newlands in Cape Town or Adelaide Oval it has a great backcloth of mountains embracing it on one side. More immediately, the cricket bowl has a surround of saman trees. A deep blue sky caps the many variegated greens, browns and reds of hillsides, trees and flowers. Nature, so generous in her favours, had at that time still defied the efforts of those who sought to make a successful grass wicket, though two experimental ones lay to the side of the jute strip, laid on a clay and sand base, on which cricket was played. On such a wicket, as in Jamaica but for different reasons, neither Hutton or Stollmeyer expected a result in the fourth Test, and so it proved. Yet the West Indian spectator, starved of so much top-class cricket in those days, seemed content to see batsman amass runs and disconsolate bowlers find salvation only in the occasional bouncer. I recall arriving a little late on the second day, finding somewhere to sit in the unreserved seats and listening to the endless chatter. An English friend and I, both living in Trinidad at the time, were the only two expatriates in the packed area and we endured with fixed smiles an endless teasing, which had a sharp edge to it, about the achievements of the West Indian side. I wrote in an article:

Cricket is everyman's delight in Trinidad. Picture the Oval at Port of Spain: the crowd is indifferent as to whether it sits on benches or astride the branches of the widespreading saman trees; the noise, kept up perpetually in a temperature of some 90°, would not disgrace a Scots crowd at Murrayfield. A fellow shouting, 'Somebo'y call me?' touts peanuts and drinks, the latter being 'iced' until honesty and the heat compel him to style them 'cool'. Everton Weekes is batting, my neighbour turns to me: 'Sir Everton, boy. Sir Donal' Bradman make plenty two hundreds, Sir Everton make two hundred now', and so indeed, he does. Presently Mr Weekes is caught and all round among the bettors is a rustle of dollar bills and a jingle of British coppers, a confusion of currency in the Eastern Caribbean. The Legislative Council is present, thanks to the Minister of Labour's proposal 'that the sound of the willow is infinitely more desirable than the sound of human voice on an occasion of this sort'; The Minister of Education has allowed the future Ramadhins and Valentines to cast aside their much-thumbed 'Caribbean Readers' and their lunchtime bats of coconut branches and to sit in the schoolboys' stand.

The West Indies amassed 681 for 8, all three W's making centuries. England's reply of 537 included centuries from May and Compton. Hutton's 44 enabled him to become the first England player to have made over 400 runs eight times in Test series. The inevitable draw followed. During the match MCC were guests at a dinner given by the West Indies Board of Control in which Sir Errol Dos Santos, the president, expressed his shock at some of the crowd behaviour, which he tried to indicate was more due to drink than to political attitudes. In this Dos Santos was being diplomatic and seeking to distance Trinidad from events in Jamaica or British Guiana, for the match in Trinidad had had its 'incidents' on the first day whose repercussions in the press were considerable. Briefly, two umpiring decisions had been matters of controversy: Graveney's catching of Holt and Spooner's of Weekes. Weekes went on to make 'two hundred now' as my neighbour in the public seats had expected of him. The England players showed some dismay, bewilderment and disbelief, and the first incident had not been helped by the umpires discussing it with all and sundry during the lunch interval. Next day J. S. Barker, a Yorkshireman long resident as a journalist in Trinidad, addressed an open letter to Hutton in the *Trinidad Guardian*. Its message was picked up by a large number of papers in the cricket-playing world and, as such, discredited the image of MCC:

Dear Len Hutton,

We in the West Indies are becoming increasingly distressed by the undercurrents of hostility and suspicion which began with your arrival in the West Indies and have been growing in strength ever since.

'We in the West Indies' means *your* admirers and supporters, not that small minority for whom the West Indies can do no wrong. It means, also, many hundreds of your fellow countrymen (and even your fellow Yorkshire-men!) whose anticipatory delight in your tour is slowly turning to dismay and embarrassment.

THE CHARGES

The charges against us are:
1. The West Indies umpiring falls below the standards of English umpiring.
2. West Indies umpiring is not only incompetent but dishonest.
3. A hostility bordering on intimidation has been directed at your team since the Test began.

To charge No. 1 we modestly plead guilty. Charge No. 2 we reject with the contempt it deserves. To charge No. 3 whilst emphatically dissociating Trinidad from it, we must also plead guilty.

Nevertheless, we submit that the astonishing departures from all canons of good taste and good sportsmanship made by certain members of your team are at once more painful to bear and easier to remedy than any of these charges – even if they were all true.

STRANGE CONDUCT

The criticizing of umpires' decisions, whatever your private opinions, the public arguments with, and even the brow-beating of these much-tried gentlemen, is not the conduct to which we are accustomed, or which we expect from men dignified by the colours of the MCC.

May I suggest that you yourself cast the first stone by seeing to it that the pleasure we find in your tour is not marred by other 'incidents'.

That England should lose a well-deserved reputation for good sportsmanship is a far more serious matter than the loss of a cricket match, even a Test Match, and will be remembered much longer than and in far more important fields of life than the cricket field.

Yours sincerely
J. S. Barker

Hutton's view, then and later, was that at no point had his players even thought the umpiring was dishonest (Charge 2). Nor did he feel the accusation of an 'astonishing departure from all the canons of good sportsmanship' was in any way justified by events. The players had been tolerant to a degree when decisions had gone against them. Only Trueman's slowness in showing concern for Ferguson in the colony game came anywhere near meeting Barker's criticisms. Hutton, as plenty of evidence after the tour testified, had gone out of his way to thank umpires. Indeed, he had done so at the Trinidad Board of

Control dinner in his reply to Dos Santos. The British press had little sympathy with Barker's views and were unanimous in praising the conduct of MCC in most difficult circumstances. Alex Bannister in the *Daily Mail* wrote that 'the general tone and behaviour of the MCC party was excellent and the conduct of the overwhelming majority of the players examplary'.

Hutton received a private letter from an English doctor working in the colony repudiating Barker's letter:

> I hope it will be some comfort to you to know that we English people here not only disagreed entirely with the substance of the letter but deplored the fact that it was published. And that the person responsible . . . should be an Englishman and a Yorkshireman is quite incomprehensible. To put himself forward as the High Priest of sportsmanship and good conduct and to charge you and your team of un-English behaviour can only be interpreted as the unseemly attempt of a journalist to 'go one better' than his fellow-scribes and by a piece of smug, sensational writing to attract to himself a little of that limelight which writers of a certain order love to bask in – even if great harm and injustice are done to others as the price of his exploits.

Although the writer spoke primarily for the English community he believed he echoed the views of many Trinidadians as well. Since Barker was English, the two letters – public and private – cut across racial boundaries. Be that as it may, damage was undoubtedly done. Those at Lord's who wished to depose Hutton on his return had, for the moment, something which they might use in evidence against him. Apart from what the *Trinidad Guardian* had to say, this leg of the tour passed off far better than had the British Guiana stage. The crowd were appreciative of the fine batting of May and Compton and the only other shadow on events was cast by some bowling of bouncers, one of which from King, hit Laker.

Finally came the return visit to Jamaica, where Hutton feared the political undertones but looked forward immensely to meeting his wife and having a few days off at Montego Bay while the side played a Jamaica Colts XI. Dorothy had arrived just before him and they were both able to enjoy a spell of luxury living, bathing and resting on the beach. Then came a 100-mile drive to Kingston and a lunch *en route* at the famous Jamaica Inn. Kingston brought him back to the real-world problems of injuries to players, the business of trying to draw level in the series and the debut of a seventeen-year-old called Gary Sobers.

Hutton, in conversation with the groundsman at Sabina Park,

agreed with him that whoever won the toss ought to make 700, privately hoping that at last it would be himself and that England might make 400. Some twenty-four hours later it was Stollmeyer who won the toss . . . and the West Indies had lost 4 wickets for 13 and come within an ace of 5 for 29 when two catches went astray.

The morning – and the rest of the day – belonged to Bailey. He had opened the bowling only because Statham was unfit, bowled against the wind, and finished up with 7 for 34. A team whose collective batting averages for the series produced a total of 448, were dismissed for 139. When the first wicket fell to Bailey in the opening over, MCC reacted with nonchalance as they did when the West Indies continued to collapse. Hutton had given instructions that they were to exercise total restraint and give no cause for complaint whatever. Ten minutes after the last wicket fell, Bailey joined Hutton as opening batsman to see out the day's play. On the next day Hutton held the innings together when it might have slipped away for not much more than the West Indies had made. Hour after hour, concentration never wavering, he met the great pace and height of King and a generous bonus of bumpers. At 194 for 5, as the day's play ended, he was 93 not out. Things had not prospered for England as a whole as they might have done, wrote one commentator.

Thursday 1 April 1954 may be seen, in retrospect, as the last of the really great days of Hutton's career as a Test batsman. He completed his nineteenth Test-century soon after play began, allowed himself the luxury of a brief onslaught on Ramadhin and then ensured that he would be there after lunch. A century partnership with Evans was followed by another one with Wardle, with whom he added 77 in an hour. He went in to tea having reached his third double-century and his third-highest score in Test cricket. He had been on the field non-stop for close on three days in grilling heat. It was an infinitely greater endurance performance than that at The Oval in 1938. He was sixteen years older, bore the responsibilities of captaincy, recognized the consequences for the side if he failed and had combatted the West Indian heat and noise. Dorothy had been among the spectators and noticed him trudging wearily into the pavilion, head down, and murmuring a 'Thank you' to some voice of congratulation. He yearned 'for a cup of tea, a change of my sweat-soaked shirt and the luxury of putting my feet up'.

Throughout the game, incident-free as it had been on the field, he had been aware of a certain hostility from officials demonstrated, for example, when some complimentary tickets for friends were torn up. Indeed, his opposite number Stollmeyer had had his own fears after the crowd's attitude towards him two months earlier. The blow-up Hutton had feared arose not from anything in the game itself but from that murmured 'thank you'. Within moments someone entered the dressing room accusing him of insulting the Chief Minister and called it 'the crowning insult'. As to the second remark, Hutton could think of no previous insults while he generously gave whatever apology was due – and more – to the Chief Minister, Alex Bustamante, whom he had failed to realize was the man offering him congratulations. The Chief Minister accepted the incident at its face value when the two men met in the evening but petty officialdom and the local press blew up the affair. Its immediate effect on Hutton was that he lost his wicket in the first over after tea, 'in such a mental whirl after the rumpus and not knowing how the trumped-up incident might end' that his concentration, so long and magnificently sustained, had gone. Next morning the Jamaica *Daily Gleaner* gave the matter full prominence, with a letter Hutton had found time to write tucked away on page 8:

I should like to assure the Chief Minister and everyone in Jamaica that never for one moment did I intend to offend the Hon. Mr Bustamante . . . It was most unfortunate that I was not at first aware of the Hon. Bustamante's presence at the entrance to the pavilion. After having batted for nearly nine hours and having concentrated on the cricket for nearly three days, I was extremely tired and was thinking only of the twenty minutes' respite from the game allowed by the tea interval. When returning to the pavilion through a mass of applauding spectators a batsman rarely singles out an individual and there is merely an undefined sound ringing pleasantly in his ears.

Had I been forewarned of the Chief Minister's presence, I should naturally have been delighted and honoured.

At the conclusion of the game I had a most friendly discussion with Mr daCosta, the President of the Kingston Cricket Club, who was Mr Bustamante's host on this occasion, and Mr Nethersole, representing the West Indies Cricket Board of Control, and the matter was dealt with and disposed of as between sportsmen.

I think it most regrettable that an unfortunate impression has been created and I hope this letter will make everyone realise that my team and myself have the greatest respect and admiration for the Hon. Mr Bustamante.

It should be added that Hutton's letter to the press had contained the name of Mr Bustamante in the third paragraph and that was deleted by the paper to leave the impression that the two men had not met in the evening.

The match ended two days later, England winning by nine wickets. The spectators, whatever may have been their earlier deficiencies, gave the victors a generous reception and the series ended on level terms, not a triumph but far more than English players or critics could have hoped for after the end of the second Test. Crawford White in the *News Chronicle* called it 'the best cricket any English side has produced since the Jardine and Chapman series'. This was high praise, and, in so far as it related to Hutton as a batsman, was an unanimous opinion. The *Yorkshire Post* declared that Hutton had 'silenced his critics . . . His leadership in exacting circumstances should make him first choice as England's captain in Australia'. *The Times* called him 'the best batsman playing today' but tempered its view of the team's success by saying that the batting 'was almost carried by one man'. 'In concentration and certainty he stood alone', wrote *Wisden*. He had scored 677 runs in the Tests, for an average of 96.71, over 40 runs ahead of any other player on the England side and superior to any West Indian batsman.

As a captain on the field, Hutton had led not only by example – Hammond had done this before the war – but also by encouragement. Tactically, he was in touch with his bowlers, changed them shrewdly and kept a close eye on his field-setting. The players themselves recognized the burden which their captain had had to carry and had shown this in the private dinner of the senior men before the third Test, in which they had declared a total support for him. Hutton, in turn, was pleased at the display of loyalty and conceded to their view that a more aggressive strategy might produce dividends.

Evans, despite a slight grievance over being forbidden to attend a party in Jamaica to which Hutton himself went, thought him 'a worthy ambassador under the most difficult and embarrassing circumstances'. Statham commented not long after the tour: 'It seems strange to remember the frantic search for a man capable of leading England while Hutton was there all the time, alone on the doorstep, just waiting for the invitation to step inside.' Even Laker, critical of Hutton's captaincy in 1953 and believing that he 'regarded spinners as a last resort', accepted that he did 'an exceedingly capable job'. Wardle regarded the whole tour as 'a resounding triumph' for Hutton and was even moved to add that his leadership both on and off the field had never been surpassed. A judgement as extravagant as this must be debatable, but it leaves one in no doubt that, of the men who served under England's first modern professional captain, there were those who had the highest opinion of him.

Only in Hutton's relationship with Trueman must there be some qualification. Both were Yorkshiremen playing in the same county team at home under another leader. To the younger man, Hutton was 'Len'. But Hutton, as Trueman's captain on tour, rightly expected to be addressed as 'skipper'. Trueman found it difficult to distinguish between the man he played with for Yorkshire in the summer of 1953 and would do again in the summer of 1954, and the man who was now his captain. When incidents occurred, both on and off the field, Hutton took a discretionary view of things recognizing, as John Arlott has put it, that Trueman 'would lose heart for bowling'. Hutton's remedy was 'to nurse him by not being over-strict and by allowing him his high spirits'. It led one press correspondent to suggest that Hutton gave 'the volcanic Freddie Trueman far too much liberty with his gestures of annoyance' while recognizing that the real tragedy – and not just for Trueman – lay in stories being circulated from island to island and magnified to unbelievable proportions.

Trueman himself looked for a more positive approach from his captain. He would write later that 'much of the trouble might have been avoided had the senior players given more guidance to the youngsters'. Hutton, as we have seen, did his best to give such guidance and perhaps Trueman demanded more than his fair share of a busy captain's time and believed he was denied it. He felt anxious and puzzled, not to say unhappy, as the tour developed. *The Times* correspondent believed that the best man 'to contain Trueman in moments of stress' was Trueman. For some years Trueman nursed his grievances and, in a BBC programme in 1964, he tried, without success, to draw Hutton's fire on the allegations that the bowler had insulted an umpire in British Guiana. Hutton was to say after the tour that the West Indies made heavy demands on young players and 'were not the ideal place to send immature English cricketers'.

Hutton's task would also have been easier had there been both a different manager and a clear definition of the manager's role. He had been asked by Swanton, acting as an intermediary for Altham, MCC treasurer, whom he would like as manager and he had suggested Griffith, the recently appointed assistant secretary of MCC who had toured the West Indies in 1947–48. The MCC Committee did not appoint him, apparently on the grounds that he could not be spared from Lord's. Instead, as we have seen, Palmer, the successful secretary-captain of Leicestershire, was appointed player-manager and given a dual role in which he was answerable to Hutton on the field. Palmer, despite a schoolmaster background, had not the sense of authority which the circumstances demanded. Swanton, not given to exaggeration and a man of sober and moderate judgement, regarded the managerial appointment as, in his experience, 'just about the worst decision ever to have come out of Lord's'. The view that the captain was essentially in charge, so emphatically established by Jardine in 1932–33, still prevailed. Yet the case was emerging, even in the 1950s, for a manager with a distinctive role to play in authority. Thirty years later, as another England tour to the West Indies in 1985–86 demonstrated, the matter remained unsolved. By 1987 the appointments of Peter Lush and Micky Stewart had established an authority on football lines.

Hutton's relationship with the West Indies players was a sound one although there were one or two instances which suggested a certain aloofness. Stollmeyer, at a party at the start of the tour, felt that Hutton wished to distance himself from the opposition and Trueman was aware that fraternization with them was not approved of by the captain. As the weeks went by, Hutton became more relaxed in his attitude and gave support to his own declared contention that two sides could 'play this game hard and yet keep firm friends'. Indeed, the more the cricketers saw forces outside their control working against them, the more a unity grew between the two teams.

Rightly, Hutton regarded the cricket as the main business. His request for fewer social occasions brought criticism both from the white community, who felt such events their due, and from the non-white one, who felt slighted. Those ready to take offence could easily imagine situations in which the captain or his players upset them. The incident with the Chief Minister of Jamaica affecting Hutton had been an instance of this. Yet no one could have striven harder to be a diplomat. Trueman, indeed, felt that Hutton tried to be 'more of a diplomat than a captain', and on the score of diplomacy he could not be faulted. As a touring captain he may at the start have lacked the authority of a Jardine or the self-confidence of an Allen, but he quickly acquired both these qualities. Had he distanced himself from the players, as Hammond had done in Australia in 1946–47, the consequences might have been enormous.

So ended what *The Times* called 'the second most controversial tour in cricket history', set against that of 1932–33. Some comparisons between the two may be made. The controversy in 1932–33 arose out of a particular policy pursued on the field by the England captain. Its consequences were political in that Australian nationalism and economic interest were sensitive to the implications of what had taken place at Adelaide in the third Test – the core of the bodyline issue. The controversy in 1953–54 was the reverse. West Indian nationalism and economic interest were being heralded off the field and the consequences affected the cricketers in that their play was inhibited by noise, riot and intimidation. Secondly, Jardine, the England captain in 1932–33, was tough enough physically and mentally to cope with a situation largely of his own making. The one who suffered was his manager, Warner. In the West Indies in 1953–54, Hutton, while displaying immense qualities of toughness and inward strength, nevertheless experienced the decline in health which would hasten the end of his career in little over a year. By contrast with Jardine, the situation had not been one of his own making. Thirdly, while the earlier tour involved those at Lord's in a string of cables with Australian cricketing officials and the risk that the tour might be called off, the later one was seen to a conclusion with no direct dialogue between MCC and the West Indian Board of Control. The British press as a whole roundly praised Hutton in their summaries of the tour. 'There is no knowing what would have happened had he been of less equable temperament', commented the *Daily Mail* correspondent, Alex Bannister, who wrote a striking tribute in his book on the tour:

I cannot see a serious competitor arising for the leadership of the tour to Australia in September – faults could be picked in Hutton's tactics, his field placings, on occasions even perhaps in a lack of positive direction to the team. In personality he does not compare with some of the captains of the past, and in the words of a team-mate he does not 'bubble'. He takes some understanding – as he himself is the first to admit. He is inclined to indulge in somewhat obscure philosophizing, and some charged him with being too tolerant of Trueman.

In spite of all criticisms, the general emerged from his battles triumphant in the end, though not unscathed and, to my mind, England owed a lot to him for his will-power and his determination, to say nothing of his skill as a cricketer.

I thought it a sheer miracle that, with so many distractions and worries off the field, Hutton was able to stand head and shoulders above any batsman on either side and to maintain his consistency and concentration. Without him England would cut a sorry figure.

A perceptive judgement came from Ian Peebles in an article in the *Sunday Times*:

It was natural that Hutton's captaincy was the subject of much discussion, especially when his particular army seemed to be heading for defeat. Although he won the last two battles he still has his critics.

In trying to assess the merits and faults of Hutton's leadership so far, the logical starting-point may well be the broad question of the relative advantages of an amateur or a professional captain. Surely the answer in modern times is the best man for the job irrespective of status.

In this case Hutton was obviously the man for the job and has brought a good ration of the bacon home. The chief criticism against him is that of undue caution and a reluctance to press home a favourable situation. These are clearly not native characteristics; for, in pre-war days, no side were so quick to scent and exploit a tactical opening as Yorkshire. Many a more pedestrian side was harried out of a seemingly impregnable position in a furious half-hour's bombardment.

The same criticism is made of his direction of the batting; for, despite a statement attributed to him, on one occasion, that he gave his batsmen no instructions, direction there must be. It does appear that his batsmen incline to imitate his example of wearing down rather than destroying the attack.

Hutton, while a magnificent player of strokes, is the greatest defensive batsman in the world. He can afford the bowler every opportunity of attack yet foil his best efforts and remain master. A less gifted player who pursues such tactics is liable to find himself hard pressed and worn out long before the bowler is worn down. Thus while Hutton, as the very foundation of our batting, should adopt the policy most suitable to himself, one would like to see him instil a rather more aggressive attitude into his supporting batsmen. It may be difficult to say to a team 'Do as I preach, not as I practise,' but captains are expected to say difficult things.

The Times, in its summary of the tour, fully recognized the burdens Hutton had carried on and off the field and saw his ability to bat as well as he did in relation to them as 'an extraordinary feat of mental and physical endurance'. The *Yorkshire Post*, in a leading article, spoke of his 'wisdom and courage' at Georgetown:

By that quietly firm decision, Mr Hutton did much for the amicable future of Tests within the West Indies. He also showed the high quality of leadership on which he had been so freely faulted. To hold the West Indies to a draw on their own grounds would be a creditable performance in any circumstances. In the circumstances of this particular series it was a personal triumph, and honour will not be withheld where it is most emphatically due.

Another leading article in the *Sydney Morning Herald* said:

Hutton and his team have gone a long way to restoring England's prestige. Certain guardians of English cricket have suggested changing the captain, but Australians will hope to see this much-shot-at general defending the Ashes in the 1954–55 series. He is a foeman worthy of our cheers.

The Australians would meet the general six months later.

From MCC came the statement that the performance of Hutton and his men in squaring the series was 'magnificent' and Hutton in part deserved 'the warmest congratulations for retaining such wonderful concentration and form in spite of all his responsibilities'.

Meanwhile, back in Pudsey, the subject of all these tributes put the final touches to his official report to MCC. It was a 15-page document in which he dealt with the problems of the tour and commented on his players. The umpiring 'except on one or two occasions, was appalling'. He attributed this to incompetence and a genuine fear of local reprisals and influences. Agreement on playing conditions, he argued, should have been fixed by the appropriate authorities before the tour began – discussions on when the new ball might be taken caused confusion and dissastisfaction. Hutton recognized that there was 'far too much jealousy between the islands' and believed the sense of difference made the task of the West Indian Board of Control extremely difficult. He commented on the broader and less definable issue of relationships between visitors and hosts. 'Our friends in the West Indies actively connected with cricket could be numbered with one hand', he wrote and this, he believed, contributed to 'a rather strained atmosphere' on occasions. His recommendation to MCC was that future captains be men of experience able to handle difficult situations and he paid a generous tribute to the role played by his manager, Palmer.

Hutton's report also dealt with the individual players. So glowing was his tribute to Bailey, his vice-captain, that he might almost have been suggesting him as a contender for the captaincy for those who looked for an amateur or sought to take the burden off Hutton himself. Bailey was 'every captain's ideal – responsive, perceptive, a tactical move ahead of his shrewdest opponent and never overawed or intimidated'. He was equally generous in his tribute to May – 'a young man always willing to learn', and to Compton – 'as senior profession-al, a great help in every way'. Of Evans he wrote: 'I feel that you know all there is to know about him.'

More significant for the future was what he said on Trueman. He was 'a character' whom the game needed and whose keenness 'was probably responsible for some of his aggressive actions on the field'. He was a man in whom there was 'no vice, envy or jealousy' and 'was most distressed' over the Georgetown umpiring incident. Of Laker,

22 The start of the MCC 1953–54 tour, Hamilton, Bermuda.

23 The England captain leads Yorkshire, at Bristol, 1954
(*P. A. – Reuter Photos Ltd*).

24 Outward-bound for Australia, MCC, 1954–55
(*Associated Newspapers Ltd*).

25 MCC *v*. South Africans at Lord's, 1955 – moments before LH had
to retire and relinquish the England captaincy (*Sport & General*).

26 Formal and informal: at Buckingham Palace, 1956
(*Evening News*).

27 At Thorniehurst, Pudsey, 1958 (LH built the seat)
(*Richard Rogers*).

28 Part of the orchestra with
Katie Boyle, Moira Lister,
Margaret Rutherford, Herman
Lindar (conductor), Edmundo
Ros, Lord Boothby, Cliff
Michelmore: the Albert Hall,
1961 (*Evening News*).

29 With the politicians: Sir Alec
Douglas-Home has tea with LH and
Sidney Hainsworth, Hull, 1965

30 Harold Wilson, as Chancellor, at
LH's graduation, Bradford, 1982
(*University of Bradford*).

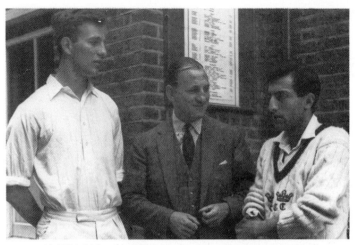

31 With Richard and the Nawab of Pataudi, University Match at Lord's, 1963 (*S & G Press Agency Ltd*).

32 LH and the business of conveyor belting.

33 The last match: Old England *v.* England Ladies at The Oval, 1973.

34 Three generations of Yorkshire opening batsmen:
Boycott, Sutcliffe, LH at Headingley, 1977 (*The Yorkshire Post*).

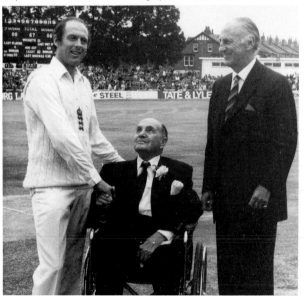

35 Other sports:
golf in the 1970s
(*LPA International
Photo Service Ltd*).

36 Baseball instruction
from a Pittsburgh Pirate,
1978.

37
Picture 21, thirty years on: Sheffield, 1983.

38
Impromptu coaching for Benjamin, 1985.

39
Seventieth birthday party with Miller, Compton and Trueman, Lord's, 1986.

40
Sir Leonard and Lady Hutton, at Kingston-on-Thames, 1987.

Hutton wrote that he had a 'strong tendency to be afraid of certain batsmen', and his greater praise was reserved for Lock. Statham, rather curiously, received the briefest report – a couple of sentences indicating improvement and endeavour. Among the other batsmen, Graveney was seen as someone who 'rather disappointed' his captain because 'at times his concentration seemed to desert him' while Watson seemed to be affected by the 'extra tension of a Test match'.

In a tour attracting extensive press interest Hutton wrote that he and his manager had been approached by journalists 'far more often than anticipated', important as a close dialogue was. Finally, he stressed the need to have a masseur throughout the tour and, in particular, someone of the quality and personality of Harold Dalton whom they had had in Jamaica.

With his report written and submitted to MCC, his duty was done and he could relax. He was a very tired man and he approached the coming English season with some physical and mental apprehension. The West Indies tour had taken a toll from which, in cricketing terms, he would never really recover.

9

Triumph Down Under

1954–55

'His triumph as a captain was complete. He fashioned the
attack which made the victory.'

John Bapty, *Yorkshire Evening Post*, 1955

Lord's on Tuesday 4 May 1954 was bleak and cold as Hutton went out
to bat for Yorkshire against MCC and was promptly bowled by
Stuart Surridge, the Surrey captain, for a single. Surridge, having
already led his county to the first two of a long run of successes in the
1950s, had watched Hutton's captaincy in the West Indies and told a
journalist that he would be regarded among the great Test captains.
Ten days later Hutton (in Yardley's absence) captained Yorkshire to
victory against Gloucestershire, carrying his bat in the second innings
in a match personally saddened by the news of the death of George
Hirst. In his tribute to the press Hutton said, 'He did more for me than
any other cricketer'. He again captained the county against Hampshire
at Bradford, making the top score of 63 in the match and welcoming
the performance of Bob Appleyard, the off-spin bowler whose 7 for
35 marked his return after being out of the game for two years with
tuberculosis.

Thereafter he played very little cricket until the first Test, still
mentally tired after the West Indies tour and physically in pain.
Mudbaths at Harrogate and rest at home brought him, a somewhat
reluctant starter, to the inaugural Test played by Pakistan in England. It

146

was a game reduced to eight hours' play by rain and in which he had the doubtful honour of his being the first wicket ever to be taken by a Pakistani in a Test match in England when bowled by Khan Mohammed for 0. Little luck came his way except for winning the toss (for a change) with a sixpence given to him by the Duke of Edinburgh when the two sides visited Buckingham Palace. Immediately after the Test he took part in Yorkshire's first-ever tie, against Leicestershire at Huddersfield, going from there to play Middlesex at Lord's.

By now it was late June and he had had barely a dozen innings all summer. Press speculation grew upon whether he would continue as the England captain. The alternative candidate was David Sheppard and 'Will it be Hutton or Sheppard?' was a typical headline. Sheppard had led both Cambridge University and Sussex, taking the county from 13th to second place in the championship in 1953. He had broken several batting records while at Cambridge and his claim to a place in the England side on merit could only marginally be disputed. He would, said his advocates, be in the tradition of amateurs from the ancient English universities. Nor would his appointment necessarily be seen as a criticism of the man in office who would be able to concentrate on his batting, though Hutton still had his critics: those who thought he lacked dynamism, those who simply opposed a professional being captain and those who thought he would assail Australia with a pace attack which would revive memories of Jardine's captaincy.

Sheppard had embarked on the studies which would lead to ordination and eventually to the bishopric of Liverpool. He would become one of the most influential men in the north of England on social issues in the 1980s, even arousing speculation that he might become Archbishop of Canterbury. In 1954, he was reading theology at Ridley Hall, Cambridge, finding time to play a reasonable amount of cricket and under pressure from some sources to declare himself as an available candidate. Bishop Sheppard has indicated, some thirty years later, how strong those pressures were. Robins, a selector, and Errol Holmes, a former Surrey captain and the son-in-law of Leveson Gower, both worked hard on his behalf, even suggesting that he went to a secret meeting at the home of Aird, the MCC secretary. He felt in a moral dilemma and consulted his tutor, Norman Sykes, the future Dean of Winchester. Sykes, a Yorkshireman and a cricket enthusiast, met Hutton through an introduction from Sheppard, and came away with the opinion that a small part of him might be relieved not to be captain but that the larger part very much wished to continue the task he had undertaken. With some reluctance, Sheppard indicated he would take leave of absence from Ridley Hall if approached by the selectors and meanwhile would let events take their course.

Hutton, for his part, chose the Middlesex match at Lord's to tell Aird that he was prepared to go to Australia, either as captain or player. On Aird's advice, he wrote a formal letter to the Board of Control saying so. This was in the nature of the man, a genuine concern not to embarrass the selectors nor to let down his country. The Board had to weigh up various arguments: his health, his responsibilities as an opening bat and the case for Sheppard.

There followed a month at the height of the season when Hutton, on medical advice, played neither for Yorkshire nor England. The selectors appointed Sheppard for the second and third Tests against Pakistan, England winning by an innings at Trent Bridge and having much the best of a rain-ruined match at Old Trafford. Peebles wrote in the *Sunday Times* that Sheppard 'batted fairly and handled his side competently, but one could not say in honesty he did anything to enhance his claims of succession. Indeed, events offered him but little scope'. Sheppard was in an unpleasant situation 'because I felt quite unsure of my position, as though I was more of a caretaker than a captain'. Robins, sensing that he was the odd man out among the selectors, was changing his ground and gave Sheppard a hint at Nottingham that his tenure was temporary: 'I feel we've been unfair to Hutton. He was in a very difficult position in the West Indies.' At the time of the third Test Hutton got back into the game with 163 against the Combined Services, batting for three hours in a trial as much of stamina as of skill. Another century, against Nottinghamshire, was sound preparation for his return to the England side for the fourth Test.

By now the controversy of the summer was resolved and he was appointed captain for the tour of Australia. It is to the credit of both the selectors and Hutton himself that he was chosen – a distinguished cricketer of uncertain health, adjudged able to triumph over physical adversity. His own enthusiasm to do the job if asked, matched by his generosity in offering to serve under another, certainly influenced the selectors and the vote in his favour was unanimous. Both Hutton and Sheppard, each a man of strong moral fibre, conducted themselves with dignity throughout the weeks of uncertainty. Neither gave press interviews nor leaked their opinions. Their attitudes reflected the best in the professional and the amateur tradition.

Hutton was automatically invited to join the selectors, a panel of three ex-England captains in Allen, Robins and Yardley, together with Ames, Palmer, and the chairman, Altham. Collectively, they represented the Board of Control appointees for the home Tests against Pakistan, together with the MCC Cricket Committee nominees. The responsibility for tours abroad for the next twenty or so years would still technically be undertaken by MCC.

C. B. Fry, who had been both captain of England and a selector before 1914, wrote:

> Hutton or an amateur?: on this subject the humpty-dumpty of 'snobbery' was enthroned on the wall. There was supposed to be a party at Lord's so rooted in the feudal past as to object to a professional captain on social grounds. And this, of course, was absolute bunkum.

Not necessarily so, Hutton thought. Fry declared himself in favour of amateurs for a different reason. They were free from the handicap of knowing that what they did or did not do might gravely affect the economic career of a fellow member of the team. Despite this argument of doubtful validity (since an amateur was equally aware of the disservice he might be rendering to a professional's pocket), he favoured the appointment of Hutton as someone recognized by everyone in the know as a 'shrewd, steady, capable captain'.

The 'shrewd, steady, capable captain' returned to lead England in the fourth Test. Pakistan's victory by 24 runs was a tremendous stimulus for the team in their first visit to England. Warner, at last no longer a selector, wrote privately to his friend Sir Robert Menzies that 'Hutton had no cricketing sense. I told them three months ago he was no captain'. Outwardly charming, Warner would use letters to friends as a vehicle for expressing unflattering opinions.

With Australia in mind, the selectors had picked a slightly experimental side against Pakistan but this scarcely excused the English collapse in their second innings. Needing 168 on the evening of the fourth day (with the fifth day available), they set off at a great pace to get the runs that evening and earn themselves, some suggested, a day off. With half an hour remaining, and seven wickets in hand, Evans went in (above Graveney) to chase the final 59 runs. The fall of his wicket heralded a collapse and ultimate defeat on the following morning. Bowes wrote that Hutton needed to do some hard thinking on tactics and strategic problems, while the skipper's batting average for the series was 6.33. Perhaps he was a shade lucky to have been appointed captain for Australia *before* the Test took place.

Hutton played very little cricket for the rest of the season and for the first time in many years failed to score a thousand runs. Meanwhile, the side for Australia was being completed and Hutton still felt acutely conscious of the wealth of experience which he faced around the selectors' table. Allen, in particular, was a formidable personality whose pronouncements on this and that player were often accepted *ex cathedra*. Yet Hutton knew what he wanted: a bevy of fast bowlers, and he argued the case (successfully) for Tyson and (unsuccessfully) for Trueman. One of the few benefits to have come out of the last Test against Pakistan had been Tyson's bowling on his Test debut.

It was an extremely large party which would leave England in September to defend the Ashes. There were twenty-three English journalists from whose efforts came millions of words of copy and nine books on the tour; seventeen cricketers (Compton flew out later to make eighteen), most of whose names will appear as this chapter proceeds; a scorer, masseur and manager. The scorer, George Duckworth, had been the England wicket-keeper of the 1920s and 1930s, the masseur, Harold Dalton, was particularly wanted by Hutton, and the manager was Geoffrey Howard. Howard had had a distinguished career as a London club cricketer, good enough to make occasional appearances for Middlesex and to be selected for the Club Cricket Conference against the West Indies in 1933. After the war he had made his mark in cricket administration as secretary of Lancashire and then of Surrey. He had managed with considerable skill MCC's tour of India, Pakistan and Ceylon in 1951–52 and *The Cricketer* believed his charm, personality and character 'would have just about the right influence'. He was a manager who happened to have been a good performer at a level below first-class cricket and, unlike Palmer a year earlier, could give his undivided attention to the job. All three men in their different roles were a support to Hutton. Duckworth acted as a sounding-board for ideas, served as a selector, and was a source of informed opinion; Dalton had the qualities of a psychologist; and Howard, in Hutton's opinion, 'knew exactly when it was possible to relieve a captain's burden'.

With all these men, journalists, cricketers and officials, Hutton would have to work and co-operate in different ways over the next seven months. The professional cricketers among them would earn a basic £850 with a spending allowance of £4 a week and the opportunity to qualify for a bonus.

The return to the traditional mode of travel by sea meant a long parting from families. The news cameras were there at Kingsmead to see the captain walk out of his front door with Dorothy and the boys putting a brave face on things. Next day, the docks at Tilbury were crowded with reporters all clamouring for a word from Hutton. In the midst of it all, he found time for a quiet word of re-assurance with Colin Cowdrey's parents who had come to see off their son, the youngest member of the party. Cowdrey has never forgotten Hutton's kindness and thoughtfulness at that time, not least because his father died three weeks later. Not a lot was said but it was Hutton who quietly took the bereaved young man under his wing and made him his golf partner in a match on the Sunday after their arrival. On the voyage itself Cowdrey had found it difficult to approach the senior players. Hutton let events take their course and gradually he, and the other younger ones, established a relationship with him.

The captain was concerned to strike a balance on board ship between an over-rigid training scheme and idleness. He believed the role of Dalton, as masseur, was crucial, not only in assessing a player's physical condition, but also his mental one. One aspect of what might be called 'mental training' Hutton undertook himself. He prepared his less experienced players to cope with the huge crowds before whom they would play. The setting and the circumstances would be different in Australia from the West Indies. Crowds would be less intimate and less political though just as partisan. In huge grounds, such as Melbourne and Sydney, they could envelop the player so that he might become even claustrophobic within their embrace. The roar, and then the hush, could be unnerving. 'I tried to impress on them not to lose self-control in any circumstances and to steel themselves never to allow the crowds to upset them.' Cowdrey was told to equip himself for a rough reception when he went in to bat. 'You're a young player with quite a reputation. They're going to try to rough you up a bit.' Hutton was reminded of the guidance which he had been given as a young man when the ship stopped at Naples and he took a party of players and reporters to lay a wreath on the grave of Hedley Verity in the cemetery at Caserta.

On arriving at Fremantle, Hutton gave his first press conference, creating 'a splendid impression and delighting everyone by his tact and friendliness', wrote A. G. Moyes. He had the advantage of having the Australian press on his side from the beginning – the English professional who had 'beaten the system' and become captain – and he was determined to keep it that way. The journalists were a little disarmed by his tactic of playing down MCC's strength. What they least expected to hear was the view that England had not got much bowling, nor much batting. 'We're here to learn a lot from you.' Tackled on the question of bouncers, he replied that he intended 'to play the game as laid down in the rules' and that he would not support a method of attack in which the batsman was 'in danger of serious injury'. The events of 1932–33 were less than a generation away and the captain, after the bitterness of the West Indian tour, wanted this one to be free from rancour. So it was to prove: Norman Preston wrote afterwards that 'the true spirit of cricket and good fellowship' always existed and neither crowds, umpires, nor politics caused controversy. The former South Australian player, Richard Whitington, who had become a distinguished journalist, summed up Hutton's approach to captaincy:

> In leadership the team should lack very little. Hutton went out of his way in the Coronation Test series to make friends with each member of his team, and was prepared to bestow far more encouragement than any post-war captain I have watched, except Jack Cheetham.
> I know of no finer example to cricketers playing today in every respect than the professional England has chosen as her leader.

After the preliminaries, it was time to get down to business. With his memories of the successful post-war pace attack of Lindwall and Miller, Hutton hoped that the Ashes would be retained by a similar attack based on Statham and Tyson. Early on he reached the reluctant conclusion that Bedser, ironically rested from the West Indian tour a year before to prepare for Australia, was (after shingles) unfit. After an opening victory against Western Australia, in which he himself scored 145 and retired hurt, Hutton had a chance to see his bowling combination from the pavilion as he watched the match v. the Combined XI. Against a side which admittedly contained only three of the future Australian team, Statham and Tyson collected between them 6 wickets for 89 runs in the few overs which Hutton had indicated to May, the vice-captain, they should have. Statham had already established himself over the previous four years but Tyson was something new: a fast bowler of immense pace and powerful shoulders who would break down if his extreme run were not shortened. The presence of Peter Loader and Bailey as well as Bedser ensured that neither were over-used in the matches before the first Test.

Nor, indeed, did the captain over-use himself, resting in every other game and scoring 37 and 98 against South Australia, and 102 and 87 against New South Wales, and coming to the first Test with an average of 117.25. The match against New South Wales had seen him and Cowdrey hold together both the MCC innings. Cowdrey scored a century in both innings, having yet to score one in the English County Championship.

On the Sunday, the half-way point into the match, the team were taken out in a launch to see Sydney Harbour and the Bays and feel the pull of the Pacific Ocean in their small craft. Two days later it was time to get the night train 'Spirit of Progress' to Brisbane, the progress being delayed somewhat by having to change carriages at the State border between New South Wales and Queensland because of the different gauges. Australians for nearly a century paid dearly in time for the variation of gauges which stemmed from the strong independent attitude of each of the original colonies before Federation. MCC came to Wooloongabba, the place of the gathering of the waters, where they would play first Queensland and then Australia. Hutton, still experimenting, as he had done in the West Indies, in the search for another opener, sent Cowdrey in with Simpson against Queensland but the experiment was not successful and was not repeated. He did not play against Queensland. He just watched hour after hour in a seat in front of the pavilion. Drinks were brought to him but not a word was said. That part of his temperament which made him distance himself from everyone else was working overtime. The captain was in travail: a Test series was about to be born.

It is part of the folklore of cricket that Hutton won the toss at Brisbane, put the Australians in and saw England lose by an innings and 154 runs. His decision had been carefully thought out: Australia was unsure of the English fast bowlers, the wicket might be lively in the early stages, and he was fearful of how his opening partner would face Lindwall and Miller. The night before, Moyes, in a nationwide broadcast, predicted Hutton's action and adjudged it would be a wrong one. Arlott, watching a Test in Australia for the first time, realized after three-quarters of an hour that it was clear beyond all doubt that only some terrible aberration on the part of the Australian batsmen could betray them. 'The ball would not swing. It left the pitch with far less life than it met it.' Yet all might have been well had not Evans dropped out unfit on the morning of the match, and had England held even some of the catches which went astray. Bedser, alone, had seven catches dropped off him, a series of non-events which were to prove crucial to his role in the rest of the tour. Hutton himself would look back on the English fielding as 'the worst exhibition of outfield-cricket' in his time as captain. Swanton was alone in feeling that the lack of a spin bowler was an error in selection; he still thought so when discussing the series with me in 1987. Compton, injured earlier in the match, might have filled the role but he had had little practice as such on the tour.

These misfortunes and the excellence of the wicket contributed to a defeat in which Hutton drew consolation neither from his own performance with the bat, nor even from his own family – a brother at home had gone to work in the morning 'deploring the news of Len's decision to field'. Philosophically, Hutton remarked that pitches were like wives: 'you were never sure how they were going to turn out.'

Yet all was not total tragedy for a team which Arlott immediately described as 'too pleasant a company of people to be depressed'. The bonuses included runs from Edrich and Bailey of the more senior players, and from May and Cowdrey (on his Test debut) of the younger ones. Tyson's 37 not out was useful but irrelevant: far more important was Hutton's growing confidence in his potential as a bowler, especially as Bedser had proved scarcely fit enough in bowling 37 overs. Hutton arranged for Gover, travelling as a journalist, (who finally retired from coaching at the age of 80 in 1988) to take his run in hand and shorten it. *The Times* had supported Hutton's decision to put Australia in, commenting after the defeat that 'it was not only justified but made almost inevitable by circumstances and the composition of the side'. But in the end, a captain ploughs his own furrow and Hutton remained the lonely ploughman.

Two hundred miles north of Brisbane lies tropical Rockhampton: tropical by the skin of its teeth for an abstract spire, a mile or two short of the outskirts, marks the Tropic of Capricorn. In this city of stone facades and handsome pillars with an affluence based on a pastoral and mining background Hutton ran into more trouble. In a two-day match against a Queensland Country XI he allowed the pitch to be remade after MCC had made 317. The local side looked like holding out for a draw with two wickets and two balls left. Hutton persuaded their captain to extend play and MCC secured a victory: 'not quite cricket' thought some of the locals, as MCC flew off to meet the Prime Minister's XI at Canberra, still very much a 'new town' whose development since its inception as the federal capital in 1927 had been slow. The final completion of its parliament buildings was only achieved in 1988, to coincide with Australia's bicentenary. But, as the centre of government, however incomplete in its architecture, Canberra had its own importance with the Prime Minister and the Governor-General, Sir William Slim, both present at the match. Hutton, taking the final 3 wickets of the Prime Minister's XI in 11 balls, won the match for MCC by 31 runs.

Morale at first-class level was restored against Victoria at Melbourne with a century from May, and Tyson, off a shortened run, taking 6 wickets for 68, hitting the stumps five times. Hopes, so abundantly raised, were dashed three days later in the second Test at

Sydney, when the England score stood at 88 for 8. Right up until just before lunch on the fourth day prospects of success were poor until Tyson turned his back on a bouncer from Lindwall and was hit on the head. *Wisden* would report with unconscious irony, 'Tyson won the match for England because he kept his head.' For it was this blow which, in Hutton's view, stimulated him into immense action as a bowler: 'something, perhaps a new will-power, a fresh determination. Whatever the cause, a Tyson emerged who must have been as fast as any bowler in the history of cricket.' In the Australian second innings he took 6 wickets for 85 to give England an unexpected victory. In a later age, he would have won the plaudits and goblets accorded to the 'man of the match' for his 10 wickets for 130.

The winning margin of 38 runs was even narrower than it looked. A match which Moyes called the most exciting Test ever played in Australia, kept its tension to the end. (The Brisbane tie between Australia and the West Indies was yet to come in 1961.) Harvey was joined by Bill Johnston, the last Australian, with 77 runs needed. The two of them scored half of the target and, as the runs came, the probability that they might reach it increased. To the spectators it had been a grand match to watch, though to the purists it lacked technical perfection. The success of Tyson and, to a lesser extent, of Statham, was a vindication of Hutton's policy. Arlott, though pleased with the victory, attached even more importance to the enhanced stature of May and Cowdrey than to the bowling of Tyson, 'the most important factor of the match'. Hutton, in his press interview afterwards, declared his pleasure that Tyson had fulfilled his own hopes for him and added, with a wry smile, that had he won the toss he would have put Australia in again as Morris had done to him!

No comment on that Test is complete without reference to the omission of Bedser. Hutton had agonized on whether to play him or not. The conditions were perfect for Bedser, as Swanton was not slow to point out in his reports, but the attack of shingles had left its mark and Hutton still doubted his fitness. With the support of the selection committee, the decision was taken to leave him out and, contrary to some accounts, Hutton found a moment to drop Bedser a hint that he would not be playing.

Then came Christmas, and Swanton used the brief break of five days to give his readers in the *Daily Telegraph* some thoughts on 'the burden of captaincy'. He was critical of the lack of a regular system of supervised cricket training with well organized nets, fielding practice and physical training, although he did not feel that the captain should have to organize these things; he had enough to do. Swanton argued that Hutton should be allowed to concentrate on his batting and his leadership on the field and leave the rest to others. With his breadth of vision on the game, Swanton was thinking aloud on the roles which future managers, assistant managers and coaches might play. Howard, the current manager had been given no job description on his appointment and had been left by MCC to work out the respective responsibilities between himself and Hutton. Indeed, the casual approach of MCC to his appointment makes strange reading thirty years later. Howard was told that money would be credited to an MCC account at Perth on his arrival. Nothing was done and he arranged with a bank manager there to allow him an account in his own name with an overdraft of £10,000 to be paid back when the tour was in profit. In the meantime, Howard had to pay the professionals as and when they asked for advances on their tour fee.

Between the second and the third Test MCC played an up-country match at Newcastle. Christmas was spent at the Oceanic Hotel, Coogee near Sydney, and some players recalled the captain 'enduring rather than enjoying' the high spirits after the dinner once the waiters had left them to their own devices. Hutton then went direct to Melbourne. On the morning of the first day of the third Test he was feeling unwell, with fibrositis and a cold, white as a sheet and shivering. A doctor was called and he was pronounced fit to play. Players were summoned to his bedside: 'Come on, mate' (not 'skipper'), cajoled Evans. Reluctantly, he got up and made his way to the ground.

Much more worrying to him than the state of his health was the decision he knew he had to make yet again on Bedser's selection. The critics had had their say after Sydney. Bedser was fitter now and Melbourne was very much 'his' ground where he had been so successful in two Tests four years earlier. Compton took him, at Hutton's suggestion, to inspect the wicket. The arguments for leaving him out were fast diminishing but at the last moment the captain made his decision and Bedser's name was not on the team list posted up in the dressing room. In the flurry of events – getting to the ground later than usual, debating his own fitness to play, tossing-up, preparing to open the innings – Hutton failed, on this occasion, to have that private word with Bedser which courtesy to a friend and recognition of his record demanded. What had been at Sydney non-selection related to fitness was, at Melbourne, simply non-selection. The decision may have been correct: the way it was handled was assuredly not. No man gets everything right and Sir Leonard accepted that the moment of approach should have been found. But he used his recollections of the incident to remind his biographer that he was not as tough as some people thought and that a part of him shrank from speaking to Bedser, for whom the rest of the tour bore similarities to Maurice Tate in 1932–33: a great bowler of the past flexing his muscles for Mount Gambier and Yallourn.

Swanton, with a rare error of judgement, had not expected Bedser to be left out of the third Test – 'I do not think that any sensations may be expected at this time' – and was therefore extremely critical both of the fact and the manner of his omission, feeling that some sort of accompanying statement should have been made. Arlott wrote that Bedser has been 'too great a cricketer to be treated in this way'. As to whether Bedser should have been in the original twelve or not, opinions differed. Peebles argued that, on technical grounds, Hutton had to consider him up until the two captains exchanged lists.

In the context of the morning's events, Hutton was not entirely sorry to be back in the pavilion within an hour of England's innings. He sat, someone recalled, huddled in a corner of the dressing room only recovering interest in the proceedings when Cowdrey began to bat outstandingly. In the second innings Hutton's contribution was an essential one. He made 42 in 146 minutes and incurred some mild protest from the crowd at his slowness. Had he failed, England's first innings deficit of 40 would have made defeat extremely likely. Apart from being captain, he always carried an extra dimension as an opener in that he never really had a regular partner. If Hobbs had failed, there was always Sutcliffe; if Ponsford, Woodfull. Hutton, since becoming England captain had had six different partners – Simpson, Kenyon, Bailey, Watson, Sheppard and Edrich – and would add Graveney before the tour was over. By contrast, between 1924 and 1929, Hobbs had Sutcliffe as his partner in 20 out of 21 consecutive matches; nor did Hobbs have to think about captaincy as well. In the Melbourne Test Hutton had opened with Edrich and the partnership achieved little. History has identified Edrich with Hutton because they went to the wicket together that day at The Oval in 1938 but the evidence does not support their partnerships as ones of any sustained duration or success.

In Hutton's words, 'Tyson and Statham, as a two-man team, swept England to an historic victory, and figuratively speaking, I had my hand on the Ashes'. England, 40 behind on the first innings, eventually left Australia with 240 to win in just over two days. Press opinion was that Appleyard, the off-spinner, would be brought on to a wearing pitch, but he was never needed. In 75 balls, the final 8 Australian wickets went for 36 runs. Tyson's analysis of 7 for 27 was the best second innings performance by a bowler in the long history of

England v. Australia matches. In the match as a whole, he took 9 wickets and Statham, 7. As in all great bowling partnerships, each was complementary to the other – Statham the more accurate, Tyson the faster.

For all his delight in his 'two-man team', Hutton readily acknowledged the contribution of Cowdrey, whose century in the first innings had alone held the innings together, and of May's 91 in the second. England's victory, just before lunch in front of a packed Melbourne crowd on a public holiday, had been totally unexpected. Spectators, reluctant to go home, sat on in silence. A junior member of the touring party was sent out to find champagne in a city whose shops were closed and whose licensing laws were strange. As for the captain, he 'felt like a jockey riding a runaway Derby winner'. Perhaps the trotter in which he had had himself photographed at Bunbury had been a good augury; though he was personally disappointed at not making the large scores in Australia which he had done in the West Indies. Cowdrey noticed perceptively the mental strain which Hutton imposed on himself matched to the precision, the psychological pressure, with which he used Tyson against batsmen who seemed apprehensive or in trouble. This England captain, hating to hurt an old companion-in-arms such as Bedser, had iron in his soul where opponents were concerned.

Some reference must be made to the mystery of the watered wicket. The Friday and Saturday of the third Test had been played in conditions so hot that the fierce northern winds from the desert had sustained temperatures at 94°, even at midnight. The same had been true of the Sunday, when Melbourne's highest-ever night temperature of 96° was recorded, yet on the Monday morning there were signs of watering which was, of course, contrary to the regulations. Official denials were issued while soil scientists argued that the extreme heat might have produced some sort of sweating. Long afterwards, Melbourne Cricket Club admitted there had been a genuine human error and the pitch had been watered. It says much for Anglo-Australian relations on that tour that the incident was treated in a very low key by the players themselves.

The receipts for the Test had set a new Australian record and met all expenses of the tour. Henceforth, revenues in the fourth and fifth Test were pure profit and Howard could face his 'friendly' bank manager in Perth. The assumption of profit on the tour could not necessarily have been made in advance. For one thing, the Melbourne ground was being converted for the 1956 Olympic Games and a section of the stand was not available for the public to buy seats. Furthermore, as

Bruce Harris observed in the London *Evening Standard*, cricket was being fiercely challenged by tennis as a spectator force. The plea for 'instant' cricket, with the excitement contained within a few hours, as in tennis, had not yet become urgent but in twenty years' time the cricket world would be deeply split by events in Australia associated with Kerry Packer and the emergence of World Series Cricket. Fixtures, in the pre-World Series era, followed a well tried formula. The States were played twice, there were a few up-country matches (not to be underestimated) and a couple of games in Tasmania. Tasmanians with ambitions, such as Edgar McDonald and Lindsay Badcock, had had to move to the mainland and not till 1977 would the island enter the Sheffield Shield. In 1954–55 Tasmanians were joined by four of the Australian Test side in a game at Hobart before a record crowd of over 20,000 and Tasmania itself played MCC at Launceston. Hutton played in both games, making his first half-century in a dozen innings in the second one. His handling of the Tasmanian match ensured an exciting finish despite the wide disparity between the two sides. Two declarations left Tasmania the final afternoon in which to try to save the match, and the result was in doubt till MCC won in the final quarter of an hour.

Captains must be continual speechmakers. Hutton excelled himself, by all accounts, at Adelaide where a formal reception was given in the city hall in the presence of the State Premier and the Mayor and Aldermen. One journalist called his performance 'scintillating . . . nothing marks the progress of Hutton from the rank and file of cricketers to the leadership of England more than his expanding ability as a maker of speeches'. Formality over, Hutton had earned himself a rest. Ten miles from the city centre, from which Adelaide's only remaining trams travel in a straight line past brightly coloured bungalows and gardens, lies the seaside resort of Glenelg. The team stayed at the Pier Hotel and Hutton stood down while his colleagues beat Southern Australia by an innings and 143 runs, Compton (182) and May (114) sharing in a sixth-wicket partnership of 234.

Hutton divided his time between watching the game and relaxing at his hotel. A retreat such as this ensured that he could, without giving offence, avoid meeting well-meaning people, who would want to talk cricket. His dedication to the captaincy meant that he was, as journalists noted and admired, available on the telephone from early morning till late at night. 'He met our calls as no other captain had ever done,' wrote John Bapty. At Glenelg he was able to recharge his batteries and make the mental preparations which would ensure that England won the rubber and retained the Ashes.

Australia chose to bat in the fourth Test and in temperatures over 100° Hutton managed his bowlers well, keeping no man on for more than three overs at a time, and containing Australia to 161 for 4 on the first day. The match slipped briefly from his grasp when the Australian ninth-wicket pair, Len Maddocks and Johnson, the captain, put on 92 and Australia finished up with 323. Hutton set the pattern of the England innings, his 80 being ended by a spectacular catch by Davidson at short-leg, he and Edrich having the best opening partnership of their seventeen years' association. When Australia began their second innings, 18 behind, Hutton again relied on his superb fast-bowling combination and, with some worthwhile help from Appleyard, routed them, as in Melbourne, for a score of 111. A match which had had its boring features – *The Times* correspondent, John Woodcock, wrote that he 'was thankful to be paid to watch' – ended in some considerable excitement as England's small target of 94 for a moment seemed unattainable. At 2.42 p.m. England set off to get the runs. Edrich went at 2.45, Hutton at 2.55 and Cowdrey at 3.07. Some Meteor jets thundering overhead seemed to be urging on Miller, the former fighter pilot, to do his worst. Fractionally, Hutton's iron reserve slipped and, murmuring that the Australians had 'done us' he took refuge in the dressing room, unable to watch. Moments later, he had achieved what no England captain had ever done before: led England to victory in two series against Australia and been on the field in all the matches involved. Close runners were Warner (1903–04, 1911–12) and Percy Chapman (1926, 1928–29) but theirs was not quite the same achievement for Hutton had played in all ten matches.

After the Test he paid warm tribute in a press conference to his younger men, Statham, Tyson, May and Cowdrey. He hoped he would play against Australia in 1956 and suggested that his old adversary Miller should concentrate on batting rather than continue to cause him so much trouble by bowling. Bruce Harris, the only English journalist to have been present then and in 1932–33, thought Hutton's speech was gracious and generous in victory and as acceptable to the Australians as had been his remarks at Fremantle some months earlier. He compared the relaxed atmosphere of the occasion with that of 1932–33 when England's victory had been bitterly received by Australians. Harris wrote that he thought Hutton's men the happiest bunch with whom he had toured and that the mood was a tribute to the captain.

Then it was time for jollification and a return to their hotel in Glenelg. Hutton was invited by his fellow players to consider why he was 'born so beautiful', to render 'Ilkley Moor' and to sing a tongue-twisting duet with Edrich. Rather more formally, he, May and Howard took the South Australian cricket officials out to dinner. With officialdom away, the other players and their guests consumed a vast amount of champagne, the bill for which Howard, as manager, had to settle the following morning.

After all these heady delights, the fifth Test was an anti-climax. The worst rains in fifty years in New South Wales had caused loss of life and substantial damage to property. Play did not start till the fourth day, leaving a maximum of thirteen hours, yet England, declaring at 371 for 7, forced Australia to follow on for the first time since 1938, and came within measurable distance of winning the match. With four second innings wickets left, the Australians were still 32 runs behind. Hutton kept up the pressure until there were two overs left. One he gave to Graveney, the other to himself. The tour of Australia ended, not inappropriately, with the captain dismissing Benaud off the very last ball at 5.30 on 3 March 1955. Half an hour later, farewells had been said to the New South Wales Cricket Association and presents of cigarette boxes received. By 10 o'clock the team had packed and made their way to Sydney Airport *en route* to Christchurch, New Zealand, where play was due to start in thirty-six hours. The cricketers of the 1950s were moving into the jet age.

Four matches were played in New Zealand. Against Canterbury, Hutton shared in an opening partnership of 97 in 57 balls with Graveney and in one of 60 with him in the first Test. The full New Zealand side were desperately slow in batting – Geoffrey Rabone, the captain, took over three hours to score 18 – sluggish in the field, and far less impressive than Wellington, the winners of the Plunket Shield. Wellington fielded up to the best standards of an Australian side and were well led by the future New Zealand captain, John Reid.

What would prove to be Hutton's last Test match took place at Auckland. Tyson, Statham and Appleyard dismissed New Zealand for 200. England replied in conditions which had changed considerably overnight, and a pitch affected by rain, a slow outfield and poor light made their 246 seem much more creditable than figures suggest. Hutton went in fifth and saw England through most of the remainder of the innings before being bowled for 53. At 3 o'clock on the third day, with the return of the fine weather, New Zealand went in for a second time just 46 behind. Within three-quarters of an hour they had lost 3 wickets for 13. Tyson and Statham had shared the wickets and Hutton brought on Wardle, whose 'chinaman' – the leg-break to the left-hander – dismissed Bert Sutcliffe. In a further six overs, Appleyard collected four wickets before Hutton brought back his opening bowlers, from whom one over was sufficient. New Zealand had been dismissed for 26, the lowest total in the history of Test cricket. A game with some semblance of balance at 3 o'clock, and technically at its half-way point, was over by 5 o'clock. England had won by an innings and 20 runs and the tour of Australia and New Zealand was over. Hutton had it in his heart to be sorry for New Zealand 'but a captain's duty is to strike hard and keep the pressure on'.

A leading article in the *New Zealand Herald*, no doubt written tongue in cheek, said that Hutton had lacked diplomacy in announcing that he wanted 'four wins in four matches in New Zealand'. He 'should have considered our feelings':

> What have we done that Old England should turn so furiously upon us? Hutton and his men will wander off to the beaches and the golf courses while our men slink home to make the best excuses they can at the family hearth. Can we ever forget that, for a mere 26, we were blasted off Eden Park by the very men whom we imagined, a few short years ago, to be starvelings, staggering along on the little strength they got from our food parcels?

Hutton, who had not touched his clubs on the Australian part of the tour, may be thought to have earned his game of golf. As for New Zealand, their day would come. In a year's time they would beat the West Indies on the same ground to win their first Test match. Victory against England would not come until 1978 when, curiously, it was another Yorkshireman, Geoffrey Boycott, who led England.

Hutton had not been the batsman in Australia that he had been in the West Indies a year earlier. A batting average in the Tests of 24.44 could not be compared with 96.71, though on the Australian tour as a whole he scored over 1000 runs (just behind May) and came second in the averages. In the early stages, notably against Western Australia, South Australia and New South Wales, he had been the mainstay of the batting and he had been dismissed by spectacular catches on at least three occasions in the Tests when seemingly set for a large score. A similar fate had befallen Hammond in 1946–47. But Hutton had made the runs at Adelaide when failure to do so would very probably have led to a drawn series.

Australian critics were more ready to spot a decline in his abilities than English ones. Moyes thought he was reaching for the ball without using his feet sufficiently and Hassett felt that his runs 'were generally collected in laborious fashion' by comparison with 'the certainty of earlier days'. Miller, in bowling to him, thought he saw the ball a bit later. Such comments were relative and Hutton was being measured by his own superlative standards. If he were, indeed, 'over the hill', as one observer remarked, he had climbed to the pinnacle of a very high mountain before the descent began.

As captain, Hutton, set his sights on a range of peaks which he conquered with a measure of planning and efficiency. His success in Australia stemmed from his faith in his fast bowlers and his strategic use of their talents and energies. Statham and Tyson proved a match-winning pair whom he would cajole and nurse as circumstances demanded and of whom he would require the last ounce of strength if victory beckoned. There were those who felt that more use might have been made of Appleyard and possibly Compton, but the captain could point to the fact that it was his fast bowlers who decided the day. In the crucial Test at Melbourne, Appleyard, with some success in the first innings, was simply not needed in the second.

In the wider context of planning his match strategy as a whole, he was attentive to detail, observant and thoughtful. Arlott adjudged that he weighed up everything objectively and then directed his tactics towards the most effective point. Fingleton also spotted an intenseness which was found as much in him as captain on the field as in the games in which he stood down. The intensity, for example, with which he watched Lindwall bowling for Queensland against MCC probably led, in Fingleton's view, to his decision not to submit his batsmen in the Brisbane Test to Lindwall on the first morning of play. Commentators agreed that there was a quiet ruthlessness in his leadership which was expressed in the economy of his bowling attack. He gave nothing away and was quick to spot an opponent's weakness. 'Sound and shrewd', wrote Peebles, not 'brilliant and dashing'. 'Painstaking in effort', wrote Swanton, not 'a dashing spirit'. These conservative qualities belonged essentially to a Yorkshireman and neither selectors nor critics had any right to expect the more radical ones to be displayed in his brand of leadership. He was aware that he was not captain of a great side and his caution was extended to younger players whose natural exuberance he may have stifled for the best of reasons.

Only one shadow was cast across England's success: a continued criticism of the slow over-rate. Hutton, aware of the urgency with which Harvey, in particular, attacked the bowling, encouraged Tyson to take his time rather than hasten through his overs, saying to him, 'You're doing exactly what Harvey wants you to do'. Graveney, from close quarters, thought that Hutton pushed this to the limits of acceptability by stopping Tyson just before he began his run-up to make a field change. Bedser, too, believed that Hutton carried his policy to extremes. The Australian broadcaster, Alan McGilivray, again did his sums and established that England bowled about 11½ overs an hour to Australia's 14. Hutton, in his press conference at Adelaide, rejected criticism of the over-rate. 'You can't run cricket on hockey lines. I have merely been trying to help young bowlers'; and he regarded it as a necessary process to guide such bowlers in their field-placing. Furthermore, he regarded it as a legitimate device which Bradman had employed in his own day. Allen, one of the selectors, combined his business as a stockbroker with a visit to Australia for the second, third and fourth Tests and he had watched appreciatively England's three successive victories but with dismay the over-rate at Melbourne. The last word had certainly not been said on the matter at Hutton's press conference. It would be raised by Allen at the Board of Control when he returned to England.

Hutton's relations with his team were without friction. One experienced journalist described them as warm and congenial. He found time to be with them when not playing, though his few moments of privacy and relaxation were guarded jealously. Edrich, who had been surprised at his own selection, saw his role as 'aide-de-camp, adviser and front man' with the task of bringing Hutton out. Hutton was not a natural extrovert and a certain quietness of manner may sometimes have concealed from the others what he had in mind to do. His frequently uttered 'You know what I mean' was not necessarily understood. Some of his colleagues felt that he did not, as captain, pay sufficient attention to the men not selected for the Tests, and give them some comfort or encouragement in their despondency. The Bedser incident was the classic example of non-communication and it serves as something of a pointer. May, as vice-captain, saw his own role as the link between captain and player to be very important. Cowdrey, as we have seen, had his own reasons for being grateful to Hutton but he too knew when the skipper should be left alone and not spoken to: 'His streak of isolationism may have made him the great captain he was.'

Hutton regarded the tour as his hardest task as captain despite the absence of political issues and umpiring controversies which had dogged the West Indies tour. He gave as his reasons the responsibility of selecting the side for Test matches. In England he was one of an experienced panel on which he was apt, with some modesty, to regard himself as the least equipped. On tour, he was the chairman of the selection committee. In Australia his colleagues were May, Edrich and Evans, together with the manager (the one duty which MCC had specified to Howard) and Duckworth. Somewhat surprisingly, Compton – the vice-captain on the previous tour – was not asked by Hutton to serve as a selector. Bedser was asked to be senior professional (but not a selector) but declined on the grounds that Hutton, by definition, filled the role himself. May felt, in retrospect, that meetings of the selectors were fairly informal and that Hutton saw himself as the decision maker.

His relations with Howard, the manager, were entirely cordial and he relied on his help a great deal. 'What shall we do with all these?' he asked when a load of letters of congratulations poured in after the Ashes had been won. 'I shall get a letter printed and you will "top and tail" it,' replied Howard. With the press, Hutton enjoyed a genuine and informative relationship. Nothing, many of them thought, was too much trouble. They were a formidable body which, besides all the Australians, included his predecessor Brown, three former England players in Bowes, Gover and Peebles, the editor of *Wisden*, Norman Preston, and writers either in the forefront of their profession or establishing themselves such as Arlott, John Kay, Alan Ross, Swanton, Wellings and Woodcock. From the *Yorkshire Evening Post* had come John Bapty, a friend of many years' standing. The general consensus was that he handled his press conferences with ease, humour and honesty and would be a welcome member of the press box next time MCC went to Australia.

The way in which Hutton conducted himself in public and his courtesy translated itself to the Australian crowds whose barracking (and it was noisy and prolonged at Melbourne) was without rancour and soon forgotten. The Australians warmed to a man who would line up children and sign autographs – he estimated he signed his name several thousand times on the tour – and who had pioneered the role of a professional captain of an MCC side so effectively. Democratic to the core, they cast him in a different mould from some (but by no means all) of the earlier captains of sides from 'home'. It was not the least of his achievements that he had emulated Jardine, his boyhood hero, and the Australians' anti-hero, in beating Australia in a series and employing a pace attack as had Jardine, without any of the friction or tactics which had the earlier triumph. Australians everywhere were glad that England had won after years in the doldrums. His finest hour had been 2 February 1955, and the culmination of an ambition which he could scarcely have comprehended coming his way, even as recently as four years before.

During the later stages of the tour Hutton was joined by his wife and one is again reminded that much of his reserves of strength came from the happiness of his marriage. She had been in the West Indies at a difficult time when the incident with the Jamaican Chief Minister took place. She was with him again to share in the undiluted success of his Australian enterprise. He paid tribute to her support, saying she was able to do 'everything but bat'. Yorkshire had given him permission to come home by sea, and he and Dorothy had a leisurely voyage, arriving in England early in May to be greeted with what was no less than his due, membership of MCC, following a special meeting to allow a serving professional cricketer to be elected. The tie was brought to him by the secretary as the ship docked.

To the officials of the Club of which he was now a member, the MCC captain submitted his report on the tour. It was a brief document, in contrast to that of a year earlier. There was nothing controversial to say (and if there were, he did not mention over-rates). He praised the way practice wickets were made available at Perth, the success of covered wickets and the umpiring in first-class matches. There was some mild criticism of the quality of balls used in the State and county matches and just a hint that Australian officialdom could be awkward: 'a certain amount of arrogance prevailing among several members of the Australian Board of Control, which several years of defeats will help to reduce'.

His players merited outstanding reports: 'Conduct on and off the field was excellent in every way. At all times I had excellent co-operation.' He made a plea for hotels where players would not be besieged by hangers-on – 'the bigger the hotel in most cases, the less desirable for a team'. No 'end of term' report was written on the captain himself and the comments of two journalists may serve instead. John Bapty of the *Yorkshire Evening Post* wrote: 'His triumph as a captain was complete. He fashioned the attack which made the victory.' E. M. Wellings, in the London *Evening Standard* said: 'He was a magnificent success.'

Hutton's seven months of concentration and commitment had been conducted in the best traditions of the principles of hard work and disciplined endeavour on which he had been brought up, but they had exacted a heavy price. Nature made its claims on this far from robust man and he returned home weary and worn.

10

New Horizons

1955–88

The most influential man to have watched Hutton leading England in Australia proved to be Gubby Allen who, on his return, and to his own surprise, was appointed chairman of the selectors. He declared himself optimistic about English prospects for the immediate future but pessimistic about the slow over-rate which England had employed under Hutton. When he and his fellow selectors – Ames, Sellers and Wilfred Wooller – met in April 1955 they endorsed the wish of the Board of Control that 'time-wasting' be reduced. They appointed Hutton captain for the whole series against South Africa, the only precedent for this mark of confidence being that of Fry in 1912, and they sought from him an assurance that 'he would do his utmost to prevent "time-wasting" and generally to speed up the team in the field'. Hutton agreed that he would speak to his team before the first Test and his appointment was announced on 23 May. To the cricket world, the horizon was set fair with Hutton in command against the only Test country he had yet to meet as leader.

He himself was not so sure of his future as he faced the Yorkshire climate in early spring in considerable pain. His season had just begun and, 'my form was as spasmodic as my appearances'. A half-century against Somerset on a bitterly cold day was the prelude to his appearance at Lord's as captain of MCC against the South Africans. For the first time he was a member of the club as well as being its captain. He fielded on the first day and came in to bat on the Saturday evening to a great reception. On the Monday morning he could not get to the ground, so stricken was he with lumbago. A decision had to be made and the captain of England wrote to the chairman of selectors announcing his retirement from international cricket and doubting whether he could even continue in the first-class game.

> It is with a sad heart that I have to write this letter to you. For some considerable time now when playing in England I have suffered from rheumatic pains. During the past three weeks I have been far worse than ever before. On my return home from Australia I felt fit and well but after a few days' cricket in this climate my pains returned.

The selectors were disappointed rather than surprised, and they invited him to become a co-opted member of their committee and appointed May in his place. The game at Lord's, his last there, proved to be the first of the season's 'lasts'. For a few more weeks he trailed around the county grounds of England, a shadow of his former greatness and plagued with persistent back trouble. In the match against Lancashire at Old Trafford a young amateur, Kenneth Standring, making his county debut, bowled him for two and he took his farewell of the Roses contests. A half-century against Sussex was Yorkshire's highest individual score in a lost match at Hove but a duck in the second innings was the prelude to 0 and 1 against Surrey at The Oval. The match was his last appearance on that ground in first-class cricket and the last time he would play before a crowd of Test match proportions. Surrey and Yorkshire were contenders for the Championship which Surrey won narrowly for the fourth year running, and the match had its own unique quality in that the new and the former England captains – May and Hutton – each played under their official county captains, Surridge and Yardley. During the Surrey match, Hutton and his MCC team were guests of MCC at a celebration dinner at the Dorchester Hotel.

Hutton's last half-century before a Yorkshire crowd was made at Hull against Kent though another one at Northampton suggested that he might return to form and fitness. On Monday 27 June at Trent Bridge he took 194 runs off the Nottinghamshire bowlers in five hours with three sixes and 24 fours, his final hundred runs coming in an hour. It would be his last century in first-class cricket and his last catch dismissed Hardstaff, one of his batting partners in the

1938 marathon at The Oval and a player several years senior to him in age.

Three days later against Hampshire he was hardly able to move from his hotel to the ground and, in the almost rural setting of cricket at Dean Park, Bournemouth before the chestnuts, the conifers and the retired colonels a great England player passed unobtrusively from the scene. When the South Africans came to Bramall Lane Yorkshire would have been glad of him to meet the pace of Peter Heine but it was not to be and he played no more in 1955. In September, the Yorkshire Committee voted to give him £8 a match for each of the fifteen he had missed.

In the following January, after seeing a specialist, Hutton finally retired from first-class cricket. The announcement on the BBC News was followed by a tribute from H. S. Altham who declared that 'a great chapter in the history of cricket is closed'. He had, as a batsman, represented in his person 'the complete development of modern techniques, confronting the problems posed by bowlers and the field dispositions which supported them'. As a captain, he had revealed 'a very shrewd brain and a complete devotion'. John Arlott paid another tribute on the following evening: 'It often seemed in the lean years after the war that he stood alone – except perhaps for Compton – between England and overwhelming defeat by Australia.' As a captain, he had the Yorkshireman's quality of resistance: 'If he could not win a match, he was not going to give it away.'

Soon afterwards, Hutton was himself broadcasting with Brian Johnston in an unscripted programme on The Ashes. His invitation from Christopher Rowland, the producer, came with the comment, 'I need hardly tell you that any programme in which you appear will be of the greatest interest to our audiences'. Johnston was the host when the BBC featured a dinner in Hutton's honour in February 1956 given by the National Sporting Club in the Café Royal, London. The speakers were Sir Norman Birkett, Tommy Trinder, the comedian, and Hutton. Collectively, they earned the BBC minute: 'speeches of high calibre and not just platitudes'.

For the next few years, Hutton was much in demand as a broadcaster. Wilfed Pickles asked him to take part in a programme on his own stage career; there was a link-up with John Arlott (in London) and Gary Sobers (in Barbados) in *Saturday Night on the Light*; he was on the panel of *Does the Team Think?* and he contributed to programmes on other cricketers, such as Miller and Worrell. Roy Plomley invited him in 1959 to choose his records on *Desert Island Discs*. Hutton told his interviewer that he hated the idea of being on a desert island, even more so when denied a set of carpenter's tools. Faced with the usual choice of one book, he found it difficult to decide between his old favourite, Boswell's *Johnson* or Cardus' *Summer Game*. In the end he compromised by choosing Altham's *History of Cricket*. His choice of music included songs by Harry Belafonte and Maxine Daniels.

Television claimed him when Ethel Goldsack, a dedicated and gifted teacher of deaf children, found that her cricket hero was among her surprise guests on *This is your Life*, while his appearance on a panel led to an internal BBC minute from the producer, 'All my colleagues, not to mention the press, were full of praise for the way he handled the questions'. For an appearance in August 1961 at Lime Grove Studios in *Sportsview* he earned his highest BBC fee, 25 guineas.

The five years from 1956 to 1961 were the ones in which he most frequently broadcast. He had sometimes turned down invitations in earlier years when he regarded the playing of cricket as his top priority. But the playing days were over and he has left it on record that he ended his career with Yorkshire as much with a sense of relief as of regret. J. M. Kilburn, who had watched him over so many years, wrote that 'the playing routine was losing its attraction: he had completed an exhausting journey'. He fitted less easily into the Yorkshire dressing room in the 1950s than in the 1930s. The young man who had sat in the market-place listening to the wisdom of his elders found it harder to play the role of Socrates himself, and he believed the players of the 1950s listened less than he had done. They themselves felt they could not talk with ease about their cricketing problems. Ray Illingworth – future captain of England and of Yorkshire – thought that Hutton's response was 'mickey-taking' when asked for advice, and had to be told that to understand him was an acquired taste. Hutton once said of Hammond that from him you received instruction in the best possible way – 'like a man planing a piece of wood, the master-craftsman doing it for you to watch'. Like Hammond, he taught by example rather than by exposition. The model pupil did not become a natural teacher of his art as, for example, Arthur Mitchell had become. The pre-war Yorkshire player was a gifted coach in the post-war years, able to hold an audience of schoolboys in a classroom with chalk and talk as much as in the nets. Hutton did not have these qualities.

In 1956 he put Yorkshire cricket behind him as the pattern of his life changed. No longer did he travel up and down the land, nor spend the night in hotels in Taunton or Chelmsford, Hove or Cardiff or eat countless chicken salads in pavilions. Instead when April came the

Huttons had their first family holiday abroad, going to Switzerland. Just a few weeks after his father's last game for Yorkshire, Richard had won a bat autographed by the two Test teams of 1955 for the best batting average at Wood Hall preparatory school, and the London evening *Star* featured the event as the lead story in its daily Diary. Their father took Richard and John to The Oval to see the fifth Test, the first time the boys had seen where their father had made his record score.

Both boys had begun to cope with having a famous father and having their own cricket prowess reported upon from time to time. Even cricket in the garden at Kingsmead with a tennis ball and the occasional broken window would be an item of interest to some reporter. At the end of the summer term Richard had left his preparatory school and in the autumn he went to Repton. His parents had made the choice on the advice of his preparatory school headmaster and in the knowledge that John Eggar, the former Derbyshire player, was associated with the cricket there as a master. Repton was a school with an outstanding cricket record. Repton cricketers had included Fry (whose grandson was a contemporary of Richard's there), John Crawford, Bryan Valentine and Donald Carr. In a sense, their presence in the mythology of Repton cricket made it easier for Richard Hutton when he arrived since great names were no novelty.

By 1959 he had won his place in the 1st XI as a batsman, scoring over 700 runs and making 140 against Malvern. In the following year he had established himself as an opening batsman and his 166 against Uppingham was the highest score in public school cricket in the season. His performance won him selection for the two Schools matches at Lord's, the Rest against Southern Schools and the Public Schools against the Combined Services. His father was there to see him open the innings for the Rest, with a half-century and displaying, wrote E. M. Wellings, the schools correspondent for *Wisden*, 'movement and mannerisms which proclaimed him unmistakably the son of Sir Leonard'. 'Once again', Movietone News relentlessly told thousands in their local cinema, 'a famous name makes work for the scoreboard'.

In 1961 Richard Hutton captained the Repton XI and, with Guy Turner, shared in an opening partnership of 268 against Uppingham, beating the 227 which the same pair had scored against Uppingham the year before. He also had had the temerity to get his father lbw for 3 when they met in the Repton match against MCC. 'Some wretched Repton "beak" putting his finger up straightaway', recalled a spectator who had come to see Sir Leonard bat. He scored over a thousand runs in the school season, beating a record set up by Crawford and which was itself beaten in 1987, and topped the averages in both batting and bowling. He was a batsman strong off the front foot and was among several boys who impressed Wellings in the two Lord's matches in what was regarded as a vintage year for public schools cricket. Hutton, like many fathers, was concerned with his boys' careers. A parental approach to St Catherine's College, Oxford asking if they would welcome a cricketer proved fruitless and his elder son went up to Christ's College, Cambridge. Of the two ancient universities, Cambridge in recent years has taken a more benevolent attitude to the selection of men of distinguished athletic talent than has Oxford. Of the five or six public school boys whom Wellings placed top of the list in 1961, Richard Hutton alone would go on to play for England.

Richard went up to Cambridge with the double pressure of being the outstanding schoolboy of the previous summer and Sir Leonard's son, but in the company of future England captains Tony Lewis and Mike Brearley he established himself in the 1962 side as an attacking batsman and a fast-medium seam bowler, winning a Blue as a freshman. What gave the family especial pride was his debut for Yorkshire in the Roses match at Old Trafford. By now he had come to terms with the inevitable adjectival phrase, 'the son of Sir Leonard', which accompanied his name in press reports. The strain was less at Cambridge than in Yorkshire and he had a distinguished season for the University in 1963, a year which brought the first suggestions that he might one day play for England. There was a family party at the Royal Hotel, Scarborough to celebrate his 21st birthday while playing in the Festival. In his last year at Cambridge he was the leading bowler, achieving considerable pace though he had yet to accomplish much for Yorkshire and it would be some years before he established himself securely in the Yorkshire side.

In 1971 Richard won the first of his five England caps when he appeared against Pakistan at Lord's making a Test debut infinitely more distinguished than that of his father thirty-four years earlier, scoring an unbeaten half-century and taking two wickets. In the Oval Test against India, Richard scored 81 off the spinners. Pleased as he was, Sir Leonard could barely watch – so Richard was told. It was a role reversal of the 1950s. *Wisden* recorded that Richard's 'off-driving recalled his famous father as he played in the classic manner' and he and Alan Knott established a seventh-wicket record of 103 for England against India. The Huttons, father and son, were the sixth such pair to play for England. To make further comparisons between them is unfair and irrelevant. Richard had given a good enough answer at The Oval to the man who told his father to his face that the son 'wasn't good enough'.

The Huttons as parents had always been aware of the pressures upon the boys of their father's name. Bradman's son, indeed, had changed his surname and Hammond – retired before his son Roger was born – preferred to talk to the boy about his prowess with Bristol Rovers than his cricketing reputation. Richard Hutton, and in due course, his brother John, would both pursue careers as accountants and become very much their own men. A family move away from Yorkshire with the boys' interests partly in mind happened, as we shall see, in 1959.

Richard's cricket, after his days with Yorkshire were over, continued as an enjoyable sideline through the Cricketer Cup and MCC out-matches. John, who followed his brother to Repton in 1960, was in the XI for three years, became captain, and in 1964 he appeared at Lord's for the Southern Schools and for H. S. Altham's Public Schools XI. Thereafter he turned to golf, appearing only occasionally on the cricket field in Cricketer Cup matches.

The cricket played by his two sons was some consolation to their father for ending a career, as he was only too well aware and frequently reminded, at an age when Jack Hobbs still had another hundred centuries to score. John had also been encouraged in his golf by his father who, like many a sportsman, found it a relaxation. Leonard Hutton had begun to play as a teenager when given a set of clubs by Lord Milton during a Yorkshire end-of-season golfing occasion at Malton. It was a game he could play without the feeling that 'half the world would read about my mistakes in the morning papers'. It had served as therapy when getting his injured arm into action and it would prove an assest in his later years in business. At his best, his handicap was down to 3. 1962, for example, found him playing in the Pro-Am two-day event at Sunningdale. His London home backed on to a golf course and there he often played until declining abilities in the mid-1980s made him a reluctant performer.

Soon after Richard had gone to Repton the Huttons left their Pudsey home in Woodhall Park Grove and moved a mile or two away to a larger house, Thorniehurst, in Galloway Lane, with a paddock where Hutton's carpentry skills were resurrected to build a garden bench. The house had originally been built by his grandfather in 1875 and happened to come on the market. It was to this new home that a letter from the Prime Minister, Sir Anthony Eden, arrived on 9 May, 1956 stating that he had it in mind to submit Hutton's name to the Queen 'with a recommendation that Her Majesty may be graciously pleased to approve that the honour of knighthood be conferred'. Hutton was overwhelmed by the offer, and 'it took time for the fact to sink in'. He replied appropriately and the announcement came in the Birthday Honours three weeks later.

There were many other distinguished and famous names honoured at the same time – Lord Cherwell, Churchill's war-time scientific adviser, the historian Arnold Toynbee, the actress Peggy Ashcroft, and the show jumper Pat Smythe among them. Fellow knights included Basil Blackwell, the publisher, Brigadier Alick Buchanan-Smith and Tom Williamson, secretary of the General and Municipal Workers Union. The list also included a K.C.V.O. for Anthony Blunt, the art historian, an honour that the sovereign would withdraw from its recipient when his espionage was revealed. In a typical catholic collection of the great, the good, the long-serving, and the humble who were honoured by the Queen, Hutton's name was the principal one identified in the press headlines and on the BBC. On 10 July, the Hutton family went to Buckingham Place for the investiture and theirs was the photograph all the papers carried the next day – Sir Leonard in his grey topper, Lady Hutton in navy blue, the boys in grey suits. Afterwards, they had lunch with Dame Peggy Ashcroft who had been at the same investiture. On the following day, the family went home so that Sir Leonard could attend the Northern Cricket Society dinner on the eve of Headingley Test match in which his former opening partner, Washbrook, returned to the England side and contributed 98 to a great England victory.

One of the first functions which Hutton attended in his new role as an elder statesman of the game was the centenary in 1957 of cricket at Old Trafford. He had been away from first-class cricket for two years but he played an innings of 76 for MCC against Lancashire which, the commentators agreed, rolled back the years:

> His stance as he awaited each ball was still a model of ease, neat elegance and perfection of balance. His judgement seemed so immediate and unerring that it belied his long absence from the game. His defence was so compact and effortless, the feet always in position so swiftly and so correctly, that it was again as of old as if each ball had been forejudged uncannily by some cricketer's act of clairvoyance.

This is to select a paragraph from the long tribute paid to him by Denys Rowbotham in the *Manchester Guardian*, in whose pages Neville Cardus had garlanded so many cricketers of Hutton's generation and earlier. In the course of the innings for the few spectators on a bitterly cold day whose dedication he rewarded, he became the tenth man to score 40,000 runs in first-class cricket; and only Hammond, in that company, bettered by less than a run his career average of 55.54. In the evening Viscount Monckton and Sir Norman Birkett, two eloquent lawyers both with a passion for cricket, spoke at the dinner in Manchester Town Hall. Sir Leonard Hutton had composed his own piece of eloquence for the occasion earlier in the day. The tragedy was, as someone remarked, that he was still only forty. He had played barely a dozen years of cricket at the highest level after his Oval triumph in 1938. In 1960, he played against Cambridge University, and for MCC against Ireland, scoring 89 before departing 'stumped Calhoun bowled Huey', a very Irish way for a Yorkshire-man to end his first-class career. Without him MCC's score of 183 would have looked very thin.

Occasions such as those at Old Trafford, Eastbourne and Dublin were ones in which Hutton might have permitted himself to look over his shoulder at the past. But, as a family man, he was perfectly aware that it must be to the future that he looked. When the site of his sports business in Bradford was taken over for extensions to the St George's Town Hall he decided not to accept the offer of alternative premises – a decision, he said later, 'which might have been right or wrong'.

He had begun to write for the London *Evening News* and he would be on their staff until 1963. More and more he found himself travelling south and another decision was taken after much thought: to leave Pudsey and buy a house in North London. To the boys it would make less difference since they were both away at school, though Richard did not want to leave Yorkshire. Dorothy too was at first reluctant to leave Thorniehurst, a house and garden which they had had for such a short time, on which they had done so much work and for which she had further plans. Nevertheless in 1959 the move was made, at first to rented accommodation in Ennismore Gardens in the West End and then to Kingston-on-Thames on London's south-west fringe; scarcely North London but there was a golf course nearby and some new properties were being built. A mortgage was taken out – for the first time – and the intention was to stay for ten years or so and then return to Yorkshire. No sooner had the move been made when Hutton was approached by a businessman with an offer of further employment which would make continued residence in London an advantage. Twenty-five years later, when Sir Leonard had retired from this second career and his sons were both married and living nearby, the wish or need to move back north had long disappeared. Instead, there would be annual 'pilgrimages' usually when England were playing at Headingley.

The businessman, Sidney Hainsworth, was born in Pudsey, and educated at the Grammar School and at Leeds University. He had served in the same officer-cadet battalion as Herbert Sutcliffe during the first world war and he was best man at Sutcliffe's wedding in Pudsey Parish Church in 1921. The two men were friends for over sixty years and Sutcliffe's allegiance to cricket from the centre was matched by that of Hainsworth from the sidelines. The one would be the means of introducing Hutton to a cricket career, and the other to a business one. Hainsworth invited Hutton in 1960 to join the firm of J. H. Fenner and Co. (Holdings) Ltd of which he was chairman and managing director. Fenner's were (and are) power transmission engineers, manufacturing equipment such as pulleys, power belts and gearboxes which make it possible for machinery in the coal-mining industry to operate. They are suppliers to the industry throughout the world and in the 1960s had embarked on a policy of expansion through the opening of regional depots in the United Kingdom and subsidiary development abroad.

Dr Hainsworth talked to me in the study of his home a few miles from Hull: an active man, older than the century, surrounded by his papers and files and, as president of the firm, with a continuing interest in its affairs. A call to head office in Hull brought an immediate answer to a small point which had escaped his prodigious memory.

I had seen the special qualities which would make Hutton a success in business. He was a man of disciplined behaviour, with a wonderful control of his feelings and a good judge of people. I had marked him down for years: he had this streak of commonsense. We could not train him in mechanical engineering, but we could teach him the rudiments of our trade and we could take him to see people who mattered to us. A formula was worked out: Sir Leonard would talk cricket agreeably to Fenner's associates for a few minutes then we took over and he would slip into the background. We insisted that he should not try to sell. His business was to create an atmosphere where someone else could sell.

As a formula it served, and in the early days it was the basis of Hutton's role with Fenner's. At first he was employed only in the United Kingdom. When a new branch opened, for example in Ipswich in 1962 or in Leicester in 1963, he was asked to cut the tape and tour the exhibition of products on sale. The following year saw him at the MG factory in Abingdon where the fitting of Fenner Mechanical

Rubber Products on to the new MGB model gave the cars 'as smooth a performance as a long Hutton innings'. Always there was the link to be established somehow, however laboured the pun, between the great cricketer and the firm's products. Hutton, often with Lady Hutton, would be found talking to area managers, technicians, sales staff. This was what was expected. As a colleague remarked, 'He did have a way with people and he did not make the mistake of talking for too long. He had a dry humour though a habit of going off at a tangent – a cricket story, having begun, might be left unfinished.' Hainsworth's choice of Hutton to join the firm was very much an individual decision and some of his fellow directors had doubted his wisdom in the matter. They came to be genuinely surprised at Hutton's quiet mastery of the marketing side of the business which he gradually acquired and by his new-found familiarity with the language of pulleys and wedge belts, though one commented that Hutton did not really understand much of what he heard but was a good listener and conveyed the right impression: 'We paid him not to look bored.'

Hainsworth would use Hutton's services in other public relations directions: a visitor had to be met at Heathrow on behalf of the firm, or a politician with cricketing interests chatted to or approached. Both Sir Alec Douglas-Home and Harold Wilson (as they then were) crossed his path. Hainsworth had a strong sense of civic pride and associated himself with the Hull Literary and Philosophical Society, of which he was president. Sir Leonard with Lady Hutton would be there at the Society's annual reception and dinner with the Lord Mayor and the Bishop, or looking after John Arlott who had been invited to open the winter season with a paper on poetry. His presence would be essential at the annual Social and Sports Club Dinner. All in all, there was a lot of travelling: a not unfamiliar pattern to one who had been on the county cricket circuit for so long. And always there was the obligatory photograph for the local press or the in-house magazine, *V-Belt*, smiling and being gracious in a dinner jacket or city suit.

Hainsworth may have been a hard taskmaster but he also took a genuine delight in the cricketer's company. His devotion to the game itself was expressed in two practical ways: through the matches played by his own XI from 1958 onwards as benefit occasions for Yorkshire players, and through the introduction of the Fenner Trophy. S. B. Hainsworth's XI was captained throughout the 1960s by Hutton, and Hainsworth would invite such distinguished players as the West Indians Sir Garfield Sobers, Clive Lloyd, Wesley Hall, Seymour

Nurse, Charlie Griffith, and Roy Gilchrist, the South African Eddie
Barlow and the Australian Neil Hawke, to play against Yorkshire
XIs. Crowds of 4000 and more would watch on Fenner's own ground
at Marfleet. Among typical encounters were those of 1967 and 1968.
In 1967 Yorkshire declared at 205 for 5 and Hainsworth's XI replied
with 180 (Hutton 43). A year later, Yorkshire declared at 184 for 4
(Close 64) and the opposition scored 149 for 7 with 'a circumspect 33
from Hutton'. For a dozen years these annual matches took place,
putting sums of about £400 in the pockets of beneficiaries such as Fred
Trueman, Ray Illingworth, Ken Taylor, Jimmy Binks and Vic
Wilson. One year was devoted to the benefit of Percy Holmes, the
former Yorkshire cricketer, and another raised money for the Herbert
Sutcliffe Gates at Headingley.

They were, of course, festival occasions as much enjoyed for the
cricket as the *après*, but for Hutton there was a certain tension. He was
on show for the firm and the old sense of obligation returned. Once,
as a world cricketer, he had had to make runs for the small boys taken
along by their fathers: now he had to because Fenner's staff and
employees expected he would. By 1970, he was content to be a
spectator sitting in a deck chair with the management. Cricket for
Hainsworth's XI was part of the job. More relaxing were the
occasional games he played over the years for the Authors against the
National Book League (an annual encounter), for the Duke of
Norfolk's XI against the visiting tourists, for Old England, and for
MCC in matches against schools.

Hainsworth's other contribution, The Fenner Trophy, was launched
in 1971 to replace the long-established Yorkshire match against MCC
in the Scarborough Festival by three one-day matches. Towards the
end of the 1960s, the Festival had lost some of its appeal. Touring sides
no longer came and the fine balance between cricket which was
entertaining yet positive seemed to have been lost. Hainsworth saw
that it must change. As one member of the firm said, 'When he is not
thinking Fenner he is thinking cricket, and in the sacred name of
advertising he persuaded the Board to donate a Fenner Trophy with
suitable sponsorship for Yorkshire and three invited counties to
contest as a knock-out competition.' The one-day game, by now
established through the Gillette Cup and the John Player League, had
made another conquest.

The Festival, under a fresh guise, was an instant success, attracting
crowds of over 35,000 annually and bringing a different idiom to an
historic occasion. There were still tents, still fishermen to be watched
on the quayside in the evening, still musical shows, but the image of

Leveson Gower had gone for ever. Hainsworth, with his thrusting vision of what the future demanded, had taken his place. The name of Fenner would last for the 1970s and Yorkshire would win the trophy by 2 runs in its final year of 1981 in a fittingly exciting end to the competition. Other sponsors would take Fenner's place but the success of the Scarborough Festival – new-style – had been assured.

In the first Fenner Trophy competition in 1971 Richard Hutton appeared in the Yorkshire XI. A year later he was again in the side when Yorkshire won in the final against Lancashire. Sir Leonard was always present at trophy matches. It would be his job to look after the firm's guests and from time to time he would adjudicate the man of the match award. In 1976 he was president of the Festival in its centenary year. The young professional from Pudsey who had first met Dorothy there over forty years earlier had become the lineal inheritor of Leveson Gower; Sir Henry would have been surprised but quite pleased. Nor was the advance just in cricketing terms. In 1973 Sir Leonard had been appointed a non-executive director of Fenner International Ltd, a recognition of his services to the company urged by Hainsworth in the face of some opposition.

In the same year in which he joined the Board, the new company director played his own last game, for an Old England XI against the England Ladies' XI at The Oval. The ladies' side had won the first World Cup competition defeating Australia in the final at Edgbaston. On 26 August 1973 they took on the men's side led by Compton and including Simpson, Arthur Wellard, Evans, Roly Jenkins, Harold Gimblett and Derek Shackleton. Batting first, the England Ladies made 171 for 6 in their allowed 45 overs, to which the Old England Men (with an allowance of 35 overs) replied with 174 for 4, winning in the last over. Hutton, in his 34, wrote Tony Pawson (who also played in the match), 'showed how well he could have adapted to limited-over cricket . . . It was a drive over extra cover that gave him particular pleasure and a lofting straight drive that brought his downfall'. Sir Leonard recalled how flat and fast were the ladies' throws to the stumps.

We have seen what part he played in the business and social interests of Fenner in Britain. While the formula of talking cricket was preserved, he gradually acquired enough technical knowledge to talk convincingly to potential customers. He replaced a certain pessimism towards the marketing of a product with a burning optimism and was, in Hainsworth's view, 'ready to sell'. The intricacies of the Fenalplast impact testing machine held fewer terrors for him and Hainsworth, who had always visualized an eventual role for him in the firm's links with overseas cricketing countries, sent him to Rhodesia on the first of many overseas visits. Then, in 1970, he visited India and Australia. He had never played cricket in India but his name was known and he was given mass press coverage during his two weeks there. He had to be the diplomat, with questions on politics and race coming his way; and also the salesman, with as he said, 'smart and clever businessmen' posing commercial queries. In Australia, he was acting for his firm in the face of fierce Japanese competition in the New South Wales coalfields and he wrote in his report to Fenner's on his return:

> They used a good deal of Fenaplast belting, and they're very pleased with it. It has a good reputation out there. I didn't hear one complaint about the quality or service.
>
> You can play golf or snooker with an Australian executive and he will never talk shop. He saves that for the office. And when we get down to business he wants to know how good the product is, and how much it costs. Australians seem to get on well with North Country men. We speak the same language.

Four years later, in 1974, he was again on a promotional tour, which took him back again to India and South Africa and in which he called on India's prime minister, Mrs Indira Gandhi. Their conversation was on both world problems and on cricket, Sir Leonard being 'impressed by her knowledge of the game and her recognition of its unifying factor in India's national life'. At a colliery in Bengal he was persuaded to play cricket and, in borrowed gear and walking shoes, played an innings (of 34) in India – which was more than Bradman ever did. At Bombay he met Duleepsinhji, the nephew of Ranji.

His visit to South Africa immediately afterwards was to a country no longer within the circle of Test cricket. Hutton's relationships with South African cricketers were personally friendly and he was strongly in sympathy with those who deplored the effect of politics upon cricket and the ban upon South Africa as a Test match country. His popularity among the South African coal-mining community may be illustrated by the story of the man with an automatic tie rack. Hutton was intrigued, as we all would be, by his dialling a number, and the tie being released but his admiration had to be quickly tempered by the determination of his host to give him the gadget to take home. He was able to take Lady Hutton with him on this trip, she staying on with friends while he went on to Australia for the firm. Another visit to Australia came in 1977 to coincide with the Centenary Test at Melbourne at which he was an official guest.

By now, he was travelling abroad, often with his wife, for Fenner virtually every year. In 1978 came his first visit to the United States – and from there on to Australia again and home via South Africa where Richard was working. Dr Hainsworth commented on the United States part of Hutton's tour:

> There were doubts about sending him to a non-cricketing country, and we thought his usefulness would be confined to countries where his name was known. We were wrong! He was welcomed by many English engineers working in the pits, invited to their homes, plied with questions about cricket and introduced to the Americans as the Babe Ruth of cricket.

This identification with baseball led to a session with Phil Garner, third baseman of the Pittsburg Pirates, and an introduction to the skills of the game. Sir Leonard ruefully compared Garner's contract of $360,000 per year with cricketers' salaries. The *Carlsbad Current-Argus* reported his visit to the Potash Open Golf Tournament in New Mexico in a piece so engaging that its cricket inaccuracies may be excused:

> One of England's most famous sportsmen, Sir Leonard Hutton, will brighten this week's 17th annual Potash Capital Open Golf Tournament as an informal featured speaker at a cocktail party for contestants and sponsors.
>
> Hutton's fame in England derives from his exploits in one of the country's biggest sports, cricket. He is regarded among the best batsmen who ever played world-class cricket. Some say the best.
>
> Yorkshire, largest county in England and equivalent to a state in this country, insists that its cricketers be county natives and does not import outsiders. Hutton went on from those beginnings to represent Great Britain in 1937, at the tender age of 21, in a test match against New Zealand – considered a high honor.
>
> In a famous 1938 test match against Australia, he established a world record of 374 runs and still holds England's all-time high individual scoring record in first-class cricket.
>
> Sir Leonard is the English answer to Babe Ruth. Scoring 100 runs, referred to as a 'century', in one innings is considered a great milestone in a cricketer's life. He scored 129 such centuries.

He proved entirely acceptable to American business and golfing circles and there were visits thereafter almost every year until he retired. 'He certainly earned his money and served us well', said one executive. By now he was a businessman of some twenty years' experience and a director for several of them. His ability to sell had been acknowledged by his colleagues and his success in the field was unquestioned. Only in the Board Room was he less happy. Some directors felt that his lack of technical knowledge made him contribute little to debate and Hainsworth thought that he found the meetings boring.

Towards the end of his time with Fenner, the firm arranged for Sir Leonard and his wife to visit Australia while England was playing five Test matches between November 1982 and January 1983 – closely scheduled so that England might then compete with Australia and New Zealand in the Benson and Hedges World Cup Series. Hutton's programme allowed him to see most of the Tests while fitting in the various engagements which his firm had arranged for him. On the rest day in the first Test at Perth, for example, he was collected from his hotel at 7.30 a.m. to spend a day with Western Collieries Ltd, visiting mines in three places, lunching with local officials and politicians and attending a dinner in the evening – a fifteen-hour day on duty. On the next day he had to leave the ground when Derek Randall and Bob Taylor were staging an England recovery to attend a reception for customers and distributors of Power Transmission. He was able to see the second and third Tests at Brisbane and Adelaide. England lost on both occasions primarily because there was no effective answer to the Australian fast bowling. At Adelaide 17 wickets were taken by Geoff Lawson, Jeff Thomson and Rodney Hogg. Apart from Bob Willis, England had no comparable answer. Hutton reflected on the men he had used thirty years earlier.

During the last Test at Sydney there were opportunities to play golf at the Royal Sydney Golf Club and to meet more Fenner officials before flying back to England early in January. It had been an enjoyable two months with plenty of good cricket to watch, not too many demands being made by his employers, and with the company of his wife. His career with Fenner would soon be over and younger men would have to tackle the problem of selling to the Australian coal-mining industry. As a senior executive in the Sydney office wrote to him, 'potential orders for conveyor belting are fought over pretty hard these days'. Hutton had done his share of the fighting and of being the VIP expected to meet new people day after day. In 1984, when he retired from Fenner at the age of 68, he had completed almost a quarter of a century with the firm. He left behind a reputation as a reliable, hard-working businessman who knew his job. He was, in the view of Hainsworth, 'one of the best investments Fenner made'. He had spent more years marketing conveyor belts for them than making runs for England and Yorkshire.

The pressures of work for Fenner made it difficult for Hutton to give time to his role as an England selector when, in 1975, he joined Alec Bedser, Ken Barrington and the umpire Charles Elliott in selecting the England teams to play against Australia in 1975 and the West Indies in 1976. If a request came at short notice to meet some visitor on behalf of the firm, then that took priority and a plan to watch a player in a county game had to be abandoned. When a conference at Dusseldorf made it impossible for him to fulfil his obligations at Bristol as a selector, he thought it time to resign and he stood down in 1977 in favour of John Murray, the former England wicket-keeper.

Selectors, in Hutton's view, had to be readily available and he felt unable to meet what was required. One must regret that such a sound judge of a cricketer was able to achieve so little in this aspect of the game and his employers – keen enough to use his name – must bear a little of the responsibility for not realizing that a conflict of interest existed. Gubby Allen's employers, for example, had insisted he should accept an invitation to become the chairman of selectors and he remained in office for six years. Yet one must add that Sir Leonard was a reluctant selector. He did not enjoy the committee side of the job and he took exception to the approaches which Barrington was making to persuade Boycott to resume playing for England.

It was as a journalist rather than as a selector that he made a more sustained contribution to cricket after he had retired from playing. While he was still captain of England, he had written, with the permission of the authorities, a weekly article in the London Sunday paper, the *News of the World*. In a thousand words or so he would comment on the contemporary scene, reminisce a little, give an occasional story from 'the inside' and, above all, write without malice. Some of the material found a more permanent home in his second book, *Just my story* published in 1956 and put together by R. J. Hayter from recordings on tape. John Arlott called it 'illuminating in its revelations of the worries of any Test captain' and a record of hard-won success which compelled respect.

In 1958–59, Hutton made his fourth visit to Australia, as a correspondent for the *Evening News* with the MCC party led by May, his successor. He thought that May had taken out a strong side though they were to lose the series by four matches to none. In his view, defeat was attributable to the disciplinary absence of Wardle from the party while the team became 'demoralized and shattered by the fierce controversies centred on throwing, dragging and umpiring'. He was not a member of the National Union of Journalists and, while he worked for the *Evening News*, he was required to have an accredited member with him, though the journalist concerned felt that Hutton could do the job better.

During the tour he made a typically cryptic approach to Michael Davie who was reporting for the *Observer* with the remark, 'You've got a typewriter. When I was batting, I had a bat.' It led to his joining the *Observer* staff and becoming his own man as a reporter though his non-membership of NUJ meant that much of what he wrote carried a low profile.

He was of the generation of cricketers who read their Cardus and Robertson-Glasgow. Neither writer was to every cricketer's taste. The comparison between an innings someone might play and the music of Beethoven (Cardus's preference) or lines from Virgil (Robertson-Glasgow's speciality) might not seem apparent to a player whose first reaction was that neither the Germans nor the Romans played the game. Cautiously, came the realization that a new art-form was being pursued; that evocative language, musical analogies, and classical allusions might even enhance the word-picture being conveyed of a dreary day between the showers at Southend, let alone that of a full house at Lord's with pennants flying, runs flowing, beer in the Tavern and the Australians in retreat.

These were the two cricket writers, Sir Leonard told me, who appealed to him most. When he began to compose his own pieces for the *Observer*, typewriter on the attack, something of the style of each of them could be found. An obituary on Duckworth, who died in 1966, has the Cardus touch:

> George Duckworth came from Lancashire. Anyone who did not realize this after being in his company for ten minutes was either illiterate or a fool. God Almighty decided some 64 years ago that Lancashire needed a wicket-keeper. I don't think He had England in mind; I think He was primarily concerned with Lancashire.

Another, on Lord Constantine, in 1971, had something of Robertson-Glasgow's gift of conveying what he meant in a tightly written but demonstrative paragraph:

> He moved as only a West Indian can move. He ran as though his feet did not touch the ground. His limbs appeared boneless. He coiled them from time to time and then darted and sprang like a panther, gathering the ball for a throw at the wicket. At that he had no peer.

New Horizons

An internal note in the *Observer* files spoke of the 'wry wisdom he brought to the international cricket scene and of his illuminating comments on Test matches'. In 1984 the West Indies became the first touring side to win all five Test matches in England. The convincing way in which they won the second Test at Lord's, through an outstanding double-century by Gordon Greenidge, led Hutton to reflect upon West Indian cricket as he had known it. At that stage – and half a summer of further success remained – he rated the West Indies just below the 1948 Australians but the greatest West Indies side ever and Greenidge the 'best West Indies opening bat I have seen'. Of Viv Richards and of Greenidge he wrote:

Richards is a genius. He plays far more across the line of the ball than any other great player I have seen. He is not too good a model to copy for the young cricketer. Good length, six to eight inches outside the off stump, is the place to bowl at him. Greenidge is much more correct. The young batsman could learn from the way he started his innings last Tuesday, slowly building until, as the day wore on, it became impossible to bowl to him.

So far as the West Indies bowlers were concerned, he commented:

Constantine and Martindale were fast bowlers of the highest class, but I think Joel Garner and Malcolm Marshall are better, and along with a fit Holding form a bowling combination which no batsman can relish. Charlie Griffith and Wesley Hall were both fine bowlers, worth their place in any Test side. They were almost unplayable on a pitch with a little life. I rate these two very highly indeed.

In 1986 during the second Test match between England and New Zealand at Trent Bridge he wrote on some of the players to whom England would have to look in the late 1980s:

I have been impressed with England's bowling on a placid and pleasant batting pitch at Nottingham: it is some time since I last saw an England attack with this potential for improvement. Thomas is full of talent, quick and with a good action. He must improve his direction and vary his pace. He is young and so full of spirit that I believe England have a possible high-class all-rounder.

Small, too, can develop and is a very useful bowler off his shorter run, while Pringle improved with almost every match, bowling with little luck in this particular Test. Of the other tour candidates (for Australia in

1986–87), I would take Foster because the basics are right. Jarvis is having an impressive season but he is only 21, and I have no wish to see him bowled into the ground.

He wrote very little after 1986 but the *Observer* asked him to comment on the bicentenary match between MCC and the Rest of the World in 1987. Fifty years earlier he had made a century in the 150th anniversary celebrations. Now he allowed his readers to share in his own delight in dining next to Everton Weekes and Ray Lindwall, in getting their autographs for a grandson, in meeting Bill Ponsford who had made a couple of quadruple-centuries when Hutton was still at Littlemoor Council School, and in greeting Bill Brown, whose autograph the young Hutton, in his first season in the Yorkshire side, had obtained. He compared Mike Gatting to Patsy Hendren and rated Sunil Gavaskar, who marked his final appearance in first-class cricket with an innings of 188, 'as one of the best half dozen batsmen of my time'.

Two or three years before he gave up regular journalism, Hutton had published his third book, *Fifty Years in Cricket*. He acknowledged the help of his old friend Alex Bannister and it carried a foreword by his son Richard which was a charming essay reflecting the relationship between a famous father and a highly talented son and demonstrating the happiness of the Hutton family circle. The book itself, while marginally repetitive on the earlier years, offered a serious study of his years as England captain. John Arlott called it 'a model cricket autobiography' and the book of 'a wise man who can look both success and failure in the face and in each instance turn away, with that familiar wry grin, and back to whatever human matter concerns him at the moment'.

The book concluded with some thoughts on the game as Hutton saw it in 1984. Central to those thoughts was his judgment on the circumstances of Yorkshire's cricket. From the sidelines he had watched the fortunes of Yorkshire: in the 'sixties, the rise of Boycott; in the 'seventies, the county's lack of success; in the 'eighties, tragic drama. 'Nothing in my cricketing life has saddened me more than the decline and fall of Yorkshire,' he wrote. He recognized contributory factors such as Yorkshire's continuing commitment to home-grown players, the widening gulf between county standards and that of the Yorkshire leagues (the county nursery) and the lack of a sufficiently strong bowling attack. But the real issue was between those who worshipped at the shrine of individualism, 'a purblind loyalty and enthusiasm for Boycott', and those who sought the restoration of the collective allegiance to team and captain which had been essential to the tradition of his own Yorkshire.

For Boycott himself, Hutton had a certain sympathy and a closer understanding of his problem than others might – 'there were occasions during my own career when I experienced some of the fervour which has surrounded Geoffrey' – and he accepted that the Yorkshire of the post-1960s offered no one else to hero-worship. In the 1930s, he 'would have been one of several titans, each enjoying a share of the public adulation'. Boycott, the accumulator of runs for their own sake (or that of his supporters), had become the instrument of controversy, the focal point of discontent and even the symbol of defeat. Cricket has offered few greater paradoxes than the Yorkshire side of 1983, bottom of the county championship, containing within it one of the world's greatest batsmen.

When events were brought to a head by the dismissal of Boycott at the end of that disastrous season and his reinstatement in the bitterness of mood and weather at Harrogate in January 1984, Hutton had no doubts where he stood. He voted with the minority in support of the Committee's policy to dismiss Boycott and he voted in support of the besieged General and Cricket Committees. He deplored the departure from the scene of Yardley, the county president, and Michael Crawford, the chairman, and of the massive expertise which the outgoing Cricket Committee represented. He noted the names of those who campaigned so fervently for Boycott and commented cynically: 'If there are former players of note among their numbers, it has escaped my notice.' In the debate as a whole, Hutton stood for the virtues which had served the Yorkshire of his day: strong leadership, team loyalty, self-discipline and an informed administration.

Three years later, in 1987, Boycott finally left Yorkshire after the new committee decided not to offer him another one-year contract. He had scored 10,000 more runs for Yorkshire than had Hutton and played for many more seasons. The one man had left Yorkshire aching to score even more, the other had made enough to satisfy him. The one had received the mock accolade of 'knighthood' from his fervent supporters and, with some irony, from his critics; the other had won the genuine award for chivalry. To compare them is to compare greatness with greatness, dedication with dedication, but vaunting ambition with zealous ardour and lust with love.

One of the major changes in cricket after Hutton retired was the introduction of the one-day game. It had been popular during the second world war and he had played, as we have seen, in some of the representative one-day matches. Changes in the game were considered and rejected by an Advisory Committee set up by MCC in 1942, though a Select Commitee under Sir Stanley Jackson recommended that the possibility of a knock-out competition of three-day matches be investigated. Ten years went by before the Altham Committee in 1956 made the first proposals for a one-day knock-out competition. Washbrook, alone of Hutton's contemporaries as a professional, served on the Altham Committee. Since, at the time, Hutton had a little more leisure, having retired and not yet taken up work with Fenner, his absence from a Committee which met only five times seems a distinct loss, especially as MCC had recently elected him to its ranks. Of the seventeen names on it, half a dozen had a very tenuous connection with the playing of the first-class game. In later years, a monthly informal lunch at Lord's, with the then MCC secretary, Griffith, and other retired cricketers, provided him with an opportunity to contribute some views.

When the one-day competitions began in 1963, seven years after the Altham recommendations, Hutton was in sympathy with them – 'with the possible exception of the 40-over contests which deny basic abilities'. 'I would have enjoyed playing in the one-day internationals and the major domestic competitions, particularly in front of a full house at Lord's.' Instead, he was sometimes a reporter on such occasions and he was also much in demand as an adjudicator of the man of the match award, latterly preferring to be at The Oval or Lord's since he had less distance to travel. One recalls him adjudicating at Lord's, at the end of the 1986 Natwest Final, trying, without much success, to make his voice heard over a rather inefficient loudspeaker while noisy crowds cheered the new heroes.

Another vignette comes to mind. In 1987 he was adjudicating the match between the Combined Universities and Middlesex. Rain had stopped play and the sparse crowd had scattered to the bars and refreshment rooms. Sir Leonard bought a cup of tea in the Long Room, saw the TV showing some game taking place elsewhere, took his cup over to the screen and became completely absorbed. Cricket, sixty years on, still had its hold on him.

Through the years after his retirement from the game, Hutton continued to be found attending functions with a sporting association. Sometimes, as we have noticed, they would be linked to his work with Fenner. Others were quite independent of his employers, among the earliest of which was an appearance at a Radio Exhibition in Liverpool in 1955 for the gramophone company, 'His Master's Voice', for which he was paid a fee of £30. By no means all were remunerated. To a little village fete at Dinton in Buckinghamshire, raising money for a new cricket pavilion, he gave an autographed bat for the raffle. Among his more unusual public appearances was taking part in the Royal Philharmonic Orchestra's 1961 Christmas concert in the Royal Albert Hall playing the rattle in a performance of Haydn's 'Toy Symphony in C' in company with others in public life such as Lord Boothby, Edmundo Ross and Margaret Rutherford. Typical of a wide range of activities which claimed his presence was a golfing day with the National Coal Board, a dinner followed by boxing at the Anglo-American Sporting Club, a dinner-dance at Englefield Cricket Club, and a dinner given by the Sheffield Cricket Lovers' Society on the thirtieth anniversary of the Ashes victory of 1953.

The year after 1955 also brought some further recognition of his achievements. The knighthood remained the high point of distinction and he had greatly appreciated being elected a life member of MCC. Later, there came the presidency of the Forty Club to follow in a distinguished line which included Sir Pelham Warner, Sir Jack Hobbs, Sir George Allen and Herbert Sutcliffe. Surrey, Yorkshire and Pudsey St Lawrence took their cue from MCC and all elected him to life membership. In 1985 he became, for the second time, president of the Scarborough Festival.

In 1980 he was one of some 200 former England and Australian players who gathered at Lord's for the Centenary Test. The cricket itself was diminished by the lack of play on a sunny and breezy Saturday afternoon because of rain in the morning, and millions saw on television an incident which did the game no credit. The crowd in a mood of disappointment tinged with anger, were placated by the band of the Royal Marines heralding the appearance of the cricketers of the past. None got greater applause than Hutton and the cheers, as he was recognized, rose to a tremendous crescendo. His presence gave cricket back something of what it had lost that day in the public image.

A similar occasion took place when he was invited to Australia in December 1984 to celebrate the centenary of Test cricket at Adelaide together with twenty-one other men who had led their countries on that ground. Ian Johnson took him on a lap of honour round the ground. 'Will the crowd throw things at me?' Hutton quipped. He saw the West Indies win their eleventh consecutive victory but the cricket as a whole did not measure up to the occasion.

A more unusual distinction was the conferment of the honorary degree of Master of Arts which the University of Bradford awarded him in 1982, the public orator declaiming his feats and acknowledging his own support as a schoolboy at Trent Bridge. In his visits to

Fenner's at Cambridge and the Parks at Oxford, Hutton had always enjoyed the atmosphere of a university city and he had a high respect for academic attainment. It was fitting that he should become Sir Leonard Hutton, MA.

Fame never left Sir Leonard alone. He took no steps to conceal his address – it was there in *Who's Who* for all to read. Requests for autographs pursued him, though he resented receiving the occasional book which had to be re-wrapped and taken to the post office, without even a reimbursement of postage. His home, set in the stockbroker belt with the Surrey hills and the Sussex Weald not far away, was a far cry from the little Moravian community of his Yorkshire forebears. Yet the Yorkshire associations were not forgotten. In the 1980s he felt a renewed affection for Pudsey which he demonstrated in his visits. The strained relationship between the England player and an earlier generation of Pudsey St Lawrence officials gave way to a warmth of feeling between himself and a later generation, symbolized by Keith Moss, the chairman in the 1980s. The regular visits to Leeds would include watching the Headingley Test and seeing his sister and sister-in-law in Fulneck and Pudsey. In 1987 he drove north to switch on the Christmas lights at Pudsey, preferring the comparative calmness of the A1 and the homeliness of Little Chefs to the pace of the M1 and the bustle of motorway restaurants. For a man who had come to dislike long journeys, especially in winter, it was a recognition of his loyalty to his roots.

By 1967 he was the last survivor of the four cricketing brothers of the pre-war Pudsey St Lawrence side, and the deaths of cricketing colleagues increased with the passing of the years. In 1978 came that of Herbert Sutcliffe whom he had known as long as he had known his parents and brothers and who led him 'through those early years of doubt and decision to the promised land'. So wrote Sir Leonard in the *Observer* of the man who had coached him, encouraged him, extolled him to the point of embarrassment and partnered him. Nine years later, in 1987, came the death of another of the pre-war Yorkshire side, Bill Bowes. Hutton wrote:

> Defining him in modern terms is not easy. There was a little of Willis in him and a lot of Hadlee. Yorkshire were so lucky in the 1930s to have Bowes and Verity in their dressing room. Both were so good with young players, helping them in every possible way; nothing was ever too much trouble for either of these great cricketers if it meant bringing along a career.

> Bill loved his conjurer's tricks, especially with cards, and regularly

helped at children's parties and local charities. He would often use me as a tester, asking me if I could spot the sleight of the hand. There was so much kindness and humour in the man.

He and Lady Hutton went north for Bowes's funeral, Hutton paying his tribute, as he had done at Hedley Verity's grave in Italy over 30 years earlier, to the second of the two men who had been the lynch-pin of Yorkshire's attack in the 1930s and his own very personal friends and counsellors.

In 1986, Sir Leonard reached his 70th birthday, celebrated by an appearance on the pavilion balcony at Headingley and a drink with old friends and foes at Lord's. Nowadays seventy is seen as no great age and his great contemporary Bradman was at the time a very spry and active seventy-eight-year-old but Hutton was a little scarred and worn by the nagging pains of arthritis and bronchitis. Those who saw him, not long after, on TV as part of Denis Compton's *This is your Life* felt that he showed his years. Sunshine was a great palliative and in the same year he and Lady Hutton had plenty of it as guests of the Kenya Kongonis Cricket Club.

By now both Richard and John were married and living nearby. In 1975 Richard had married Charmaine, daughter of Ben Brocklehurst, the former Somerset captain and managing director of *The Cricketer*, and John had married Judith Osborne in 1982. There were two pairs of grandchildren – Benjamin and Oliver; Robert and Michael. The closeness of his family and advancing age gradually led Sir Leonard to travel less far afield especially after he and Lady Hutton were lucky to escape serious injury on the A40 when driving from Cheltenham to Oxford in very bad conditions. Both decided that the time had come to confine most of their engagements to the London area. Plenty of invitations near to hand still came their way – in 1987 alone, to the fifth Test at The Oval, to the final of the Cricketer Cup and to Lord's for the bicentenary celebrations of MCC. Fifty years earlier in the 150th MCC anniversary matches, the young Hutton had made a century in the North against the South match, stayed in the Great Western Hotel at Paddington Station and 'felt grateful to be asked to play'. Now, at the bicentenary dinner in May, as a life member of MCC, he was, if not among the distinguished company at top table, very close to it, and certainly the most distinguished cricketer in the room.

A few weeks later, he was again at Lord's to see Yorkshire's first Cup Final win in eighteen years, beating Northamptonshire in the Benson and Hedges competition. The man who had felt awkward about

leading an MCC side when he was not even a member, joined MCC
in more bicentenary celebrations at the Guildhall and, as we have seen,
was present throughout the match between MCC and the Rest of the
World. By then, the old inhibitions about Lord's had entirely gone.
The Secretary of MCC, Colonel John Stephenson, would remember
him as 'a great friend of the MCC (who) knew all the staff and always
took time to talk to everyone he met'. A week later, after all the
captains and kings, the Gavaskars and Borders, had departed from
that regal scene, he was at Lord's to watch the Yorkshire village of
Treeton Welfare play in the national village final against Longparish.
'Magnificent fielding, so keen, so enthusiastic', he said to his biographer that evening. The grassroots of the game, as he had written in
an article thirty years earlier, were 'the village green'.

Shortly after the 1987 season had ended doubts were raised about
the future of the Oval. Not only did Sir Leonard contribute to the
correspondence in the press but one of his grandsons did also.
Eight-year-old Oliver wrote to the *Daily Telegraph*:

> I saw my grandfathers letters in the telegraph about the Oval being closed
> down. But how can I beat my grandfathers record without the Oval. I
> hope they can get enough money to save it.

Oliver, who was watching a video of *The Bradman Era* when I
visited his home and whose school art work consisted entirely of
drawings of cricketers, seems destined to maintain the family traditions. His father, Richard, had just returned from an MCC tour of
Bermuda as player-manager. For two or three weeks after the end of
the English 1987 season Sir Leonard therefore had a personal interest
in the press reports of that tour before the bombardment in the
English winter of 1987–88 of the World Cup, the Test series against
Pakistan and against New Zealand and the bicentennial Test in 1988,
celebrating the discovery of Australia. He wondered whether the
crisis over umpiring in the Pakistan series might make it rival his own
visit to the West Indies in 1953–54 for the title of 'the second most
controversial tour' in cricket history. The first week in May 1988 was
full of interest for him. On the Tuesday he attended the 70th birthday
celebrations of Denis Compton; on the Wednesday he was at MCC's
dinner at Lord's to welcome the West Indians and on the Friday the
Worcestershire batsman Graeme Hick scored 405 not out, to displace
Hutton's 364 as the highest score ever made in England in the
twentieth century. In July the celebrations of the 50th anniversary of
those 364 runs began with a dinner given during the Headingley Test
by Yorkshire CCC and Pudsey CC. The top table alone offered a

glittering array of cricketing talent, John Warr spoke at his inimitable best and – so lengthy were the proceedings – Fred Trueman began speaking on a Thursday and finished on a Friday. The guest of honour had been 'at the wicket' for almost as many hours as the marathon innings itself. A programme compiled by Yorkshire TV during the day was shown in the late evening. Four weeks later, by day and date, came the actual 50th anniversary. The press and the cameras gathered at the Oval, Sir Leonard was accompanied to the wicket by Alec Bedser to stand on the very spot where Bradman had congratulated him in 1938. The sun was shining 'just like it was on the day', he said, 'and it hasn't changed a lot here. The gasometer is still there, made in Leeds, you know. The grass isn't as brown as it was. No use trying to shine the ball after an hour in my day. Waste of time.' His old colleague, Joe Hardstaff, was there able to reminisce with him at the lunch given by the *Observer* to launch the first edition of this biography.

Whether Sir Leonard liked it or not, that innings at the Oval in 1938 had been the personal landmark, as his grandson had recognised, which had shaped the course of his life and laid the foundations of his fame, if not his fortune. 'Hardly a day goes by,' he once said, 'without someone asking me about what happened on August 23, 1938'.

In 1989 there was another visit north when he and his biographer were asked 'in tandem' to the celebrations of the centenary of the Tofts Road ground at Pudsey. During the day, Richard Hutton captained an MCC side against the club and in the evening Sir Leonard graced the dinner with his presence while I made the response on his behalf. 'It was nice to see some old friends, some of whom I had not seen for years,' he wrote afterwards. These links with his roots were further strengthened when he was elected president of Yorkshire CCC in January 1990, following the decision of the general committee not to nominate Viscount Mountgarret for a further term. There were those who believed that Yorkshire would best be served by a president who was not in any way closely involved with the politics of the club and who would be a respected figure-head. A phone call secured his agreement to nomination. Sir Leonard gave a pledge to watch the team whenever he could. He attended the pre-season lunch at Headingley and he was present at Yorkshire's matches with Kent and Sussex, a welcome visitor in the dressing-room, the manager recalled. He regarded the honour bestowed on him as great a one as his knighthood and his election won universal approval. 'Everyone liked him,' said a committee member, 'and he would never say anything if he felt it might be political'. Geoffrey Boycott thought that 'the members felt comfortable with him'.

Another interest which claimed his attention in the last two years of his life was the 'Save the Oval' campaign of which he became patron. He attended a number of functions and the Oval, indeed, was the ground where he watched a lot of cricket in his last few summers. Twice, in 1990, his '364' became a news item. In an extraordinary game at the Oval, Neil Fairbrother scored 366 in Lancashire's total of 863 in response to Surrey's 707 for 9 wickets declared. Fairbrother's innings exceeded Hutton's to become the highest individual score at the Oval. For good measure, the ubiquitous 364 asserted itself as the Lancashire record third-wicket partnership of Fairbrother and Michael Atherton. Afterwards Sir Leonard and Fairbrother jointly signed four bats to be auctioned for charity. Then, in July 1990, Graham Gooch scored 333 in the Test match against India at Lord's, dismissed soon after tea on the second day. He had made the third highest Test score by an Englishman, eclipsed by Hammond's 336 against New Zealand and by Hutton. Sir Leonard was there, making a move to leave the ground (John Woodcock observed) when Gooch neared his record – 'Not that he would have resented losing it (but) anxious lest he should have to face the press'.

A few weeks later he was present at the Oval Test against India and on Saturday 1 September he saw Lancashire beat Northamptonshire rather easily in the NatWest final at Lord's. 1990 was a grand summer for English cricket – glorious weather and a renaissance in the achievements of the England side. Five days after the Lord's match, on 6 September, the same day in which the English party for Australia was announced, Sir Leonard Hutton died. It was a time of great political crisis, and world news about events in the Middle East dominated the media, but space was found on television, radio and in the press to give extensive coverage to his career. His formal obituary in *The Times* commanded half-a-page. He was 'the last of the great players on a bad pitch and exquisitely accomplished on a good one. As England's captain, he was determined, shrewdly cautious and undefeated'. There was almost a full page of assessments and tributes, perhaps the warmest of which was that of Ray Illingworth, a former captain of both Yorkshire and England: 'He was simply God to me as a kid when I followed him all round the Bradford League playing with Pudsey St Lawrence. He was the best player I ever encountered, a class apart.'

The *Yorkshire Post* carried the banner headline, 'Death of a Legend'.

Column after column recorded his achievements with the valedictory salutation that:

> his magnificence was inescapable. Thousands upon thousands of fervent admirers gave him their confidence and approbation; thundered their applause as the loveliest off-drive of modern times left the fieldsmen in the covers immobile; raised their ovation on the completion of another century or another innings of precious memory.

Sir Leonard Hutton's funeral took place at St Peter's Church, Kingston-on-Thames, on the following Thursday. Autumn had not yet set in and it was a day of warm sunshine; of the warmth which had helped to keep him in the south when so much of his heart had still lain in Pudsey and in Yorkshire. It was an occasion both of private grief and of public affection for a much-loved English sportsman.

11

Len Hutton

'He sees cricket as a career, a way of life, a matter for
concentrated attention; a thing to study, to master.'
Howard Marshall, BBC broadcast, 1952

There is a sense in which Leonard Hutton may be thought of as the
puritan in twentieth-century English cricket. From the Moravian
community in which he was brought up he acquired sound puritan
precepts of diligence, discipline and endeavour. The game he chose to
play was therefore pursued as an enterprise to be undertaken on these
lines – as Howard Marshall said, 'a matter for concentrated attention; a
thing to study, to master'. When J. M. Kilburn wrote that 'we have
been inclined to demand endless repetition and anything less than your
best we have tended to regard as failure', this was adding the puritan
burden of obligation of which Hutton was always aware, while in his
own precepts to young cricketers there is a note of puritan rebuke: 'If
things go wrong, don't blame your coach. Look nearer home for the
cause.' His captaincy of England had the qualities of toughness and
conviction displayed by the puritan entrepreneur. In all he did there
was a single-minded determination which, as Denis Compton noted,
even his fiercest critics could not deny.

When he retired from playing in 1956, the jurists vied with one
another in finding the telling phrase, the judgement that posterity
would expect, a definition of his craftsmanship, his place in the lineage

of the great. 'He was one of the best batsmen of all time, whether in technique or in the mental and moral resources that must accompany batting', declared H. S. Altham. 'His faultless judgement of length and his easy rhythm', wrote E. W. Swanton, 'were the hall-marks of his batting'. Neville Cardus saw him as an exemplar of 'the classical unities of batsmanship'. Much of what was said had already been said in the preceding twenty years, for it was the essence of Hutton that what he could do in the 1950s he could do potentially in the 1930s. Cardus had written in 1937: 'a grave interference with destiny will occur if Hutton does not develop into one of the finest opening batsmen in the records of the game.' Kilburn had said in the same year, 'England will have in him a cricketer for joy and pride for many years to come, and the possibilities in his realm of achievement seem quite beyond computation'. The skills had been learnt in the Yorkshire nursery and, although not always displayed to their fullest in the earlier years, the passage of time would see him develop a freedom of range and strokeplay which he would relate to the needs of a situation. Only the hook, reluctantly pressed into service, was more a penance than a pleasure.

What, then, were the expectations of those who watched: the devotees of Headingley on a chill May morning, partisan Sydney-siders on the Hill, Jamaicans brought up on George Headley, Gloucestershire men who knew only Hammond, Ovalites who had acclaimed Hobbs? They would see him walk to the wicket absorbed in thought, working out the day's demands, ready to embark on an exercise in concentration and patience which would be sustained, if need be, for several hours. They would note a harmony of bat and body, moving as if in unison, the bat an extension of the arms, so that each stroke was played with perfect positioning from the uplift of the bat to its full continuation. They would admire his footwork, his economy of movement, his tidiness. His batting was Baroque rather than Rococo, a concern for balance and wholeness rather than florid ornamentation. It was a matter of geometry in which the lines and angles were calculated to place the ball, a matter of algebra in solving the equation between bat and ball, a matter of arithmetic in deciding what to do with the ball or whether to do anything with it at all. And, if Art and Mathematics seemed too academic for all but the purist, tents for the scholar rather than the spectator, then exposition was enough. There was the off-drive, the anvil of his batting, and cuts timed so late that the ball had almost won its immunity before being dispatched. If the going were hard, the wicket difficult, the spinners making the most of turning and lifting conditions, he would play a dead bat so effectively that the ball would abandon its challenge and sink, without a whimper, to his feet. No one Fred Trueman ever saw could bat as well on any sort of wicket. No one Ray Lindwall ever saw knew so precisely when not to play the ball. The bat might be fractionally angled in the pick-up but who cared, except perhaps an expectant bowler who moved the ball in late. Did he really play slow bowlers too much from the crease? The film *Maestro*, which the BBC made in 1988, brought the evidence back for photographic consideration: certainly not at The Oval in 1938: sometimes in the post-war years.

Some dared to find him dull if he were not immediately entertaining. They would fail to realize that he was interpreting the role of the opening batsman in the way he thought best – wearing down the bowlers and the seam of the ball. He was taking stock of the wicket, the weather and the atmosphere before putting his imprint on the game. Then he was ready to go in search of half-volleys. It could be argued that he did not always make the fullest use of his talents. Tom Graveney and Denis Compton could both remember days when, in Graveney's words, 'he let the half-volleys go by', and, in Compton's, 'trundlers who ought to have been shivering in their boots would be treated with respect'. For all that, it would be Compton, of all his contemporaries, who paid Hutton the fullest tribute: 'He was faultlessly correct to the last detail, particularly in defence, and he is unquestionably one of the immortals to be put alongside Hobbs and Hammond.'

Hutton carried greater responsibilites as an England batsman than did Hammond – 1950–51 asked more of the leading scorer than did 1928–29 – and he ran very close to him in runs and centuries at Test level. He was half a generation younger and their partnership of 264 at 88 runs an hour at The Oval a few days before the outbreak of war must stand as a symbol rather than a fact of comparison. The older man had been the high priest of England's batting in the dozen years before the war, the younger one, in barely a dozen after it. Fortunate were those players and spectators who saw them both bat together, in that game, as Compton did: 'for a while we sat on the dressing room balcony drinking the heady wine of Hammond and Hutton, and forgetting Hitler.'

Long before either Compton or Hutton had made a run, except in short pants, Cardus had offered an evaluation of the twenty-four-year-old Hammond: 'there is no going beyond perfection.' For Cardus, to whom cricketers in general got worse, Hammond was as brightly burnished as any of the players of the Golden Age. C. B. Fry, one of that band himself, was still observing the game after both Hammond and Hutton had retired and he called Hammond 'the greatest batsman of them all'. John Arlott made even stronger claims for Hobbs: 'Those who played with him and against him generally considered him – in all conditions, on all pitches and against all types of bowling – the finest.' Then there are the Antipodean voices proclaiming Bradman with figures none of the others can match. When writing my biography of Hammond I sought Sir Leonard's opinion of him. The reply was immediate and unequivocal: 'I find it hard to rate anyone higher.' A man cannot with ease nominate himself for an Oscar and one senses Hutton would have been embarrassed were he placed above any of these contestants in some speculative list. Aggregates of runs will distance the leaders from the pack but they do not establish absolute judgements. Let Hutton, with the great men of his or any other generation, have his *alpha*.

The examiners identified him very early in his career. Pre-war players such as Alf Gover could recall his name being mentioned on the county circuit by the Yorkshire professionals who would go out of their way 'to tell us that this was the star of the future'. And they also recalled the modesty with which Hutton sustained a position that cannot have been easy. It is as much to his credit as it is to his colleagues' that he established a warm relationship within their ranks. Opponents, Reg Sinfield for example, found him 'a pleasure to play against'. After the war he never quite regained that ease in the context of Yorkshire, and his relationships with fellow players there took on a different perspective. He who had been so willing to learn found it harder to teach. Advice did not flow readily from his lips and he felt that a later generation lacked the humility and the dedication of his own. As a consequence, he did not emerge as the strong personality in the Yorkshire dressing room which the county needed in the post-Sellers era.

In one way those who got to know him best, whether at county or Test level, were those who opened the batting with him. They came closest to him in the demonstration of his craft, though the experience could be intimidating. His county colleague Lowson probably failed to blossom as he should have done because he was over-conscious of his partner at the other end. If Hutton had, as his Australian opponent Sidney Barnes remarked, 'an imperious air' at the wicket, it was a legacy from his partnerships with Sutcliffe. Cyril Washbrook made a point of telling me that 'Hutton was an admirable opening partner in every way who never tried to dominate the way the game should be played'.

Good county man as Hutton was (he was never the temperamental prima donna in the Yorkshire side) it would be at Test level that qualities beyond the ability to bat would be demonstrated. There was some mild surprise among other professionals when he became the England captain, but it would not be they who made barbed attacks on his leadership. From the receipt of the first bunch of insulting anonymous letters to the return of the amateur England captains in May, Cowdrey, Dexter and Smith, he was entitled to think that his was seen as a parvenu appointment. The collective voice of censure saw him as cautious and defensive, proving nothing by beating India, creating disaster and discord in the West Indies, winning the Ashes by attrition and retaining them by a slower over-rate and even (this was 1954) losing to Pakistan.

To set against these jibes Hutton would offer a leadership which was quietly effective rather than demonstrative, and a tenacity of will which embodied total dedication and sheer hard work. The sum total of these virtuous endeavours was the reward of victory but a breakdown in health. He had not found it easy to share his worries, delegate his responsibilities and discuss his policies. Swanton, who was a more outspoken critic than many, acknowledged the burden Hutton carried and recognized that the only two other England captains in the twentieth century carrying a similar responsibility as batsmen, Hammond and MacLaren, were not successful leaders. The critics, even Swanton, came to accept that Hutton was the exception. Nor did he allow the burden of captaincy to affect his performances as a batsman – and here the critics were toppled from one of their favourite planks. His batting average of 53.68 when England captain was only marginally below that of 57.82 when he was not. On the score of runs and averages, in and out of office, he and Hammond ran very much in harness.

Hutton, at the time of his appointment, was far removed from the traditional England captain who had probably led his school or university side and, almost definitely, his county. As the Australian Jack Fingleton observed, English professionals were trained to be led rather than to lead. Hutton had to learn the job from scratch, and perhaps the hardest lesson was in man-management. He was lucky in that the men under him were willing enough to accept the authority of someone who was, in effect, an officer commissioned from the ranks. No irreparable conflict took place between him and any of his players though a strained relationship lasted for some time with Trueman. Human nature being what it is, he had his preferences but, as a colleague indicated, 'no favouritism'. Some of those for whom he had less regard as cricketers were aware of his judgement of them, Laker particularly, and even a player as distinguished as Graveney found him a difficult man to understand. To them in conversation he could adopt the same parrying tactics as he did with journalists but with less reason for so doing. He was not as mentally tough as some thought, and the Bedser incident at Melbourne would have caused less anguish to a leader of sterner mould. Hutton had some of Jardine's qualities but by no means all of them.

Tactics came easier than man-management. He was, remarked Norman Yardley, 'sound rather than venturesome'. He set fields and chose bowlers to save runs as a primary objective. He was painstaking in his field-setting and whether or not this be seen as a device to keep down runs, it made for slow cricket, as did his preference for fast bowlers. All the time he was concerned about how to remove a batsman. When a new man came in, as Peter May observed, 'he would put himself in the incoming batsman's place and think about his worries and decide whom he would like least to face'. A view supported by the Australian captain, Ian Johnson: 'he had a fine capacity for seeing the weakness in his opponents.' Alf Gover observed with admiration the way in which he intimidated batsmen by the range of pressure he imposed. All this produced a captaincy on the field which gave no quarter.

Another side of his captaincy was demonstrated in his conduct on the two overseas tours. In retrospect, MCC's visit to the West Indies may be seen to have happened at a period of transition. The imperial relationship was giving way to an international one and the letter 'I' in ICC would change its meaning in 1965. Colonies were aspiring to nationhood: a white West Indian society was conceding power to a coloured one and the Grants and Stollmeyers would have no successors on the cricket field. Linked to this was social change. Riot and disorder in sporting arenas would soon make bottle-throwing seem no more than an unruly picnic gone wrong, though cricket would escape lightly compared with football. Umpires who expected obeisance from players would be clinging to an antediluvian pipe-dream. In more ways than being England's first professional captain, Hutton was exploring uncharted waters and the man who had trained for Dieppe had a chance to show his courage at Georgetown. No remotely similar problems faced him in Australia. The lessons in diplomacy which he had learnt the hard way in the West Indies, were expressed in an easy relationship with the Australian people as a whole. It was a measure of his achievements in that country that he could win both the Ashes and the goodwill of the public. His opposite number, Johnson, had 'a very high regard for him as a person' and saw him as 'a fine captain by any standards'. The qualities of an ambassador abroad, which Sir Donald Bradman regarded as so essential for a touring captain, he displayed in full measure.

Some twenty-five years later in 1979, Alan Gibson in his book on England captains nudged himself into a decision as to who was the greatest and he wrote, 'Yes, I would plump for Sir Leonard'. The writer A. A. Thomson gave a high place to the dignity with which Hutton conducted himself – the captaincy issue in 1954 is just one instance – and to the loyalty which he inspired. One of his closest observers was Ian Peebles who saw him as 'a straightforward practitioner who did a very good job' while the Australian journalist, Ray Robinson, wrote that in the 'acid test of captaincy – how a skipper acts when the game is running against his side – he won full marks'. If his had been a pragmatic appointment in 1952, pragmatism had triumphed. No series in twenty-three Test matches was lost and the Ashes were won. His admirers rejoiced and his critics mellowed. No England captain, before or since, with the exception of Peter May and possibly Graham Gooch, can match his achievements both as captain and batsman.

Hutton was a man who set himself goals, as Fingleton, playing against him in 1938, noticed. Once the captaincy came his way there was simply a fresh set of goals to be achieved. Kilburn, with unconscious prophecy, had seen him in the pre-war years as 'the knight with all his tournaments before him'. When the knighthood duly came and the tournaments were over, it was the climax of twenty years in which he had been at the centre of the English cricket stage. In the middle 1930s it had been difficult to separate his name from that of Sutcliffe. 'If you were to ask a stranger to name a Bradford League Club he would probably plump for Pudsey St Lawrence and tell you that Herbert Sutcliffe and Len Hutton learnt their cricket there', wrote John Kay, the historian of Lancashire cricket. Hutton's name had been inexorably linked with that of Sutcliffe. Coaching had produced the perfect pupil, a model of his teacher when batting. Praise was bestowed to the point of embarrassment. Then came what Swanton has called 'the fiasco at The Oval in 1938' – an Australian calculated Bradman would have made 727 in the same length of time – and he was a legendary figure in his own right from then onwards, as well known as Hammond had been after he returned from Australia in 1929 and Bradman after he returned there in 1930. He would play better innings (six of them, at least) but '364' would remain as much a millstone as a milestone. Nor did Sobers' 365 against Pakistan in 1958 supplant it in the popular image (except perhaps in West Indian eyes).

What came nearest to The Oval in 1938 was his Ashes' victory in 1953. 'You'd think we'd just won a war', said the wretched journalist at Pudsey. 'This is England, my dear chap, not one of those continental countries', replied his colleague. 'Do you think there'd be a turn-out like this if we'd only won a war?' Far from Pudsey another journalist was writing, 'Every cricketing generation produces at least one outstanding figure. Hutton's fame is unique.' International celebrity as Hutton was, there also was a sense in which he was a provincial hero to a generation of Yorkshiremen. 'He became a sort of god to me and remained so although I never met him', was a typical memory sustained by those who had watched him and who wrote to his biographer. Hutton was the preserve of Yorkshire and more especially Yorkshire cricket. Yet, when he came home in 1953 and all Pudsey turned out to claim him, the suspicion was already growing that he was becoming less and less one of them. Someone said, 'When tha gets ta Pudsey toneet let's 'ear a bit o' Yorksheer.' It was a sly reference to the polished 'received English' tones in which he had made his speech from the Oval balcony. Hutton gave the Pudsey crowd authentic Yorkshire but he had been perceptibly changing his accent since the war and in the manner of many another Yorkshireman who travelled far afield, he would preserve two voices, one for home consumption and one for export. 'I could be a bit of an actor', he told his biographer.

When he left Yorkshire – for good as it turned out – six years later, the provincial critics remained. Unlike some Yorkshiremen who were content to be upwardly mobile from a modest local base, Hutton seemed to them to cut himself off and identify himself with the south. The truth is less simple. When he was asked by Roy Plomley to select some records for his desert island, he chose 'The London I Love' because the city played an important part in his life and 'On Ilkley Moor Baht' 'at' because 'it brought back wonderful memories of Yorkshire, my home'. There turned out to be sound business reasons why he should live and work in the South and, as Sir Leonard observed, 'It was really no one else's business'; true, of course, but a lot of Yorkshire hero-worshippers approaching middle age felt bereft and let down. In a letter to John Arlott written in January 1966 he gave another reason why he preferred the south:

> The weather is bad here, but not as bad as Yorkshire, this is an impossibility. In January and February, they hibernate in Yorkshire. No place can be as bad as the West Riding, I should know.

The climate in the south of England and holidays in Tenerife, Majorca and Greece from time to time were some antidote to his increasing bronchitis and arthritis, a theme which more and more found its way into his conversation and correspondence as he grew older.

Hutton's health, or lack of it, had been a constant factor in his cricket career. He had more than his fair share of injuries, his wartime fracture being by far the worst, and they brought in their aftermath arthritis with almost constant pain. Added to this were the aches derived from physical and mental tensions. A more extrovert personality would have found relief in conversation, in a few drinks or, indeed, in doing whatever had to be done less single-mindedly. Achievement and fulfilment was all-in-all to Hutton, and always those stern puritan voices were calling on him to succeed. So, with a hap'orth of words and a thimbleful of alcohol – the saving grace was the frequent cigarette – he batted on. It was never meant to be a joy-ride. Yet it would be totally wrong to adjudge him a joyless man without humour. A humour very much of his own kind was never far away and might be seen in the twinkle in his blue eyes, a warm smile, the intonation of his voice or in what he said. He could be Delphic in his utterances, and instances abound of his enigmatic remarks to reporters, their questions parried with irrelevant replies. Such tactics as: 'Have you bought a new car lately?' allowed him time, while the uncertain laugh around the group played itself out, to think up the diplomatic answer. This was humour, not so much for its own sake, as with a purpose. Jokes on the field itself might be few and far between. He beckoned Compton during a demanding partnership against Australia: 'There must be easier ways of earning a living.' Among those he knew really well his humour was more immediate. Norman Yardley recalled a lunch at Headingley in 1986 at which 'Len had us in fits'. For one to be the recipient of such mirth Hutton had to be entirely at his ease. At the MCC Dinner at Lord's in 1990, he held a table of 8, mostly strangers, in captive silence and, as the mood changed, handled their questions with ease.

Humour may have lurked in the wings but he realized that, as a person, he was expected to be centre-stage. He took trouble to talk to people and many have recollections of his remembering them after a gap of years or at least giving the impression that he did so. He would respond to a Yorkshire accent and strike up a casual conversation, as a couple quite unknown to him at Wimbledon recalled. He had a natural courtesy, good manners and that winning smile, and he was not un-aware that these graces mattered; that the simple gesture gave immense pleasure. 'I got home that night to find my wife thrilled to pieces. Len, who hardly knew her, had made a special effort to walk over and shake hands', recalled a man whom he came across in business.

Len Hutton

His business friend was an accountant, and he remembered Hutton enquiring why his royalty cheque from Slazengers was late. In pursuing what was his due, Hutton was a realist. Cricket had brought him publicity and it had also brought him some prosperity. He had always had a thrifty approach to money typical of many a Yorkshireman or of his own Scottish ancestors. As a child he had become aware that there had been more of it in his grandfather's time than in his father's. He lived in a county where men talked 'brass' and he made himself better informed than his contemporaries in the cricket world on how money 'worked'. Bill Bowes thought he knew more about the stock market than any Yorkshire professional except, perhaps, Sutcliffe. His son Richard recalled that when he telephoned his father to announce his engagement, Sir Leonard's main topic of conversation was interest rates. Yet this same prudent man could send an open cheque to a Methodist Church bazaar. When the rewards had begun to come – the Australian's cheque which bought him his first house, the advertising revenues, a substantial benefit, journalism – he accepted them as a fair return for his talent. By the standards of the day, cricket had served him well.

Yet he could not be entirely assured about the future when, at the age of thirty-nine, he suddenly ceased to have a regular monthly income. Cricketers of his generation could fall on hard times after their playing days were over. Paynter died in poverty and Hammond was saved from penury by an administrative appointment at a university in South Africa. It must, therefore, be seen as something of a brave decision to sustain the expense of preparatory and public school education for both boys just at a time when his cricket career had ended and his shop was being closed. A journalist chose the moment to compare his approach to cricket to that of 'an efficient and ambitious businessman making a success of his career'. Fenner gave him the opportunity to be the businessman in reality and to demonstrate those qualities in the marketing field. One need not be surprised at this. The 'work ethic' was essential to his philosophy.

It is more than ordinarily true that Sir Leonard Hutton owed a great deal, in all his achievements, to his wife. She was as vital to her husband in his business career as in his cricket one. 'She could meet anyone and hold her own in any conversation, cricket or otherwise', commented a Fenner director. The happiness of their marriage is central to an understanding of Sir Leonard's success. Dorothy Hutton, if not quite 'the girl next door', came from a similar Yorkshire background with a brother who had played for the county: 'a sensible Yorkshire lass', remembered a contemporary of theirs. They married

205

young and faced together the twin hazards of fame and separation, either of which can tumble a marriage if the foundations are not secure. Year after year she would look after the boys over many months when their father was touring abroad, the only real link being what was in the papers, the pictures on Movietone or Pathé News or a garbled telephone conversation. She shared in the vital decisions – to send the boys to Repton and to move south. By the 1980s, with both sons in the City and the second generation destined to go to public schools, the Huttons represented a successful and almost classic example of social mobility through self-endeavour.

Sir Leonard, as he freely admitted, had much to thank cricket for. It allowed him to fulfil his talents, see the world and paint the story of his life on a wide canvas. It had accorded him the epithet of 'Great'. Greatness has no need to display itself and throughout his life he retained the quality of modesty, a judgement no one has remotely challenged. Indeed, as a person, he may be said almost to have under-valued himself. The imp of vanity could dance elsewhere. Yet great-ness is not easily relinquished and it continued to make its claims on Sir Leonard long after his playing days. He never ceased to be news: the BBC in the fiftieth year of his Oval record pursued him, and his biographer knocked at his door to unlock the portals of his life. Sport, at its best, is the safety valve of a working society and it is a common ground of dialogue among those, rich and poor, distinguished and ordinary, who follow it. It selects its heroes and makes value-judgements on them. Sir Leonard became deservedly cricket's 'verray parfit gentil knight', displaying the knightly virtues of chivalry, honour and valour.

Two centuries ago, Benjamin Hutton unwittingly followed the advice of Samuel Johnson and quit his native Scotland for England. His descendant admired the compiler of the famous dictionary. In the sense of some words of Johnson addressed to an adversary, Sir Leonard addressed himself to bowlers: by repelling their violence, defying their rage and requiring their abilities to be proved, he compiled his own folio of figures, the ledger of his life.

Statistical Appendix

Note
These statistics for Sir Leonard Hutton's career differ from those published in *Wisden*, 1956 by including the three first-class matches which he played after he retired, by including the innings of 107 against Derbyshire at Bradford in 1950 (omitted in *Wisden*, 1956, page 103) and by crediting him with bowling figures of 3–0–16–0 against New South Wales in 1946–47 which *Wisden*, 1948 wrongly attributed to Compton.

L. Hutton 1934–1960

First-class career

	Matches	Inns	Times Not Out	Runs	Highest Score	100s	50s	Avge	Catches	Overs	Maidens	Runs	Wkts	Avge	5/ Inns	10/ Match	Best Bowling
1934	16	28	2	863	196	1	5	33.19	11	103	17	379	11	34.45	–	–	3/65
1935	17	23	3	577	131	1	1	28.85	6	22.1	5	79	2	39.50	–	–	2/50
1936 Jamaica	3	5	2	123	59	–	1	41.00	3	7	0	45	1	45.00	–	–	1/22
1936	34	49	6	1282	163	1	8	29.81	27	173.3	44	479	21	22.81	–	–	4/25
1937	35	58	7	2888	271*	10	12	56.62	28	315	56	1025	28	36.60	1	–	6/76
1938	25	37	6	1874	364	6	5	60.45	14	227.1	51	576	20	28.80	1	–	5/45
1938/9 South Africa	14	19	1	1168	202	2	4	64.88	7	24	1	108	2	54.00	–	–	1/17
1939	33	52	6	2883	280*	12	8	62.67	39	†220.7	38	822	44	18.68	2	–	5/58
1945	9	16	0	782	188	2	4	48.87	3	35	0	167	5	33.40	–	–	2/12
1946	24	38	6	1552	183*	4	7	48.50	13	58	11	173	9	19.22	–	–	4/40
1946/7 Australia	14	21	3	1267	151*	3	8	70.38	5	†21	1	132	2	66.00	–	–	1/8
1947	26	44	4	2585	270*	11	7	64.62	23	109	18	344	12	28.83	–	–	3/46
1947/8 West Indies	5	10	1	578	138	2	3	64.22	6	5	1	20	0	–	–	–	–
1948	28	48	7	2654	176*	10	13	64.73	23	26	5	102	0	–	–	–	–
1948/9 South Africa	14	21	1	1477	174	5	7	73.85	8	1	0	7	0	–	–	–	–
1949	33	56	6	3429	269*	12	17	68.58	41	102	29	286	7	40.86	–	–	3/23
1950	25	40	3	2128	202*	6	11	55.51	24	28	5	90	2	45.00	–	–	2/58
1950/1 Aus/NZ	15	25	4	1382	156*	5	7	65.80	19	4	0	11	1	11.00	–	–	1/4

Table 1 — By season

1951	31	47	8	2145	194*	7	9	55.00	33	11	1	44	4	11.00	–	–	4/20
1952	28	45	3	2567	189	11	12	61.11	31	10	8	43	1	43.00	–	–	1/37
1953	27	44	5	2458	241	8	10	63.02	15	31	0	129	0	–	–	–	–
1953/4 West Indies	8	12	2	780	205	2	4	78.00	3	6	0	43	0	–	–	–	–
1954	20	28	2	912	163	2	4	35.07	7	–	–	–	–	–	–	–	–
1954/5 Aus/NZ	15	25	2	1059	145*	2	6	46.04	6	†0.6	0	2	1	2.00	–	–	1/2
1955	11	19	1	537	194	1	4	29.83	5	–	–	–	–	–	–	–	–
1957	1	2	0	101	76	–	1	50.50	–	–	–	–	–	–	–	–	–
1960	2	2	0	89	89	–	1	44.50	–	–	–	–	–	–	–	–	–
TOTAL	513	814	91	40140	364	129	179	55.51	400	‡9730	292	5106	173	29.51	4	1	6/76

Table 2 — In England / Overseas

In England	425	676	75	32306	364	105	139	53.75	343	‡9272	289	4738	166	28.54	4	1	6/76
Overseas	88	138	16	7834	205	24	40	64.21	57	‡458	3	368	7	52.57	–	–	1/2
TOTAL	513	814	91	40140	364	129	179	55.51	400	‡9730	292	5106	173	29.51	4	1	6/76

Table 3 — By country overseas

In West Indies	16	27	5	1481	205	4	8	67.31	12	18	1	108	1	108.00	–	–	1/22
South Africa	28	40	2	2645	202	10	11	69.60	15	25	1	115	2	57.50	–	–	1/17
New Zealand	6	8	0	283	69	–	3	35.37	1	3	0	7	0	–	–	–	–
Australia	38	63	9	3425	156*	10	18	63.42	29	22.6	1	138	4	34.50	–	–	1/2
TOTAL	513	814	91	40140	364	129	179	55.51	400	‡9730	292	5106	173	29.51	4	1	6/76

* = Not Out Innings   † = 8-Ball Overs   ‡ = Balls bowled

LEN HUTTON

Batting for Yorkshire

County Championship	Matches	Inns	Times Not Out	Runs	Highest Score	100s	50s	Avge	Catches
1934	14	25	1	801	196	1	4	33.37	9
1935	14	19	3	411	131	1	–	25.68	6
1936	29	43	6	1108	163	1	6	29.94	24
1937	22	36	5	1728	271★	5	7	55.74	19
1938	13	17	3	631	107	1	3	45.07	8
1939	26	40	4	2167	280★	9	6	60.19	31
1946	16	26	4	1112	171	3	5	50.54	9
1947	14	23	1	1551	270★	6	4	73.00	13
1948	14	22	5	1565	176★	8	4	92.05	11
1949	22	38	5	2098	269★	6	11	63.57	35
1950	14	21	2	1125	156	4	4	59.21	15
1951	17	26	5	1222	194★	5	4	58.19	20
1952	17	26	1	1482	189	7	6	59.28	16
1953	14	21	1	1149	178	4	4	57.45	4
1954	13	19	2	676	149★	1	4	39.76	6
1955	10	18	0	535	194	1	4	29.72	5
TOTAL	269	420	48	19361	280★	63	76	52.04	231

Other v.									
Lancashire	1	1	0	26	26	–	–	26.00	1
Universities	24	32	4	1400	180	5	5	50.00	12
Tourists	15	23	1	1381	183★	6	5	62.77	14
Jamaica	3	5	2	123	59	–	1	41.00	3
Scotland	3	3	1	270	146★	1	1	135.00	2
MCC	23	39	6	1834	161	8	8	55.57	14
RAF	1	2	0	128	73	–	2	64.00	–
Combined Services	1	1	0	163	163	1	–	163.00	–
Middlesex	1	1	0	121	121	1	–	121.00	1
Total	72	107	14	5446	183★	22	22	58.55	46
TOTAL	341	527	62	24807	280★	85	98	53.34	278

Statistical Appendix

Batting on English Grounds

	Matches	Inns	Times Not Out	Runs	Highest Score	100s	50s	Avge	Catches
Bath	1	1	0	3	3	–	–	3.00	1
Birmingham	8	12	3	491	158	1	2	54.55	8
Bournemouth	8	13	4	550	270*	1	2	61.11	9
Bradford	36	57	3	2824	183*	9	12	52.29	27
Brentwood	1	2	0	147	141	1	–	73.50	1
Bristol	9	15	2	450	110*	1	2	34.61	3
Cambridge	10	13	1	702	180	3	2	58.50	5
Canterbury	3	4	0	207	120	1	1	51.75	1
Cardiff	6	10	1	321	90	–	3	35.66	4
Chesterfield	6	10	2	233	84	–	2	29.12	8
Clacton	1	1	0	58	58	–	1	58.00	3
Colchester	1	2	1	167	156	1	–	167.00	1
Dover	5	7	0	348	100	1	3	49.71	5
Dublin	1	1	0	89	89	–	1	89.00	–
Eastbourne	3	4	0	164	87	–	2	41.00	–
Edinburgh	1	1	0	79	79	–	1	79.00	–
Gloucester	2	4	2	87	35*	–	–	43.50	–
Harrogate	6	6	0	392	163	2	1	65.33	6
Hove	7	13	2	748	165	4	2	68.00	4
Huddersfield	9	17	2	775	141	4	3	51.66	13
Hull	15	19	3	1012	171*	3	5	63.25	10
Ilford	3	5	1	281	124	1	1	70.20	3
Leeds	42	62	6	3192	189	15	10	57.00	28
Leicester	8	12	2	454	137	1	3	45.40	7
Lord's	52	91	9	3302	196	11	13	40.26	38
Maidstone	1	2	0	33	29	–	–	16.50	–
Manchester	24	42	4	1840	201	4	11	48.42	17
Newport	1	2	0	80	51	–	1	40.00	–
Northampton	4	7	0	269	65	–	2	38.42	8
Nottingham	14	22	3	1153	194*	4	4	60.68	11
The Oval	21	34	2	2291	364	8	7	71.59	18
Oxford	14	19	3	698	141	2	3	43.62	7
Portsmouth	1	1	0	38	38	–	–	38.00	2
Scarborough	44	78	8	4190	241	13	25	59.85	42
Sheffield	38	56	9	2756	280*	6	10	59.91	34
Southend	2	4	0	379	197	2	–	94.75	–
Stourbridge	3	5	0	118	101	1	–	29.50	6

Batting on English Grounds—contd

	Matches	Inns	Times Not Out	Runs	Highest Score	100s	50s	Avge	Catches
Swansea	2	2	0	200	197	1	–	100.00	2
Taunton	2	3	0	125	52	–	1	41.46	–
Tonbridge	1	1	0	136	136	1	–	136.00	–
Tunbridge Wells	1	2	0	106	74	–	1	53.00	2
Wellingborough	1	1	1	269	269*	1	–	—	1
Wells	1	2	0	25	16	–	–	12.50	2
Westcliff	2	4	0	216	103	1	1	54.00	2
Worcester	4	7	1	308	196	1	1	51.33	4
TOTAL	425	676	75	32306	364	105	139	53.75	343
Yorkshire Grounds	190	295	32	15141	280*	52	66	57.57	160
Other English Grounds	235	381	43	17165	364	53	73	50.78	183

Batting on Overseas Grounds

	Matches	Inns	Times Not Out	Runs	Highest Score	100s	50s	Avge	Catches
Adelaide	8	15	2	1103	156*	3	7	84.74	7
Auckland	2	2	0	122	69	–	2	61.00	1
Bloemfontein	1	1	0	134	134	1	–	134.00	2
Bridgetown	2	4	1	211	77	–	3	70.33	1
Brisbane	5	8	2	138	62*	–	1	23.00	3
Bulawayo	1	1	0	145	145	1	–	145.00	2
Cape Town	5	9	1	401	125	1	2	50.12	2
Christchurch	2	2	0	61	33	–	–	30.50	–
Dunedin	1	2	0	14	11	–	–	7.00	–
Durban	6	9	0	502	108	1	4	55.77	2
East London	2	3	0	8	5	–	–	2.66	2
Georgetown	4	6	1	424	169	2	1	84.80	1
Hobart	1	1	0	15	15	–	–	15.00	–
Johannesburg	7	9	0	813	174	4	2	90.33	4
Kimberley	1	1	0	149	149	1	–	149.00	1
Kingston	9	15	2	772	205	2	4	59.38	10
Launceston	2	3	1	133	61	–	2	66.50	–
Melbourne	9	16	2	763	151*	2	3	54.50	14
Perth	2	2	1	155	145*	1	–	155.00	2
Pietermaritzburg	1	2	1	68	53*	–	1	68.00	–
Port Elizabeth	2	3	0	280	202	1	–	93.33	–
Port of Spain	1	2	1	74	44	–	–	74.00	–
Pretoria	1	1	0	66	66	–	1	66.00	–
Salisbury	1	1	0	79	79	–	1	79.00	–
Sydney	11	18	1	1118	150	4	5	65.76	3
Wellington	1	2	0	86	57	–	1	43.00	–
TOTAL	88	138	16	7834	205	24	40	64.21	57

Batting in Test Matches

	Matches	Inns	Times Not Out	Runs	Highest Score	100s	50s	Avge	Catches
1937 New Zealand	3	5	0	127	100	1	–	25.40	2
1938 Australia	3	4	0	473	364	2	–	118.25	1
1938/9 South Africa	4	6	0	265	92	–	2	44.16	3
1939 West Indies	3	6	1	480	196	2	1	96.00	3
1946 India	3	5	1	123	67	–	1	30.75	–
1946/7 Australia	5	9	1	417	122*	1	2	52.12	1
1947 South Africa	5	10	2	344	100	1	1	43.00	5
1947/8 West Indies	2	4	0	171	60	–	2	42.75	3
1948 Australia	4	8	0	342	81	–	4	42.75	5
1948/9 South Africa	5	9	0	577	158	2	2	64.11	2
1949 New Zealand	4	6	0	469	206	2	2	78.16	2
1950 West Indies	3	6	1	333	202*	1	–	66.60	2
1950/1 Australia	5	10	4	533	156*	1	4	88.83	9
1950/1 New Zealand	2	3	0	114	57	–	1	38.00	–
1951 South Africa	5	6	2	378	100	1	2	54.00	8
1952 India	4	9	1	399	150	2	1	79.80	3
1953 Australia	5	9	1	443	145	1	3	55.37	4
1953/4 West Indies	5	8	1	677	205	2	3	96.71	1
1954 Pakistan	2	3	0	19	14	–	–	6.33	–
1954/5 Australia	5	9	0	220	80	–	1	24.44	2
1954/5 New Zealand	2	3	0	67	33	–	1	22.33	1
Home	44	77	9	3930	364	13	15	57.79	35
Overseas	35	61	6	3041	205	6	18	55.29	22
TOTAL	79	138	15	6971	364	19	33	56.67	57
Australia	27	49	6	2428	364	5	14	56.46	22
India	7	11	2	522	150	2	2	58.00	3
New Zealand	11	17	0	777	206	3	4	51.51	5
Pakistan	2	3	0	19	14	–	–	6.33	–
South Africa	19	34	4	1564	158	4	7	52.13	18
West Indies	13	24	3	1661	205	5	6	79.09	9
TOTAL	79	138	15	6971	364	19	33	56.67	57

Batting in England

	Matches	Inns	Times Not Out	Runs	Highest Score	100s	50s	Avge	Catches
Yorkshire									
Derbyshire	14	20	3	865	271★	2	4	50.88	12
Essex	19	32	4	1802	197	7	6	64.35	18
Glamorgan	15	22	2	1063	197	2	7	53.15	12
Gloucestershire	18	30	4	927	110★	2	5	35.65	9
Hampshire	16	25	5	1055	280★	2	3	52.75	20
Kent	20	30	1	1592	189	5	9	54.89	15
Lancashire	27	44	5	1763	201	5	5	45.20	19
Leicestershire	15	22	4	990	153	3	5	55.00	10
Middlesex	24	38	3	1608	133	6	5	45.94	21
Northamptonshire	12	18	3	1179	269★	4	5	78.60	17
Nottinghamshire	12	17	4	948	194★	4	1	72.92	10
Somerset	11	17	1	823	141	3	3	51.43	9
Surrey	17	28	0	1286	163	5	4	45.92	13
Sussex	20	32	5	1942	177	8	9	71.92	16
Warwickshire	17	25	2	820	158	2	3	35.65	13
Worcestershire	14	22	2	845	196	4	2	42.25	16
M.C.C.	23	39	6	1834	161	8	8	55.57	14
Oxford University	14	19	3	698	141	2	3	43.62	6
Cambridge University	10	13	1	702	180	3	2	58.50	5
Australia	5	9	0	296	84	0	3	32.88	2
South Africa	3	3	0	351	156	2	1	117.00	9
New Zealand	3	5	0	345	167	2	0	69.00	2
India	2	2	1	189	183★	1	0	189.00	2
West Indies	2	4	0	200	104	1	1	50.00	3
Scotland	3	3	1	270	146★	1	1	135.00	2
R.A.F.	1	2	0	128	73	0	2	64.00	–
Combined Services	1	1	0	163	163	1	0	163.00	–
TOTAL Yorkshire	338	522	60	24684	280★	85	97	53.42	275
Others									
England	44	77	9	3930	364	13	15	57.79	35
M.C.C.	4	6	1	308	89	–	4	61.60	–
North	4	8	0	510	102	2	4	43.50	3
Rest	1	2	0	68	50	–	1	34.00	1
Players	12	22	3	1070	241	2	7	56.31	16

Batting in England—contd

	Matches	Inns	Times Not Out	Runs	Highest Score	100s	50s	Avge	Catches
England XI	12	20	1	809	104	1	5	42.57	7
HDG Leveson Gower's XI	5	10	1	537	188	1	4	59.66	5
TN Pearce's XI	3	6	0	282	102	1	1	47.00	1
M.C.C.	1	2	0	108	73	–	1	54.00	–
LC Stevens's XI	1	1	0	0	0	–	–	0.00	–
TOTAL in England	425	676	75	32306	364	105	139	53.75	343

Centuries in first-class cricket (129)

196	Yorkshire	v	Worcestershire	Worcester	1934
131	Yorkshire	v	Middlesex	Leeds	1935
163	Yorkshire	v	Surrey	Leeds	1936
271*	Yorkshire	v	Derbyshire	Sheffield	1937
161	Yorkshire	v	M.C.C.	Lord's	1937
153	Yorkshire	v	Leicestershire	Hull	1937
136	Yorkshire	v	Kent	Tonbridge	1937
135	Yorkshire	v	New Zealanders	Leeds	1937
124	Yorkshire	v	Essex	Ilford	1937
121	Yorkshire	v	Middlesex	The Oval	1937
102	North	v	South	Lord's	1937
101	Yorkshire	v	Worcestershire	Stourbridge	1937
100	England	v	New Zealand	Manchester	1937
364	England	v	Australia	The Oval	1938
180	Yorkshire	v	Cambridge University	Cambridge	1938
141	Yorkshire	v	Oxford University	Oxford	1938
107	Yorkshire	v	Sussex	Leeds	1938
106*	Yorkshire	v	M.C.C.	Scarborough	1938
100	England	v	Australia	Nottingham	1938
202	M.C.C.	v	Eastern Province	Port Elizabeth	1938/9
149	M.C.C.	v	Griqualand West	Kimberley	1938/9
148	M.C.C.	v	Combined Transvaal	Johannesburg	1938/9
145	M.C.C.	v	Rhodesia	Bulawayo	1938/9
108	M.C.C.	v	Natal	Durban	1938/9
280*	Yorkshire	v	Hampshire	Sheffield	1939

Centuries in first-class cricket (129)—contd

196	England	v West Indies	Lord's	1939
177	Yorkshire	v Sussex	Scarborough	1939
165*	England	v West Indies	The Oval	1939
158	Yorkshire	v Warwickshire	Birmingham	1939
151	Yorkshire	v Surrey	Leeds	1939
144	Yorkshire	v Glamorgan	Bradford	1939
109	Yorkshire	v Worcestershire	Bradford	1939
105*	Yorkshire	v Lancashire	Leeds	1939
103	Yorkshire	v Sussex	Hove	1939
102	Yorkshire	v Cambridge University	Cambridge	1939
100	Yorkshire	v Kent	Dover	1939
188	HDG Leveson Gower's XI	v New Zealanders	Scarborough	1945
104	An England XI	v Australian Services	Lord's	1945
183*	Yorkshire	v Indians	Bradford	1946
171*	Yorkshire	v Northamptonshire	Hull	1946
111	Yorkshire	v Leicestershire	Leeds	1946
101	Yorkshire	v Surrey	The Oval	1946
151*	M.C.C.	v Victoria	Melbourne	1946/7
136	M.C.C.	v South Australia	Adelaide	1946/7
122*	England	v Australia	Sydney	1946/7
270*	Yorkshire	v Hampshire	Bournemouth	1947
197 104 }	Yorkshire	v Essex	Southend	1947
197	Yorkshire	v Glamorgan	Swansea	1947
137	Yorkshire	v Leicestershire	Leicester	1947
137	Yorkshire	v South Africans	Sheffield	1947
120*	Yorkshire	v Cambridge University	Cambridge	1947
107	Yorkshire	v M.C.C.	Scarborough	1947
106	Yorkshire	v Sussex	Bradford	1947
103	Yorkshire	v Oxford University	Oxford	1947
100	England	v South Africa	Leeds	1947
138	M.C.C.	v British Guiana	Georgetown	1947/8
128	M.C.C.	v Jamaica	Kingston	1947/8
176*	Yorkshire	v Sussex	Sheffield	1948
155	Yorkshire	v Sussex	Hove	1948
144*	Yorkshire	v Essex	Leeds	1948
133	Yorkshire	v Middlesex	Lord's	1948
132*	Players	v Gentlemen	Lord's	1948
107*	Yorkshire	v M.C.C.	Scarborough	1948
104	Yorkshire	v Lancashire	Manchester	1948

Centuries in first-class cricket (129)—contd

103	Yorkshire	v Essex	Westcliff	1948
100*	Yorkshire	v Northamptonshire	Huddersfield	1948
100	Yorkshire	v Lancashire	Leeds	1948
174	M.C.C.	v Transvaal	Johannesburg	1948/9
158	England	v South Africa	Johannesburg	1948/9
134	M.C.C.	v Orange Free State	Bloemfontein	1948/9
125	M.C.C.	v Cape Province	Cape Town	1948/9
123	England	v South Africa	Johannesburg	1948/9
269*	Yorkshire	v Northamptonshire	Wellingborough	1949
206	England	v New Zealand	The Oval	1949
201	Yorkshire	v Lancashire	Manchester	1949
167	Yorkshire	v New Zealanders	Bradford	1949
165 / 100	Yorkshire	v Sussex	Hove	1949
147	Yorkshire	v M.C.C.	Scarborough	1949
146*	Yorkshire	v Scotland	Hull	1949
113	Yorkshire	v Middlesex	Lord's	1949
104	Yorkshire	v Northamptonshire	Bradford	1949
101	England	v New Zealand	Leeds	1949
101	North	v South	Scarborough	1949
202*	England	v West Indies	The Oval	1950
156	Yorkshire	v Essex	Colchester	1950
153	Yorkshire	v Nottinghamshire	Nottingham	1950
141	Yorkshire	v Somerset	Huddersfield	1950
107	Yorkshire	v West Indians	Sheffield	1950
107	Yorkshire	v Derbyshire	Bradford	1950
156*	England	v Australia	Adelaide	1950/1
150	M.C.C.	v New South Wales	Sydney	1950/1
128	M.C.C.	v Victoria	Melbourne	1950/1
126	M.C.C.	v South Australia	Adelaide	1950/1
112	M.C.C.	v New South Wales	Sydney	1950/1
194*	Yorkshire	v Nottinghamshire	Nottingham	1951
151	Yorkshire	v Surrey	The Oval	1951
156	Yorkshire	v South Africans	Sheffield	1951
141	Yorkshire	v Essex	Brentwood	1951
117	Yorkshire	v Middlesex	Lord's	1951
110*	Yorkshire	v Gloucestershire	Bristol	1951
100	England	v South Africa	Leeds	1951
189	Yorkshire	v Kent	Leeds	1952
152	Yorkshire	v Lancashire	Leeds	1952

Centuries in first-class cricket (129)—contd

150	England	v	India	Lord's	1952
132	Yorkshire	v	Middlesex	Lord's	1952
120	Yorkshire	v	Kent	Canterbury	1952
119	Yorkshire	v	Somerset	Huddersfield	1952
108	Yorkshire	v	Gloucestershire	Harrogate	1952
104	England	v	India	Manchester	1952
104	Yorkshire	v	Surrey	The Oval	1952
103 } 107 }	Yorkshire	v	M.C.C.	Scarborough	1952
241	Players	v	Gentlemen	Scarborough	1953
178	Yorkshire	v	Somerset	Leeds	1953
145	England	v	Australia	Lord's	1953
125	Yorkshire	v	Warwickshire	Bradford	1953
103*	Yorkshire	v	M.C.C.	Scarborough	1953
102	TN Pearce's XI	v	Australians	Scarborough	1953
100*	Yorkshire	v	Kent	Scarborough	1953
100	Yorkshire	v	Worcestershire	Huddersfield	1953
205	England	v	West Indies	Kingston	1953/4
169	England	v	West Indies	Georgetown	1953/4
163	Yorkshire	v	Combined Services	Harrogate	1954
149*	Yorkshire	v	Nottinghamshire	Bradford	1954
145*	M.C.C.	v	Western Australia	Perth	1954/5
102	M.C.C.	v	New South Wales	Sydney	1954/5
194	Yorkshire	v	Nottinghamshire	Nottingham	1955

Wicket Partnerships over 175

267	1st	W Barber	Yorkshire	v	Kent	Leeds	1934
247	4th	M Leyland	Yorkshire	v	Essex	Hull	1936
230	1st	H Sutcliffe	Yorkshire	v	Surrey	Leeds	1936
191	3rd	M Leyland	Yorkshire	v	Surrey	Leeds	1936
315	1st	H Sutcliffe	Yorkshire	v	Leicestershire	Hull	1937
233	3rd	M Leyland	Yorkshire	v	Worcestershire	Stourbridge	1937
181	1st	H Sutcliffe	Yorkshire	v	Derbyshire	Sheffield	1937
191*	5th	C Turner					
219	1st	CJ Barnett					
382	2nd	M Leyland	England	v	Australia	The Oval	1938
215	6th	J Hardstaff					
230	2nd	A Mitchell	Yorkshire	v	Cambridge University	Cambridge	1938
177	2nd	W Barber	Yorkshire	v	Oxford University	Oxford	1938
263	1st	WJ Edrich	M.C.C.	v	Griqualand West	Kimberley	1938/9
207	1st	WJ Edrich	M.C.C.	v	Natal	Durban	1938/9
177	2nd	E Paynter	M.C.C.	v	Eastern Province	Port Elizabeth	1938/9
264	3rd	WR Hammond	England	v	West Indies	The Oval	1939
315	1st	H Sutcliffe	Yorkshire	v	Hampshire	Sheffield	1939
178*	2nd	W Barber					
248	4th	DCS Compton	England	v	West Indies	Lord's	1939
240	3rd	M Leyland	Yorkshire	v	Surrey	Leeds	1939
228	3rd	M Leyland	Yorkshire	v	Surrey	The Oval	1939

175	4th	W Barber	Yorkshire	v	Sussex	Scarborough	1939
203	1st	C Washbrook	HDG Leveson Gower's XI	v	New Zealanders	Scarborough	1945
240	1st	C Washbrook	M.C.C.	v	South Australia	Adelaide	1946/7
273	5th	NWD Yardley	Yorkshire	v	Hampshire	Bournemouth	1947
196	2nd	GA Smithson	Yorkshire	v	Leicestershire	Leicester	1947
192	3rd	W Watson	Yorkshire	v	Essex	Southend	1947
189	1st	H Halliday	Yorkshire	v	Essex	Southend	1947
176	5th	A Coxon	Yorkshire	v	Sussex	Sheffield	1948
359	1st	C Washbrook	England	v	South Africa	Johannesburg	1948/9
206	2nd	RT Simpson	M.C.C.	v	Transvaal	Johannesburg	1948/9
191	3rd	DCS Compton	M.C.C.	v	Cape Province	Cape Town	1948/9
261*	2nd	JV Wilson	Yorkshire	v	Scotland	Hull	1949
218	2nd	WJ Edrich	England	v	New Zealand	The Oval	1949
185	2nd	JV Wilson	Yorkshire	v	Nottinghamshire	Nottingham	1950
178	2nd	H Halliday	Yorkshire	v	Somerset	Huddersfield	1950
236	3rd	RT Simpson	M.C.C.	v	New South Wales	Sydney	1950/1
196	6th	TE Bailey	M.C.C.	v	Victoria	Melbourne	1950/1
286	1st	FA Lowson	Yorkshire	v	South Africa	Sheffield	1951
199	3rd	EJ Lester	Yorkshire	v	Nottinghamshire	Nottingham	1951
197	1st	FA Lowson	Yorkshire	v	Surrey	The Oval	1951
245	1st	FA Lowson	Yorkshire	v	Lancashire	Leeds	1952
203	1st	FA Lowson	Yorkshire	v	Somerset	Huddersfield	1952
201	4th	WHH Sutcliffe	Yorkshire	v	Kent	Canterbury	1952
194	2nd	R Illingworth	Yorkshire	v	Combined Services	Harrogate	1954

A Note on Sources

Manuscript

Minutes of the General and Cricket Committee of Yorkshire CCC at Headingley, Leeds

Minutes and letter files of MCC at Lord's

Broadcasts, Correspondence and Internal Memorandum at the Written Archive Centre of the BBC, Caversham, Reading

'Scrapbooks' in the possession of Sir Leonard and Lady Hutton

Newspapers

The first-class career of Sir Leonard Hutton was reported in every newspaper which regarded cricket as part of its sporting province. The fullest account of his career with Yorkshire, including 2nd XI matches and those for Pudsey St Lawrence, may be found in the following: the Bradford *Telegraph and Argus*, the *Leeds Mercury*, the *Pudsey and Stanningley News*: the *Yorkshire Evening Post*; the *Yorkshire Post*.

The principal sources for all newspapers is the British Museum Newspaper Section at Colindale, North London.

Books and Journals

Wisden Cricketers' Almanack (the apostrophe after '*Wisden*' disappeared in 1938) is an essential source from 1934 onwards. The more important references, other than to matches themselves, are listed in the Index to *Wisden, 1964–1984* (ed. Derek Barnard). The *Wisden*s for 1950 and 1956 contain tributes to Sir Leonard Hutton by V. G. J. Jenkins and Sir Neville Cardus respectively.

The Cricketer was the principal cricket journal during his playing years and there are few cricket books which do not carry some reference to him in their index.

Sir Leonard's business career with Fenner is frequently mentioned in the in-house magazine, *V-Belt*, retained in the firm's offices in Hull.

Sir Leonard Hutton wrote at various times for the *Evening News*, The *Observer*, the *Star* and the *News of the World*. He published three volumes of memoirs in which he was assisted by the writer indicated in brackets below:

Cricket is my Life (Thomas Moult), 1949
Just my story (R. J. Hayter), 1956
Fifty years in Cricket (Alex Bannister), 1984

While no full-scale biography of him has been written, there have been several shorter contributions:

J. M. Kilburn, Len Hutton, (32pp), 1950
Brian Trevor, Len Hutton, (49pp), 1951
Laurence Kitchin, Len Hutton, (64pp), 1953
A. A. Thomson, Hutton and Washbrook (275pp), 1963

Index

Index

226

Index

Index

Index

Index